THE BIG TWO

SOVIET–AMERICAN PERCEPTIONS OF FOREIGN POLICY

This is the first Volume in the Pegasus series,
"American Involvement in the World,"
of which Lloyd C. Gardner is General Editor.

ANATOL RAPOPORT

THE BIG

Two

SOVIET–AMERICAN
PERCEPTIONS OF FOREIGN POLICY

PEGASUS · NEW YORK

A Division of The Bobbs-Merrill Company, Inc., Publishers

Grateful acknowledgment is made to the following authors, publishers, and periodicals who have permitted the use of copyrighted material in this book:

Commentary (copyright © 1969 by the American Jewish Committee) and
    H. Stuart Hughes, for quotations from "The Second Year of the Cold War."
Doubleday & Company, for the extract of the Rosenberg espionage trial documents, from *Invitation to an Inquest,* by Walter and Miriam Schneir.
Herbert Feis and Princeton University Press, for excerpts from *Between War
    and Peace.*
Gabriel Kolko for material from *The Roots of American Empire* (Beacon Press)
    and *The Politics of War* (Random House).
Greenleaf Classics, for the excerpts from *Report on U.S. Senate Hearings: The
    Truth About Vietnam,* Edited by Earl Kemp and Frank Robinson.
George F. Kennan and *Foreign Affairs* for the quotations from "The Sources of
    Soviet Conduct," by Mr. "X."
Frederick A. Praeger, Inc., and the author, for quotations from *Expansion and
    Co-Existence,* by Adam Ulam.
Walter Lippman and Atlantic-Little, Brown and Company, for material from
    U.S. Foreign Policy: Shield of the Republic (copyright © 1943 by Walter
    Lippmann).

To Claire Adler

CONTENTS

CHAPTER 1

The Power of Life and Death

Most of the older states evolved. The United States of America and the Union of Soviet Socialist Republics were declared into existence, each by a group of men. Each group had definite ideas about the nature of the state they were creating. In each case the ideas were rooted in a certain philosophy of society and, in the case of the Bolsheviks who created the Soviet State, also in a philosophy of history.

The Founding Fathers of the United States were inspired by the political ideas originating in England and France in the seventeenth and eighteenth centuries. The main theme of these ideas was that a society is a covenant entered into by individuals who "are created equal and endowed with certain . . . rights." Governments, then, are instruments created by individuals to promote certain ends sought by individuals, "life, liberty, and the pursuit of happiness." Governments have a right to exist only as long as they are not "destructive of these ends." In particular, a government that suppresses basic rights of individuals is a tyranny and thereby loses its legitimacy. This concept of legitimacy was in sharp contradiction with an older concept embodied in the so-called divine right of kings, a rationalization of absolute monarchy.

An absolute monarch had the power of life and death over his subjects, and this power was considered to be "natural," because it emanated from God who was Himself an absolute monarch. To the Founding Fathers, it was unthinkable that a government founded on the principles that they carefully spelled out, much less *individuals* in that government, would ever have the power of life and death over the citizenry.

The Bolsheviks were inspired by ideas originating in German philosophy, particularly those of G. W. F. Hegel, later developed by Karl Marx. These ideas stemmed from an evolutionary theory of human society and led to an entirely different conception of government, more properly of the state. The point of departure in this view is not the individual, born "free and equal," but society. Human societies arose in the process of cooperation between men, necessitated by the conditions of human existence. At first no governments were needed to enforce cooperation. The need for government arose as a consequence of advancing technology and the attendant division of labor. It was then that men, engaged in differentiated tasks, entered into certain social relations with each other. These relations were determined by particular modes of production characteristic of various stages of technology. Eventually these relations became exploitative and societies were stratified into classes; for example, freemen and slaves, patricians and plebeians, lords and serfs. Governments arose not as a consequence of explicit covenants between "free individuals" but as institutions by means of which the dominant or exploiting classes kept the exploited classes in subjugation.

Forms of exploitation changed with the modes of production. At one stage the exploited class were the slaves, at another bondsmen, at another wage laborers. However, with the introduction of the industrial mode of production, an end of the exploitative systems could be foreseen. It was predicted that the exploited class of the capitalist system (the industrial workers) would seize political power and by socializing the means of production would eliminate the *basis* of exploitation. Thereby the state would lose its function (for want of an exploited class) and would "wither away." Then and only then would men become really free and masters of their own historical destiny.

The Bolsheviks viewed tyranny as a consequence of an exploitative economic system of which political systems were only derivatives. Consequently they did not view the "dictatorship of the proletariat," envisaged as a transition period between capitalism and socialism, as a form of tyranny but only as a temporary instrument to be used in organizing the new nonexploitative social order. They could not imagine that this interim government, entrusted with the task of transforming society into a humane one, much less that individuals in this government, would ever wield the power of life and death over the citizenry.

Today both Americans and Russians are living under governments that have absolute power of life and death over them. In the U.S.S.R. this power was for a time actually wielded arbitrarily and massively by one man who had at his disposal a vast organization functioning like Murder, Inc. However, I am not referring to this overt form of social pathology. I am referring to another form of it in both the Soviet Union and the United States, namely the absolute power of life and death invested in the few individuals at the controls of the vast military machines, which, once set in motion, can obliterate hundreds of millions of lives in a few hours.

There is no appeal against this suspended sentence of death. The sentence was not pronounced by any court and does not constitute punishment for any crime. Nevertheless it hangs over everyone. Moreover, this power of life and death over millions in the hands of a few individuals is considered to be "natural," as the divine right of kings was once viewed. Americans are quick to point out many despotic features of the Soviet regime, and Communist theoreticians go to great lengths to expose the dictatorial features of monopoly capitalism. It does not occur to many, however, to brand as tyranny the absolute power of life and death in the hands of the few who can, by just pronouncing a few words, destroy entire populations. The reason is not far to seek. To each population only the *other* machine of total destruction appears as a threat. Their own machine appears as a *protection* against the threat. This way of thinking is a holdover from past history. There was a time when the security of a nation could be said to depend on the efficacy of its armed might. That was the time of marching armies and fixed fortresses, of declared wars, and of mobilized national effort "in defense of the country."

The meaning of war has completely changed, but the perceptions of war have by and large remained the same. New, completely unprecedented situations are fitted into old frameworks of thought. For example, the power to declare war is vested by the United States Constitution in Congress; command over the United States armed forces is vested in the President. The former is the power to *define* a situation as war; the latter is the power to *conduct* war. Traditionally, definition of the situation came before action, and so it was assumed that the President could conduct a war only when the state of war was already defined by Congress. Now, *acts* of war define a state of war: the power to "define" a situation as a state of war by a declaration has lost all meaning. Nevertheless the President can still order acts of war. Therefore the power "to make war" has been in effect usurped by the Presidency.

In former times this sort of usurpation of power might have led to impeachment. In our day it appears to most as an inevitable consequence of "the international situation" or, better said, it does not appear as an usurpation of power except to few. It is therefore pointless to apply legalistic arguments to the effect that the political system of the United States has lost all resemblance to the system envisaged by the founders of the republic. There is no escaping the conclusion that a political system reflects the *de facto* rather than the *de jure* power relations of a society. The constitutional definitions of these relations may or may not reflect the actual ones. In any case, reassertions or redefinitions of power relations are not likely to change their basic character.

One reason why the absolute power of life and death in the hands of the President (and of his counterpart in the Soviet Union) is not generally perceived as such is because it is assumed that its use will not be governed by whim. The implication is that the issue is not absolute power as such but its arbitrary use. But what is whim? What we call whim is an apparently accidentally triggered psychological impulse. Yet, whether we view an impulse as triggered "accidentally" or not depends on the state of our knowledge. If we are ignorant of the chain of events culminating in the impulse, we may attribute the resulting action to "whim" when it may in fact be consequential; or we may view it as "rational" when it may really be an impulsive reaction. Executions ordered by absolute rulers may seem to us to have been governed by whim, but to the rulers and their advisers they doubtless appeared to be governed by "reasons of state." The genocidal actions of recent times have been rationalized in a similar manner: the inmates of Auschwitz and Treblinka were killed in order to solve what appeared to the leaders of Germany an otherwise insoluble problem, namely the removal of what was thought to be a mortal threat to the Aryan race; the inhabitants of Hiroshima and Nagasaki were killed (it was said) to save American lives, or, as some maintained later, in order to demonstrate to the Russians the extent of American military might. During 1938 the number of executions in the Soviet Union reached several thousand daily. Depending on one's anchorage of assumptions, these mass killings may appear as manifestations of homicidal mania or as a political necessity.

We know that a nuclear war can be initiated once the perceptions of events by people empowered to set the war machine in motion assume certain patterns. There is no doubt that, once these patterns are formed, the actions undertaken will appear as a political necessity to the President (or his opposite number), to their associates, and perhaps even to the majority of the populations to be exterminated. To the extent, however, that we do not know whether the triggering patterns will in fact form, we *must* attribute their formation to "accident," and so recognize the situation as governed by whim, that is, as a psychological accident. For instance, whether a nuclear war between the United States and the Soviet Union was to occur in October 1962 depended on what patterns formed in the brains of John F. Kennedy (and his advisers) and of Nikita S. Khrushchev (and his advisers). The rest of us had nothing, *but absolutely* nothing, to say in this matter. Thus all the arguments to the effect that John F. Kennedy was elected by secret ballot or that Nikita S. Khrushchev was representing the interests of the toiling masses have no bearing whatsoever on the question of whether these men and their associates possessed absolute power of life and death over the populations of the United States, the Soviet Union, and many other countries. They did. And their successors do. Similarly, all arguments to the effect that this power is wielded with full awareness of the awesome responsibility that it entails are irrelevant to the question whether the use of this power depends on whim. It does. The chain of events leading to the "decision" originates (if we pursue the analysis far enough) in a "psychological accident."

It stands to reason that the danger of an explosion (to which the outbreak of a nuclear war can be likened) resides not in the triggering mechanism, like a carelessly tossed match, but in the mass of explosives. Precautions about throwing matches will not remove the danger. It takes only one such toss; and as long as the risk is not reduced to zero, the explosion will *certainly* occur sooner or later. During the Cuban missile crisis, estimates of the "probability of nuclear war" among the participants in the decisions ranged between one-third and one-half. There is, of course, no way of checking these figures against the "real probability." There is, in fact, no way of determining the "real probability" of a unique event. At any rate, these "probabilities," however estimated, are of no consequence to the fundamental situation. As long as the nuclear arsenals exist, our lives depend on what happens in the brains of a few individuals.

The macabre absurdity of the situation has been pointed out so frequently that it is embarrassing to call attention to it, like repeating what everyone knows. Besides, although the "dangers of the nuclear age" are universally and piously recognized, recommendations directed at removing the danger simply and straightforwardly, by dismantling the machines of total destruction, are of no avail. People empowered to make decisions of this sort are governed by perceptions which make such recommendations appear as products of wishful thinking and the arguments in favor of them as hopelessly naive. Attempts to change these perceptions of the rulers are likewise doomed to failure. A radical change of perceptions involves the abandonment of accustomed frameworks of thought, and this task is almost impossible for most people—especially those involved in decisions and action rather than in conceptual analysis.

It must be kept in mind, however, that power can be exercised by a few individuals over the many only when perceptions are shared. This is especially true of modern "democracies" where "consent of the governed" is still a reality, however disparate the interests of the rulers and those of the ruled may have become. Clearly, the American people at least have *de jure* power to change the policies of their government. That they do not have *de facto* power to do this is a consequence of the fact that most of them share the perceptions of their rulers: what the rulers perceive as necessary or impossible, the ruled perceive likewise. This is especially true in matters related to foreign policy, because in these matters the image of the government as the protector of the whole nation rather than of special interests is most firmly imbedded. Since 1965, however, it is no longer true that "politics stops at the water's edge" in the United States. Not since the Civil War has the United States been torn by strife as it is today on issues of foreign policy. I believe that the more visible and violent internal racial strife is a by-product of the other, because it was the costs of the Vietnam war effort that led to the scuttling of the measures already undertaken to prevent the outbreak of domestic racial strife.

We shall examine the events that have brought into being the present threats to man and his works. These are events that mark the history of the relations between the two nuclear superpowers, particularly from the time when they found themselves the only major military powers emerging from World War II. Our emphasis, however, will not be so much on the events themselves (these have already been described in great detail by historians and experts on international relations) but on the *perceptions* of those events. In order to make sense of these perceptions, we shall have to go somewhat afield of our subject. In particular, we shall have to examine older perceptions of foreign policy prevailing in the two countries, out of which the present perceptions have grown. And in order to understand *these*, we shall have to place the subject in even broader perspective. Thus, in the next chapter, I shall attempt to define some broad types of conceptual frameworks governing thinking about international relations in the hope of shedding some light on the way U.S. and Soviet leaders think about them. In Chapters 3 and 4 I shall take an excursion into history to trace the origins of a particular conception of international relations (the "realist") which has played a prominent role in the development of Soviet-American relations.

In citing events I have relied heavily on scholars who have reconstructed them from primary sources. I have therefore contributed nothing to the factual aspect of the subject. I hope I have contributed to a better understanding of the situation in which we find ourselves, always a prerequisite of effective action.

CHAPTER 2

Conceptions of
International Relations

In traditional studies of international relations, nations or states are pictured as actors with specific needs, desires, goals, rights, and claims. Relations among these actors revolve around "issues." Such studies state, for instance, that, in the nineteenth century, Russia wanted to control the Dardanelles; the United States wanted to keep the continental powers out of the Western Hemisphere; Germany wanted to build and control a railway from Berlin to Baghdad; and so on. "International relations," according to this conception, is an account of how states or their leaders conducted their diplomacy and military strategy in pursuit of these "wants." The underlying assumption was that foreign policies were designed and modified consciously and deliberately by statesmen to satisfy specific needs of a specific state at a specific time.

Related to this traditional approach is the "realist" view (so designated by its adherents). In that model, diplomilitary strategy is also consciously and deliberately designed, but, strictly speaking, there are no specific issues. Each state simply seeks to preserve its power against the encroachments of other states, or to extend it at the expense of other states. If by an "issue" we mean something that can be settled, then this struggle for power is not really an issue.

Note that the realist view does not invalidate or ignore the classical or traditional approach. It is rather a particular generalization of it. One can examine the intercourse among a group

of states in a given time period and arrive at a conclusion that
the common denominator of all the specific issues that governed
their policies was the pursuit of power. Or one can start with
the assumption that states pursue only one goal, namely power,
and, in the light of this assumption, examine all the specific issues that arise in the intercourse among states.

The realist position is not the only one consistent with the
traditional approach. One can avoid making the assumption that
issues are merely manifestations of a struggle for power. Instead
one can assume that each issue is important in its own right and
that conflicts among states stem from particular disputes. One
could then come to a conclusion (or at least a conjecture) that if
some machinery were available for settling disputes (e.g., a
World Court or the like) conflicts among states could be resolved or kept within bounds.

Another conception of international relations puts *ideologies*
at the center of interest. In this view, not states but portions of
humanity—carriers of different religions, philosophies, or
outlooks—are in conflict. The one all-important issue then is:
"Which way of life (religion, social system) shall prevail?" States,
in this view, are institutional means of conducting the conflict.
Again, it is not necessary to discard or ignore the first two approaches in order to subscribe to the ideological conception of
international relations. The difference is only a matter of emphasis. The ideologist can, and usually does, consider the struggle for power in its own right as well as the details of diplomatic strategy. However, in the ideological model, the designers
of policies no longer appear as "free" as in the traditional or
realist models. The range of their policies is limited by their
ideologies. For example, realists criticize some aspects of U.S.
foreign policy on the ground that, in it, strategic considerations
are subordinated to ideological or moralistic ones, and, as a
consequence, certain options are foreclosed. Specifically, the
escalation of the war in Vietnam has been criticized by many
political analysts of the realist persuasion on the grounds that it
was dictated by ideological rather than sound strategic considerations; in other words, that it was a wrong war at a wrong time.

Some see an ideologically determined component in Soviet
foreign policy. They argue that some options are foreclosed to

the Russians. Thus, it might have been in Russia's national interest to come to terms with the United States, to participate in
the Baruch or the Marshall Plans, to "behave" in the United
Nations, or to allow Western-type regimes to be established in
Eastern Europe. However, it is argued, it was impossible for the
Russians to pursue such courses, even with the view of using the
reduction of tensions to build up strength for a future power
confrontation. The reason advanced why the Russians could not
pursue an accommodation policy with the West was that they
were ideologically fixated on the irreconcilable struggle between
two abstractions, socialism and capitalism, and so viewed all
proposals emanating from the West (even those that could be
taken advantage of) as traps to be avoided at all costs.

Pushed to the extreme, the ideological conception of international relations becomes the crude image of an apocalyptic
struggle between Good and Evil, found in the Soviet diatribes
against the West and in the clichés of American crusading
anti-Communists.

At least two different conclusions can be drawn from the
ideological model of international relations. One conclusion is
that the struggle between incompatible ideologies must end in a
triumph of one "world order" over the other. Another possible
conclusion is that the global conflict could be resolved by "ideological disarmament," by an insight on the part of each side into
the genesis of the other's ideology, a recognition of its legitimacy within its own sphere, and a cultivation of attitudes of
mutual tolerance. Needless to say, such a conclusion is of little
relevance to, say, the pure realist view, where not ideological
commitments but a struggle for power is assumed to underlie
international conflict.

Finally, there is a so-called *systemic* view of international relations. An example is found in the theories of Lewis F. Richardson. Richardson was a British meteorologist who devoted some
thirty years to an attempt to construct a mathematical theory of
international relations. The best known of his writings relate to
the study of arms races.[1] His point of departure was Thucydides'
observation that the Peloponnesian War (Sparta vs. Athens) was
a result of an escalation of mutual fear. Sparta suspected aggressive intentions on the part of Athens, and vice versa. As each

took measures to protect itself against the other, each confirmed the other's suspicions, since the measures, even if they were purely defensive in intent, were interpreted as preparations to attack.

Richardson applied this model to a study of the arms race between the Allies (Russia, France, and England) and the Central Powers (Germany and Austro-Hungary). He found that the growth of the arms budgets of the two blocs could be accurately fitted by a solution of a pair of differential equations. The equations themselves were statements in mathematical language of what Thucydides said in plain language: the level of armaments of one side stimulated an increase of armaments by the other.

The advantage of a mathematical model is that it enables the investigator to test his theory by examining quantitative relations (a much more rigorous test than a comparison between the predictions of a theory and grossly perceived events). Another, perhaps more significant, advantage of a mathematical theory is that it sometimes leads to unforeseen conclusions. Richardson's model led to the conclusion that an "equilibrium" in an arms race is unlikely. Conceivably the inhibiting factors in an arms race (e.g., costs) might lead to a stabilization. Whether or not this happens, however, depends on the parameters of the mutually stimulating and self-inhibiting systems described by Richardson's equations. Having estimated these parameters in the case of the arms race of 1909–1914, Richardson showed that the system was unstable. The process *had* to escalate in one direction or the other: either toward an "explosion," as Richardson interpreted the outbreak of World War I, or, on the contrary, toward disarmament. The actual course would depend on the initial conditions relating to the armament levels at some point in time and on the amount of "cooperation" existing (which Richardson estimated by the volume of interbloc trade). It turned out that the conditions at the start of the race determined its course in the "positive" direction, that is, toward war.

Richardson's systemic model of "international relations" is interesting not because it is a faithful model (it is too crude for that) and not because it fathoms the "true nature" of international relations (it is too limited for that). The model is interesting because it adds to the theory of internation conflict another dimension, usually neglected in the other models. In the systemic view, neither the strategic calculations of statesmen nor the immediate "causes" of conflict (the "issues") play any part. The international system becomes a system in the physicist's sense, a portion of the world governed by certain laws, like a mechanical, a thermodynamic, or an electromagnetic system. The events are propelled not by wills of conscious individuals but by the dynamic properties of the system itself. This does not mean, of course, that either the rationality or the "free will" of statesmen, military leaders, and so on, is necessarily denied. The decision makers may have choices, and they may make them in accordance with rational principles; but the system is simply too massive to be affected by these individual decisions. The decisions sum into a grand "resultant force" whose magnitude and direction derive from the nature of the system and from its interaction with other systems rather than from the goals pursued by the decision makers. In a somewhat similar way, a molecule of a gas moves in accordance with the impulses it receives individually, but the entire gas behaves according to the gross laws of thermodynamics, wherein the paths of individual molecules are "washed out."

Note that the systemic concept of international relations may also lead to the "balance of power" solution of international conflict. In this version, wars are consequences of disturbed balance, and the surest (perhaps the only) insurance against war is the preservation of a "balance of power" among the states. In the light of Richardson's theoretical results, it would appear that the stability of a "balanced" system depends on the magnitude of certain parameters. Therefore, in order to implement the balance of power, measures must be taken to keep these parameters within a safe range (if this is possible).

The particular context chosen by Richardson may or may not be a relevant one. The systemic point of view, however, deserves to be seriously examined with regard to international relations.

Another good example of the systemic view is Lenin's theory of imperialism, a global application of Marx's theory of capitalist dynamics. According to this theory, capitalist economies must expand because of diminishing rates of return on capital

investment. In the search for new markets, sources of raw materials, and cheap labor, capitalists of industrialized countries
carve out colonies and spheres of influence in the underdeveloped world. Since, according to Lenin's theory, states are instruments for implementing the interests of ruling classes, the states,
backing different groups of capitalists, come into conflict. Here,
then, the roots of war between capitalist states are to be sought:
not in the intrigues and machinations of diplomats, not in a
struggle between ideologies (all capitalists subscribe essentially
to the same ideology), but in the dynamics of capitalist economics. From this formulation one can deduce that, in order to abolish wars, one must abolish capitalism.

Needless to say, most studies of international relations reflect
mixtures of these various approaches. This is especially true in
recent writings, since, to a serious observer of world politics, it
must now be clear that all of the factors mentioned play some
part. The struggle for power among sovereign states is too obvious to be missed. Specific issues and clashing ideologies provide contexts for the struggle. Military technology is propelled
by its own dynamics and creates problems for the makers of foreign policies. So does global economics.

One observes, however, that the traditional and the realist
views still dominate most of the writings of U.S. and Western
academic experts on international relations. This is not surprising, since the materials on which the writings are based are
largely records of diplomatic exchanges, policy papers, and the
like. The realist generalization is practically forced upon anyone
who views these sources as the basic data of political and military history.

Soviet writings, of course, adhere to the Leninist theory of
imperialism, essentially a systemic view. They make a good sup-
plement to the views of Western experts. The latter tend to neglect the economic underpinnings of international conflicts, especially as they are reflected in the present conflict between the
United States and the Soviet Union.

To forestall misunderstanding, a word should be said about
the numerous approving references by Soviet military authors to
the ideas of Karl von Clausewitz, the foremost exponent of the
realist conception of international relations. These references

can be all traced to Lenin's positive evaluation of Clausewitz's philosophy of war.[2] One ought not conclude on that account that Soviet theories of international relations are rooted in Clausewitzian conceptions, which remain, after all, incompatible with Marxist-Leninist philosophy. Agreement with Clausewitz on the part of Soviet authors reflects rather an insistence on the political genesis of war (one of Clausewitz's fundamental assumptions) as well as a categorical rejection of so-called "idealist" conceptions, such as that war stems from the pugnacity of human nature, or that it is nature's instrument for insuring the survival of the fittest.

On the other hand, the incompatibility of Clausewitzian and Marxist conceptions did not prevent Soviet leaders, least of all Stalin, from conducting Soviet foreign policy in realist style, as distinct from describing it in those terms.[3]

Emphasis on arms races and on the autonomous role of the military establishments is left to mavericks like Richardson and, in America, to the sharp critics of U.S. foreign policy. There are no publicly visible opposite numbers of these critics in the Soviet Union. However, other variants of the systemic approach, involving analyses of global economics, content analysis of mass media, and the like, are receiving increasing attention in the United States.

CHAPTER 3

The Legacy Of Clausewitz

American perceptions of the relations between the United States and the Soviet Union have undergone a steady shift from the ideological view to the realist one. The shift is pictured by some writers[1] as a maturation process reflecting a realization on the part of the United States leaders of the proper role of a great power. It will serve our purpose to see how the realist view of international relations became dominant in world politics.

Some historians tell us that the political history of Europe begins at the close of the Thirty Years' War in 1648. It was then that the "community of sovereign states" became clearly discernible. In common parlance, a community is an aggregate of people who are aware of each other as persons and who share a common fate and a set of common values. The European political system that emerged from the Thirty Years' War had some aspects of a community if we take its members to be the assorted monarchs, princes, and princelings, each with a delineated domain. They were all aware of each other. The common values that they shared concerned, first of all, the undisputed sovereignty of each in his own realm and, second, the recognition that each was justified in his efforts both to protect this sovereignty against encroachments by others and to try to extend this sovereignty by encroaching on that of others.

That there is no necessary contradiction in this conception of a "community" is evidenced by the existence of a "business

community," say in the United States. The right of individual
firms to compete with each other not only is recognized by the
"community" but is even held to be indispensable for its existence. The result of the competition is often analogous to the
encroachment on "sovereignty," as, for instance, when one firm
conquers a portion of another's market. Formally instituted or
tacitly assumed "rules of fair competition" may impose bounds
on the extent of such encroachments, as when the American
competitive system is presumably protected by antitrust laws.
The efficacy of such laws or unwritten rules of "fair competition" does not concern us here. The important thing is that the
concept of "fair competition" does exist in the business community. A similar concept underlay the European "community of
states."

This concept was not prominent in the politics of Europe
before 1648. Throughout the Middle Ages, political thought in
Europe was dominated by the idea of restoring the Roman Em-
pire or of finding its successor. In fact, until 1453, the "Roman
Empire" had a formal existence: the eastern portion based on
Byzantium. After the capture of Constantinople by the Turks,
the Grand Duke of Moscow declared himself "emperor" (czar =
Caesar) with the dictum: "The First Rome was in Rome, the
Second in Constantinople, the Third is in Moscow, and there
will be no Fourth."

In the West, the "Holy Roman Empire of the German Nation" lived on at least as a concept, occasionally emerging into a
semblance of political reality. From our historical perspective
we see the so-called "religious wars" of the sixteenth and seventeenth centuries as political wars dominated by the clash of the
concept of empire with that of a community of sovereign states,
the religious issues being the ideological expression of that
conflict. Adherents of the empire were mostly Catholics at-
tempting to suppress the newly emergent independent realms of
those princes who used the Reformation to break away from
clerical authority. That the religious lines were not sharply
drawn is evidenced by France's support of the Protestant cause
in the Thirty Years' War. Although Catholic, France was the
strongest sovereign state on the continent and had an understandable vested interest in sovereignty.

The reason why 1648 is chosen (I think justifiably) as a turning point in the history of European international relations is that thereafter the character of the power struggle changed. Wars became *fractionated*. Alliances and blocs continued to be formed, but for the most part on an *ad hoc* basis. Essentially, the individual states became the competitors, and from the competition the concept of the sovereign *state* (later of the nation) and of the community of states arose.

Military historians sometimes refer to the period of 1648–1792 as the epoch of "cabinet wars" or "dynastic wars." Both terms are fairly descriptive of the international relations of the time. The states that emerged from the Thirty Years' War were absolute or near-absolute monarchies. Consequently, policy was guided almost exclusively by the perceived personal interests of ruling princes. These interests were not unlike those of competing modern business firms: to maintain viability (solvency), to increase it, if possible, and to reap the benefits of possession. What profit is to the modern commercial firm, "power" was to the prince.

Competition manifested itself in wars. Wars were fought to secure the domains already in possession and to enlarge them if possible. Since claims to territories were frequently supported by geneological considerations, the *casus belli* was frequently a dynastic one: Who is the "legitimate" ruler or successor?

To the extent that the success of a particular war depended on the alignment of forces (i.e., coalitions) and on the strategic considerations of the moment, decisions to wage war had to be based on calculations of contingencies ("What will Saxony do? Can we expect the neutrality of Savoy?"). These calculations were made in the cabinets of the princes, somewhat as decisions of business policy are made in the meeting rooms of business executives.

It must be kept in mind that the highly trained, gaudily dressed armies of the eighteenth century were very expensive instruments and could not be easily replaced if lost. A prince without an army was like a bankrupt businessman. For this reason, campaigns were often conducted so as to avoid pitched battles. Capitulation in the face of defeat was not a disgrace. Indeed, since wars were fought for limited, sometimes trivial objectives, capitulation was a far more desirable conclusion to a war than "fighting to the last man." The former course involved no more than certain political concessions. The latter course would deprive the loser of his well-nigh irreplaceable army.

Frequently the peace treaty formula was *status quo ante bellum*. No state risked annihilation as a result of losing a war. The rulers were well aware that the enemies of today could be the allies of tomorrow. There was then a community of interest among the competing princes, namely the preservation of the system. We do not know to what extent they were explicitly aware of this community of interests. However, its existence became manifest in the idea of the "balance of power," a determination to conduct the game in such a way as to prevent the concentration of power in any state or combination of states such that would enable it (or them) to intimidate the rest. The continuation of the system was thought to depend on the preservation of this balance of power. As for the maintenance of the system itself, it was identified with the preservation of order, the conservative ideal. It stands to reason that the princes and their supporting aristocracies were conservative, as is any privileged class. They were well adjusted to the system under which they lived.

The common people of Europe at that time were predomi nantly peasants. Their lives went on practically untouched by the machinations in the chancelleries, by wars and their outcomes. Occasionally an army along its line of march damaged the lives of the people who were in the way. The damage was due largely to the parasitic character of armies in general, not to the attitudes of a particular army toward the local population. It was, therefore, of little importance whether the army was "friendly" or "hostile." Often the people did not even know which it was. Nor did the outcome of a war have much effect on civilian populations. Even if a province passed from the possession of one prince to that of another, it made little difference in the lives of the inhabitants.

But the last decade of the eighteenth century witnessed events that resulted in a new concept of war, and consequently in a new kind of international relations. The ideas that came to dominate the last quarter of the eighteenth century had germinated during the so-called Enlightenment, mostly in France and in England. These ideas challenged the prevailing religious and social dogmas. They led to the overthrow of belief as the foundation of knowledge and of privilege based on birth as the foundation of social order. The rapidly accelerating growth of industry, trade, travel, and science brought people who lived by these activities into prominence and eventually to political power. The emergence of the middle classes to power seems "natural" in historical prospective, but, at the time, the men at the top of the old social pyramid perceived events as a dissolution of "natural" order and a descent into social chaos. They reacted with violence and so instigated violence in the revolutionary class and its allies.

It was against such a backdrop that the regicide of Louis XVI in 1793 was a signal for intervention by monarchs intent on snuffing out the danger to the established social order. Prussia invaded France. To their astonishment, the Prussians were soundly beaten. To understand why this happened helps to understand the subsequent development of the European politicomilitary system.

The eighteenth century battle was an extension of parade ground exercises. The outcome of a battle frequently depended on the successful execution of standard maneuvers. The successful execution of a maneuver depended, in turn, on the degree to which the men had been trained. Prussian soldiers were the best trained in Europe. By far the most important aspect of this training was the elimination from the soldier's psychological makeup of everything but the impulse to obey the shouted command. This is not easy to achieve. We know, however, that the suppression of self-preserving reactions can be effected in various ways. In the Prussian army, it was accomplished by terror. Frederick II is especially clear on this point.

"If a soldier," he wrote, "during an action looks about as if to flee, or so much as sets a foot outside the line, the non-commissioned officer standing behind him will run him through with his bayonet."[2]

The eighteenth century soldier was steadfast. What he lacked was a self-generated motivation to fight. He had nothing to fight for, nor was he ever told that he had anything to fight for. In-

deed, what could he be told? The concept of patriotism simply
did not exist in eighteenth century continental Europe, when
states were not nations, properly speaking, but fiefdoms.

The French Revolution changed all that. The French soldier
of the Revolutionary Army (later the Grande Armée) fought at
first to save the Revolution, later for the glory of France. Now,
it is not certain whether the different psychological makeup of
the French soldier (compared with that of the Prussian or the
Austrian) would in itself have made the decisive difference. If
belief in what one is fighting for makes for bravery in battle, so
does the absolute inhibition to disobey a command. The Prussian
soldiers did not often break ranks and run. However, another
factor entered the picture which, perhaps, was decisive. The
positively motivated French fighting men could apply tactics
which the automata of the Prussian and Austrian armies could
not. As has been said, the blindly obedient eighteenth century
soldier was taught to obey the voice of command. Without the
voice of command he could do nothing. For this reason the bat-
talions of the eighteenth century had to fight in closely packed
ranks. Also, probably for this reason, they wore bright
uniforms—to be immediately detected by their own officers in
case they did try to leave their posts. The soldiers, wrote Frederick II, "must fear their officers more than any danger."[3] The
French were not under that compulsion. They developed tactics
incomparably more flexible than the parade ground tactics of
the Princes' armies. Against the tirailleurs, the close-order drill
battalion could do next to nothing.

There was yet another reason why the armies of the monarchies were no match for the French. As has been said, they were
standing armies, highly trained and irreplaceable. The French
army was an expendable "citizen" army, limited in size only by
the male population of France. Aware that his own manpower
was virtually inexhaustible, Napoleon had no worries about the
costs of engagements and so attacked with a fury unknown in
the eighteenth century. He revolutionized the use of artillery,
promoting it to a prominence on a par with the infantry and the
cavalry. The bloodiness of Napoleonic battles testified to the
tremendous advance in the "art of war."

The sudden change in the conduct of warfare undertaken by

one power (France) made shambles of the eighteenth century system based on the "balance of power." Napoleon was not just another prince, taking opportunities as they came. He was, to begin with, no prince. Second, his aim was to organize all of Europe into a new political entity under the domination of France. He had himself crowned emperor and emphasized the source of new "legitimacy" by taking the crown from the hands of Pope Pius VI and putting it on his own head. Thereby he thought he introduced a new political era: another resurrection of the Empire, but now a secular one, dominated by the bourgeoisie, especially, of course, the French bourgeoisie.

There was no military establishment in Europe able to stop Napoleon's mass armies. A counterforce came from two quarters *outside* the old continental establishment. One was England, already primarily a bourgeois nation, which saw the threat to its own source of power, namely trade. (Napoleon's "continental system" could have excluded England's business interests from the continent.) England had no army to speak of, but she had a navy for which the French navy was no match. Another counterforce came from an altogether unexpected quarter. The very element that imbued the French army with its tremendous energy (a positive motivation of the individual soldier to fight) began to inspire *popular* resistance against the French, first in Spain, then in Russia. The total war, reintroduced for the first time since the Thirty Years' War by Napoleon, now made the French armies appear as "foreign invaders" and stimulated in the people of invaded countries the same feelings of patriotism that had made the French invading armies invincible. No longer was war simply a contest between professionals, conducted like a sport or a chess tournament according to the rules of the profession. There was now an issue, which the populations of the invaded countries saw affecting their lives. Nationalism was born.

The foremost military thinker of the time, Karl von Clausewitz, recognized the significance of this new factor in the politicomilitary evolution of Europe. In his magnum opus, *On War,* Clausewitz begins his analysis by an attempt to reveal the "true nature of war." He states in effect what war *would* be if it were not influenced by "extraneous factors," such as the time it takes to execute intended acts, imperfect knowledge of the state of affairs, human frailty, indecision, and so on. He lumped all these factors under the term "friction," an obvious allusion to the factors that conceal from superficial observation the underlying fundamental laws of motion.

Clausewitz's conception of war is a consequence of his definition of war. "War," he wrote, "is an act of violence intended to compel our opponent to fulfill our will."[4]

For Clausewitz, "we" and the "opponent" are states; and the instrument at the disposal of a state, enabling it to impose its will on another state, is the army. Once the army is destroyed or disabled, the state served by that army becomes helpless and must submit to the will of the victorious state. It follows, according to Clausewitz, that war in its "pure" or absolute form would always be a war to the finish, i.e., would end in complete victory of one state over another.

It must be observed in this conception that war-to-the-finish is not to be confused with "total war." The latter is a twentieth century conception in which the slaughter of civilians has become a "natural" ingredient of war. Clausewitz still saw war as a contest exclusively between armed forces, and battles strictly circumscribed in time and place. He did, however, perceive the changed character of war instigated by the French Revolution and the reaction to it, namely the infusion of nationalism into war as a primary motivation for fighting. He believed that this development removed the constraints that had prevented war from unfolding according to its "true nature."

Clausewitz also saw war as an instrument for gaining *political* ends. Whereas the political ends of the eighteenth century were simply the desires or ambitions (often trivial ones) of princes and princelings, nineteenth century (nationalist) wars were instigated by the aspirations of *states,* presumably reflecting the aspirations of their entire populations. Imbedded in the "essence of war," as Clausewitz understood it, was the "essence of the state," which he saw as a fusion of millions of wills into a single will pitted against other such wills. It seemed to Clausewitz that the era of the Napoleonic wars with its colossal toll of casualties (according to the ideas of magnitude prevalent then), with its cataclysmic outcomes (that is, radical changes in political configurations), and with the sudden influx of popular participation revealed the "essence of war."

Clausewitz was passionately devoted to his profession. On one occasion, he wrote to his fiancée:

> My fatherland needs the war [against Napoleon in 1806] and—frankly speaking—only war can bring me to the happy goal. In whichever way I might like to relate my life to the rest of the world, my way takes me always across a great battle field, unless I enter upon it, no permanent happiness can be mine.[5]

And on another:

> The day after tomorrow . . . there will be a great battle, for which the entire Army is longing. I myself look forward to this day with joy as I would to my own wedding day.[6]

We should not ascribe unusual bloodthirstiness to Clausewitz (although, of course, the unconscious sources of his motivations can be subject to conjecture). What we see, rather, is a typical symptom of professional pride, the same sort of pride we observe in a dedicated craftsman, teacher, artist, or scientist. In all these instances, professional activity appears to its practitioner as a rewarding and inspiring way of life: to the craftsman, as the mastery over materials; to the teacher, as molding or stimulating young minds; to the artist, as creation of order and beauty; to the scientist, as discovery of truth. So, to Clausewitz, war appeared as a noble activity, demanding from its practitioners utmost dedication, steadfastness, and courage, and leaving considerable room for magnanimity (according to the notions still prevailing in his day). The bloody aspect of war probably appeared in this view as an inescapable tragic by-product of an intrinsically virtuous endeavor. The essential positive aspect of war appeared as the mortar that binds a country into a nation state. And the nation state appeared to people of Clausewitz's persuasion as the crowning masterpiece in the evolution of human existence. This idea was especially prevalent in nineteenth century Prussia. It is important to see why.

Prussia rose to prominence as a military power in the middle of the eighteenth century as a result of wars waged by King

Frederick II against the Austrian Empire. According to Clausewitz, Frederick's successes stemmed not only from the efficiency of his military machine, in which the "art" of eighteenth century warfare was brought to a pinnacle of perfection, but also from Frederick's presumed insight into the political nature of war. He was guided in his undertakings by meticulous matching of effort expended to the ends to be gained. Presumably Frederick knew that he could not be another Alexander or Gustavus Adolphus, military leaders who conducted "open-ended" campaigns, seemingly without upper bounds. Such unbounded goals became possible only when some new element was introduced into war by *one* power, which, as a consequence of its monopoly of the new element, finds itself in a power vacuum and expands at least for a time without constraint. When this happens, conquerors appear (the Alexanders, the Caesars, the Genghis Khans, etc.). In spite of the presumed superiority of Frederick's military machine, he was not in a position to become a "great conqueror," and, Clausewitz implies, he was quite aware of this and limited his ambitions accordingly. He pushed as far as he could, taking the opportunities that arose. In the setting of the eighteenth century, Frederick did as well as could be expected.

In the 1790s, as we have seen, a new element entered the picture—an army with *élan*, namely the French. In her confrontation with France, Prussia was beaten, at first moderately, finally decisively, as no power had been beaten in the eighteenth century. This happened in the Battles of Jena and Auerstädt (October 14, 1806). Prussia was crushed and absorbed into Napoleon's political system.

In 1812, Napoleon himself was severely beaten, but not on the battlefield. The gigantic battle of that campaign (at Borodino) left him a free access to Moscow. But then something happened unheard of in the eighteenth century: the sovereign of a country whose capital was occupied by the enemy refused to sue for peace. Alexander simply ignored Napoleon's messages. The "conqueror" found himself in an empty city ravaged by fires. No one "recognized" his victory. There was nothing left for Napoleon to do but go back the way he had come. Of the bulk of Napoleon's invading army of 600,000 that crossed the Neman in June 1812, not more than 100,000 recrossed the river in December.

Young Clausewitz was profoundly impressed by this sequence of events. Already immediately following Prussia's defeat in 1806 he had discovered the "new element" (nationalism) that made the French invincible as long as their armies had a monopoly on this new "weapon." From that time on he pressed tirelessly for military reforms in Prussia that would enable that state to incorporate the "new element" into its military establishment. From 1809 on, reforms along the lines advocated by Clausewitz (and by his mentor Scharnhorst) were being carried out. The essential feature of these reforms was the replacement of the professional standing army that had been the "political instrument" of the eighteenth century by a conscripted national army. Naturally everyone could not be a soldier all the time. But the idea that all able-bodied men should be soldiers at some time was made the foundation of European military establishments. The French did not succeed (in fact, they stopped trying) in spreading liberty, equality, and fraternity throughout Europe. They did, however, spread nationalism and were finally defeated by their own "new weapon."

The work of Clausewitz attests to the fact that the Prussians were the quickest to grasp the new principle of military power. This is not surprising. A lesson is learned most firmly when the old way leads to a traumatic failure and the new way to immediate success. And this is what happened in Prussia between 1806 and 1814.

Other European powers were soon to follow Prussia's example, and the nineteenth century system, hailed by Clausewitz, was ushered in.

In some ways, the nineteenth century system (1815-1914) resembled the previous one. Europe was still a "community of states," competing with each other for power and prestige. "Wisdom" in international relations was still embodied in the preservation of the "balance of power." That is to say, the Napoleonic explosion was seen in retrospect as something no one wanted repeated (like the religious wars of the seventeenth century). However, it occurred to no one in power that war itself was an anomaly. War continued to be viewed as a normal phase in the relations among states, a "continuation of policy by other means" in Clausewitz's immortal phrase.

When seen from the perspective of the twentieth century, the nineteenth seems relatively peaceful. Actually, however, it was the Golden Age of militarism. By militarism I refer to a complex of social attitudes that ascribe special importance to military might and to the institutions that maintain it. In the nineteenth century, militarism was highly manifest. Monarchs discarded velvet and ermine and donned military uniforms. Military parades were among the most frequent and popular public spectacles. Officers developed an elaborate code of honor (a mark of especially respected callings). They were now more than professionals, that is, people distinguished by special skills: They were now potential heroes. And the aura of heroism was extended also to the common soldier. Wars and war episodes were now celebrated in poetry (they had rarely been in the immediately preceding centuries). War poetry was now not epic, as in ancient days, but *lyrical*.[7]

It may seem paradoxical at first sight that the nineteenth century, the century of rising democratic ideals and of a steadfast belief in the perfectability of man, should also have been the century in which war was viewed more than ever in the context of glory. On further reflection, however, the militarization of Europe in the nineteenth century was related to its democratization, for the common denominator of militarism and democracy is patriotism, the identification of individual "free" persons with the state as an embodiment of a national community and of national (i.e., popular) ideals. War had become everybody's business. By the 1840s, as literacy became widespread, the horizon of the common man extended beyond his immediate environment. Increasing numbers of people read newspapers. Newspapers discussed national and international affairs preponderantly in the language of statesmen, politicians, diplomats, and generals. The way of thinking of these specialists permeated the population at large. The state with its formulated interests and ambitions became truly a *national* state.

Hegel had projected this development in the 1820s and hailed it as the manifestation of the Absolute. Clausewitz, thinking in more concrete terms, saw the truly national state to be the consequence of the changed character of war.

In Book VI of *On War* is the following remarkable passage:

> A people's War in civilized Europe is a phenomenon of the nineteenth century. It has its advocates and its opponents: the latter either considering it in a political sense as a revolutionary means, a state of anarchy declared lawful, which is as dangerous as a foreign enemy to social order at home; or on military grounds, conceiving that the result is not commensurate with the expenditure of the nation's strength. The first point does not concern us here, for we look upon a People's War merely as a means of fighting, therefore in its connection with the enemy; but with regard to the latter point, we must observe that a People's War in general is to be regarded as a consequence of the outburst which the military element of our day has made through its old formal limits; as an expansion and strengthening of the whole fermentation process which we call War. The requisition system, the immense increase in the size of Armies by means of that system, and the general liability to military service, the employment of militia, are all things which lie in the same direction, if we make the limited military system of former days our starting point; and the *levée en masse*, or arming of the people now lies also in the same direction. If the first named of these new aids to War are the natural and necessary consequences of barriers thrown down; and if they have so enormously increased the power of those who first used them, that the enemy has been carried along in the current, and obliged to adopt them likewise, this will be the case also with People-Wars. . . . If this be so, then the only question is whether this modern intensification of the military element is, upon the whole salutary for the interests of humanity or otherwise,—a question which it would be about as easy to answer as the question of War itself—we leave both to philosophers.[8]

A wealth of meaning resides in that passage, and it will serve us well to probe more deeply into it. First, note that Clausewitz dismisses the political implications of the armed nation, although he must have been well aware of them. The reason for so assuming is that Clausewitz, in advocating far-reaching reforms of Prussia's military system (which included the creation of a citizens' army), had to contend against the opposition of those who viewed the reforms as "creeping democracy," to paraphrase a later version of similar attitudes in another context. Clausewitz's political orientation was probably conservative, which, in his day, meant antidemocratic. Yet his devotion to his profession came first, and so he would accept "democratization" to the extent that it was an "aid to War."

The lesson of the Napoleonic Wars was that people's armies beat professional armies. For the military man this lesson should, Clausewitz thought, decide the issue. Next, Clausewitz viewed war as the prime mover of historical development, in the way that Hegel viewed the Absolute and that Marx was later to view the mode of production. By the phrase "barriers thrown down" Clausewitz means the unfolding of the "true nature of war," which he conceives as the struggle for supremacy of *states*. Obviously Clausewitz did not invent this conception. It was already entrenched in the minds of rulers and statesmen and had begun to pervade the consciousness of populations. Clausewitz merely expressed this idea with greatest clarity and emphasis. Finally, note that Clausewitz leaves to philosophers the question of whether the "People's War," or for that matter war itself, is "salutary for the interests of humanity." Here we have the stance of the professional, strictly circumscribing the scope of discussion to the region of his competence. This attitude will be encountered again later in Chapter 14 when we analyze the military thinking in our own day. Here it suffices to point out that the separation of technical from philosophical questions becomes impossible as soon as the technical questions transcend a certain level of generality. Nor was it possible for Clausewitz. On one or two other occasions, Clausewitz modestly disclaimed competence in "philosophy." However, judging by modern standards, Clausewitz was an exceptionally able philosopher. Probably the philosophical outlook came to him so naturally that he did not know that he was a philosopher. And it is precisely this sort of philosophy—one that is generated not by a deliberate effort to philosophize but by a profound preoccupation with substantive matters—that is likely to have the most pervasive influence. It was so with Clausewitz. His famous maxim "war is the continuation of policy by other means" remains valid for the nature of international relations (as conceived by its practitioners and chief theoreticians) when the words "war" and "policy" are interchanged.

We shall call the system of international relations that

emerged in nineteenth century Europe the *Clausewitzian sys-tem*, on the basis of the following perceptions and assumptions.

1. There exists a community of *sovereign states*—sovereign meaning that their heads or ruling bodies are responsible to no one for their actions.

2. Each state has *interests*. There is no need to inquire into the nature or genesis of such interests; they are self-evident: Each state strives to expand its domain and its influence. This primary striving can be served by realizing intermediate goals, such as capture of strategically important locations or territo-ries, formation of advantageous alliances, improvement of the fighting capabilities of the armies, etc. All of these are but means to an end: the expansion of domain, power, or influence.

3. The interests of every state are normally in conflict with those of every other state. This is a logical consequence of the tacit definition of a state's interest—expansion, since expansion is accomplished at the expense of the domains or of spheres of in-terest of others.

4. Politics (formulation of policy, statesmanship, diplomacy) is the art of bringing about situations that facilitate the pursuit of a state's interests.

5. War is a *normal* phase in the relations between states. War not only may be but ought to be waged if a sober evaluation of options suggests that the interests of a state can be served thereby. Peace should be concluded for similar reasons. Al-though hatred of the enemy is often a significant factor in the efficacy of the armed forces of a state and is, at any rate, a natu-ral concomitant of rivalry among states, it ought not in itself be a sufficient reason for fighting a war. Similarly, although glory that accrues through victories enhances the prestige of the state, and so contributes to the morale of the fighting forces, the pur-suit of glory alone is not a sufficient goal for waging a war. The primary goal of war ought to be always political. All other con-siderations are secondary.

6. At times the interests of two or more states may coincide, particularly when it is to the advantage of each to curtail or to resist the power of a third state or a combination of states. The formation of coalitions or alliances, therefore, is part of the rep-ertoire of acts at the disposal of a state in pursuit of its interests.

As in the use of war and peace, such cooperation is always subservient to the primary interests of a state.

7. The power of a state is embodied in its armed might, that is, in military technology, in the strategic and tactical skills of its commanders, and in the morale of its troops. The entire population able to bear arms contributes to the armed might of a state. Consequently a population imbued with a martial spirit is an important contributory factor to the power of a state.

These principles describe what leading statesmen, military leaders, and writers on international relations have traditionally identified with political realities. And because they acted on the basis of these principles, and instilled them into their successors, the principles were confirmed in practice.

Factors omitted or insufficiently projected in Clausewitz's conception of international relations are the following.

1. *Technology.* Certainly Clausewitz was aware of the tremendous spurt of technical innovation instigated by the scientific discoveries of the eighteenth century and by the industrial revolution. He foresaw the murderous potential of the "weapons of the future." It did not occur to him, however, that eventually the nature of weaponry would erase the meaning of the decisive battle, a key concept in his theory of war. By 1914, the machine gun, and earth works extended over scores of miles, replaced the concentration of armed strength in fortresses and removed the "decisive battle" as an important factor in war. War was turned then into an attrition process, as a result of which the victors lost as much as the vanquished. The costs of war came to exceed the political stakes for which, and only for which, according to Clausewitz, wars were to be fought.

Possibly if Clausewitz had foreseen this development, he might have drawn conclusions consistent with his theory, namely that under these circumstances war must die as an instrument of national policy. But institutions and their rationales tend to persist even when the underlying realities have made them obsolete or meaningless in the original sense. In fact, the persistence of war as an institution eventually led to a *redefinition* of its underlying concepts: pursuit of national interest, victory, etc., so as to bring them into consistency with the continuing institution.

2. *The ambiguity of the notion of "nation state."* States and nationalities were not coextensive in nineteenth century Europe. Consequently the identification of "the people" with the state (the Prussian ideal) was not realizable in many cases. Clausewitz did have a conception of a "war of national liberation" but only in the context of an already existing state. According to Clausewitz, the central government never relinquishes control over the operations and over the political aims of the war. He did not envisage a war of national liberation in which a new state comes into being. Toward the end of the nineteenth century the conception of such a war of national *emergence* gave rise to the idea of a revolutionary war, that is, a war of a people against a "legitimate" government.

3. *Long-term effects of democratization.* The democratization of Europe, that is, the involvement of the populations in politics, contributed not only to the emergence of patriotism, and so of "truly national states," but also to the questioning of the sources of power of any state, regardless of its "legitimacy" even on national grounds.

Eventually these dissonances, coupled with the dogged persistence of the Clausewitzian model in the minds of rulers and of political theorists, led to the dissolution of the Clausewitzian system in Europe.

One example illustrating each of the above points will suffice.

1. The dogma of French military doctrine up to 1914 was the primacy of attack over defense. It was firmly believed that the shock of a massed infantry charge could overwhelm any defensive position, thus winning a decisive battle and, with it, a war. The French officer corps apparently had selected for attention, among the factors contributing to victory cited by Clausewitz, the one that in their opinion marked the superiority of the French army, something called *élan*. It must be recalled that neither in manpower nor in technology (other factors cited by Clausewitz) was France a match for Germany. In the first months of World War I, French infantry troops went into battle wearing their famous scarlet pantaloons. That they were highly visible targets in that attire was no disadvantage if the enemy was going to be overwhelmed by *élan*. These tactics so severely bled the French that in 1917 it looked as if the whole concep-

tual structure based on "patriotism" was going to collapse. At any rate, the idea of national glory was killed in France on the battlefield, precisely where according to Clausewitzian concepts, it was supposed to have derived its nourishment.

2. While the British, French, and later the German empires were expanding overseas, the Austrian empire was expanding into the power vacuum left by the moribund Turkish empire in southeastern Europe. Its internal tensions were thereby aggravated by further diminishing the relative weight of its politically and socially dominant German-speaking and Hungarian-speaking populations. Consequences could not be easily foreseen without taking into account a new factor in European affairs, namely the struggles of subject peoples against "legitimate" governments.

3. Clausewitz served in Russia in 1812[9] and was, as has been said, profoundly impressed by the mobilization of national feeling against the foreign invader. But he did not foresee that eventually forces would develop within Russia directed against its ruling circles, and that the Russian empire could disintegrate under precisely the conditions that, according to his percepts, should have welded it together even more firmly. Yet the czarist rulers of Russia, and even those who replaced them as the provisional government in March 1917, persisted in thinking in terms of "victory" and "national interest." This conceptual inertia led to their demise and, for a time, removed Russia from the "community of states."

We have dealt at some length with the conceptual scheme called the "realist" school of international relations and its historical origins because, as will be shown, it has played a very special role in the relations between the U.S. and the U.S.S.R.

Before World War II neither the United States nor the Soviet Union had been members of the Clausewitzian system of international relations. When they entered into it they found themselves the *only* important members. In a way, the realist mode of thinking about international relations was "rediscovered" by Soviet and American policy makers. In their thinking, then, it appears as a *new* conceptual scheme (with all the attendant vigor) replacing a no longer serviceable one. Especially in the

United States, where within certain limits debate on foreign policy goes on even "within the establishment," one can actually witness the systematic, concerted assault by the realists on the traditional American conception of foreign policy (or what Walter Lippmann called the lack of one). The realist critique introduced internal stresses, reflected in the relations between the two superpowers. In order to understand these stresses and their effects, we must examine the conceptions of international relations that prevailed in the United States and the Soviet Union before these powers found themselves confronting one another on a global scale.

CHAPTER 4

Perceptions of American
and Soviet Foreign Policies

W e have observed that the births of both the United States and the Soviet Union were marked by a proclamation of an ideology, in the one, centered on the idea of liberty, in the other, on the idea of socialism.

In the expression of these ideologies, there was stated in each case an intention to break away from the established international system. Washington's Farewell Address is often popularly (though perhaps not quite accurately) identified with a policy of isolation. The expectations of the Bolshevik leaders were that a world proletarian revolution was imminent, and so there was no question of Soviet Russia's joining the "community of states" as a member with traditional national interests and ambitions. For example, the publication of the secret treaties entered into by the czarist government and the granting of independence to various nationalities within the Russian Empire were instances of a dramatic disavowal of what could be construed as "national interest" in the hitherto accepted sense of the word.

One need not of course resort to ideological explanations of Russia's dropping out of the "community of nations." After defeat in World War I and devastation in the Civil War, Russia simply had no wherewithal to play the international power game.

Similarly, the initial nonparticipation of the United States in the international power game is easily explained by two circumstances. First, there were no rivals on its borders with which to play the game. Second, there was plenty to do to keep Americans otherwise occupied. The continent was virtually empty except for Indian tribes that were no match for people going after land with superior fire power. Accordingly, America's "national interests" in those early decades of her existence were not circumscribed by the national interests of comparable states. There was no need for an intricate foreign policy designed and conducted by specialists in intrigue, as were the foreign policies of European states. The only tasks of American foreign policy were those of eliminating the remnants of European power from the North American continent and, somewhat later, from the entire Western Hemisphere. France and Spain being in decline (France since her defeat by England in 1763, Spain since the seventeenth century), their power in the New World dissipated of its own accord. As for England, it soon became apparent that her interests coincided with those of the United States: briefly, to keep continental powers out of the Western Hemisphere. The militarily desultory War of 1812 may have helped to drive the point home.

The issues of that war are still in dispute. Reginald Horsman argues that the United States declared war in an attempt to coerce Britian into abandoning her maritime policy, which, in turn, was a measure of self-defense in Britain's war against Napoleon.[1] In this interpretation, Britain, waging her own struggle for survival, was forced to interfere with U.S.-French trade; while the United States was responding to the pressure of her own producers, "who looked longingly at the export market [and] were suffering a commercial depression in the years before 1812."[2] Horsman concedes that the idea of conquering Canada had been present already in 1807 but only as a means of waging war, not as a reason for instigating it.

Amaury de Riencourt, on the other hand, interprets the War of 1812 as the first manifestation of the imperialist ambitions of the new republic.[3] He argues that the American frontiersman wanted not merely more land but more wooded land (he needed lumber for building and fencing) of which there was an abundance in Indiana and in Upper Canada. The main obstacles were the Indians and the British, who were suspected of incensing the Indians against the settlers. Thus in de Riencourt's interpretation, the expansion of a land empire was a primary motivation for the first international war fought by the United States.

There is, of course, no way of deciding which of the so-called "causes" was decisive or primary. For example, there is no way of putting to a test Horsman's conclusion: "Had there been no war with France, there would have been no Orders in Council, no impressment, and, in all probability, no War of 1812."[4] However, we do have partial evidence against this conclusion. The United States declared war on Britain two days after an announcement was made that the Orders would be withdrawn. Of course, the slowness of communication in those days makes it possible to conclude that Britain's concession came "too late." Yet the war went on for two and a half years. It is difficult to dismiss the conjecture that there must have been other primary reasons for waging the war besides the "freedom of the seas." It must be also kept in mind that, when a state is in an expansive phase, issues related to expansion and those related to "defense" are not usually separated in the minds of either its leaders or its public. Expansion is seen as a precondition for survival.

Whatever the expansionist aims of the War of 1812 may have been, they were not realized, but a political result was.

Britain, for reasons of her own, from then on, except for some incidents (a quarrel over the Oregon Territory and a half-hearted support of the Confederacy), accepted the hegemony of the United States in the Western Hemisphere. In fact, as Walter Lippmann pointed out (see below), without the support of the British navy, the Monroe Doctrine would have been an empty gesture. Be it as it may, the foreign policy of the United States during the remainder of the nineteenth century was conquest. But as conquest did not require conquering other established states, there was no need to develop either a diplomatic or a military virtuosity.

Forward-looking Americans simply projected the triumphal march of American expansion into the future. Already in 1789 Jedediah Morse, a Congregational minister of Boston, wrote in a book on *geography* (anticipating geopolitics of a later day):

> . . . it is well known that empire has been traveling from east to west. Probably her last and broadest seat will be America . . . the largest empire that ever existed.[5]

President John Quincy Adams wrote more explicitly:

> In looking forward to the probable course of events, it is scarcely possible to resist the conviction that the annexation of Cuba to our Federal Republic will be indispensable to the continuance and integrity of the Union itself.[6]

Commodore Perry expressed similar views on the future American role in the Pacific:

> It is self-evident that the course of coming events will ere long make it necessary for the United States to extend its jurisdiction beyond the limits of the western continent, and I assume the responsibility of urging the expedience of establishing a foothold in this quarter of the globe as a measure of positive necessity for the establishment of our maritime rights in the east.[7]

The ideological rationalization of these imperialist ambitions came to be known as Manifest Destiny, an outlook in which the United States saw itself as a bearer of a mission and its conquests as the manifestation of some cosmic purpose.

Here is an excerpt of senatorial oratory immediately following the victory of the United States over Spain.

> We will not repudiate our duty . . . We will not abandon our opportunity in the Orient. We will not renounce our part in the mission of our race, trustee under God, of the civilization of the world. . . . We will move forward to our work . . . with gratitude . . . and thanksgiving to Almighty God that He has marked us as His chosen people, henceforth to lead in the regeneration of the world. . . .
>
> Our largest trade henceforth must be with Asia. The Pacific is our ocean. The power that rules the Pacific . . . is the power that rules the world. And, with the Philippines, that power is and will forever be the American Republic.[8]

Such ideas often pervaded also the self-images of European states. Germany proclaimed its *Drang nach Osten* as a civilizing mission. Poetic justifications of the British conquests in Asia and Africa are well-known. However, in a constricted environment where every move must be closely calculated, where *ad hoc* alliances are vital for pursuing limited goals, attention is focused on matters other than missionary zeal. In particular, there is little room for missionary zeal in the realist conception of foreign policy. The mission idea typically develops during periods of unimpeded growth, as in the United States during the nineteenth century.

It is instructive to examine an echo of the Manifest Destiny in an apparently nonpolitical context. An outstanding American ideologue of the nineteenth century was Samuel Clemens, in whose works the cleavage between the old and the new worlds is most vivdly expressed. It is clearly evident already in his first major work, *Innocents Abroad.* In that book, Old Europe is seen by an American with a mixture of fascination and repugnance. The theme recurs in *A Tramp Abroad,* in *The Prince and the Pauper,* and in certain passages of *Tom Sawyer* and *Huckleberry Finn.* Its most powerful expression, however, is discernible in *A Connecticut Yankee in King Arthur's Court.* Through inexplicable circumstances, the Yankee finds himself in medieval England and proceeds to "take it over." His object is not power for power's sake. He considers himself to be an enemy of entrenched power (the Knighthood and the Established Church), and he is mortified by the plight of the common people. His object is to turn a nation of serfs into a nation of men. His weapon is technical know-how, which "naturally" inspires awe in the "natives." The Connecticut Yankee is thus pictured as a missionary from the nineteenth century to the Middle Ages. But he is transparently also a missionary from America to Europe. Young America has turned her back on Old Europe and has discovered a new fountainhead of meaning in life: making over the material world. To exercise this mastery, old prejudices, fears, and superstitions must be discarded until the heritage of the past appears for what it is: a pile of junk. Above all, the freedom and equality of men must be made a fundamental article of faith. In all of Mark Twain's writings, one finds this key theme of deep contempt for kings and bishops, for regalia and ceremony, to which he counterposed American earthy "practicality."[9]

The momentum of expansion impelled American imperial ambitions beyond the borders behind which America could be secure throughout the then foreseeable future: the two oceans, a permanently friendly Canada on the north, and an impotent Mexico on the south. At the close of the Spanish-American war, the future projected by President Adams and Commodore Perry arrived. The United States entered the race for empire.

In the popular mind, however, the role of the newcomer was not that of another contender for power. In the eyes of its citizens, the United States was thought to be beyond and above the on-going power struggles. Not *realpolitik* but the defense of a just world order was to be the basis of American participation in world affairs. It was in this spirit that the United States entered World War I. The American conception of foreign policy (regardless of the forces that propelled it) became distinctly an ideological one.

Thus arose the American notion of the "just war," the ethically asymmetrical war.[10] This notion differed radically from that prevailing among European militarists of the nineteenth century. The European militarists assumed, in effect, that all wars were equally "just" and that all belligerents were equally "right." To them war was an *institution*, somewhat in the sense, as mentioned, that competition is an institution to the businessman. And it was similarly justified. Likewise, in the way the businessman typically assumes that business success will accrue to the "better" business, so the European militarists assumed that victory in war will go to the bold, the crafty, and therefore the deserving. Those among them who thought in grandiose terms defended war as an institution through which the long-term goals of Providence are realized.[11] Of course, who are the deserving could be ascertained only in retrospect, in consequence of the results of the struggle. This "objectivity" did not prevent the militarist from being convinced that his country was the most "deserving." Inevitably, however, this conception of war as an affair of honor (a holdover from knighthood warfare) made it necessary to grant a degree of "justice" to all belligerents. Accordingly, we note honors accorded to enemy dead, protocol in the treatment of prisoners of high rank, etc.

In contrast, the American notion of the "just war" logically precluded the idea of chivalry. War, according to that notion, was *inherently* evil, senseless, and cruel. Normally nations could live in peace if it were not for some other nations or leaders, who, because of insatiable lust for power or some other indefensible motive, *instigated* war. Such nations thereby took themselves outside the community of "peaceful" nations. It then became the duty of "peaceful" nations to chastise the breachers of the peace, and that was the only justifiable reason for going to war. The enemy in a "just war" was a criminal, not simply an opponent in a test of strength. One could say that in contrast to Europeans, who viewed war as a chess game, Americans conceived war as a morality play.

The Americans' conception of war was powerfully reinforced by the events leading up to World War II. Indeed, the events were of such nature as to make the conception of the just war seem unassailable. It appeared as if the world was divided between "aggressor nations" and the others, all peace-loving nations. The former instigated wars of conquest; the latter had no choice but to resist. Under these circumstances one could not put oneself into the position of the enemy and grant that he, too, was "fighting for his country." Hence the battlefields of World War II were not fields of honor; all protocol was set aside. Slaughter of civilian populations, at least by air raids, became a commonplace practice of Americans as well as of Germans and Japanese, though the rationales of the two sides for slaughtering civilians were different. The Axis leaders, especially the Germans, regarded enemy populations as subhuman and felt no more compunction about killing them than about poisoning rats. Americans rationalized their slaughter of civilians as a regrettable military necessity. Even these misgivings were sometimes dissipated in the American conception of war as a crime, in which the enemy populations were viewed as willing accomplices.

Total victory further reinforced the idea of the "just war" in the American mind. To the average American the basis of American foreign policy seemed exceedingly simple: The United States wished to live in peace with everyone and wished everyone to live in peace with each other; and the United States was resolved to *keep* the peace throughout the world. So, if leaders or nations, because of expansionist ambitions, commit breaches of peace, then Americans will again (as they have done so successfully on previous occasions) regretfully but resolutely go to war to reestablish peace. The belief was held that war would never again be *institutionalized.* War was assumed to be inherently evil. But war against war was a duty. And since America is indisputably the most powerful (as well as the most peaceful and the most democratic) nation in the world, this duty to preserve peace, by force of arms if necessary, falls squarely upon American shoulders. "Peace is our profession" is the motto of the United States Air Force.

Before and for several years after World War II, this ideological conception of foreign policy was prevalent not only in the American popular mind but also in the thinking of U.S. policy makers. However, during and after World War II, writers on foreign policy began to challenge it.

Walter Lippmann, for example, argued that from 1812 (or 1823) until 1898 the United States had a clearly formulated foreign policy, but that from 1898 until World War II it had none, and that this lack might but for sheer luck have been disastrous.

In his book, *U.S. Foreign Policy, Shield of the Republic,* Lippmann states what he believes to be the fundamental principle of a foreign policy, in Chapter 2 which is only one page long:

> I mean by a *foreign commitment* an obligation, outside the limits of the United States, which may in the last analysis have to be met by waging war.
>
> I mean by *power* the force which is necessary to prevent such a war or to win it if it cannot be prevented. In the term *necessary* power I include the military force which can be mobilized effectively within the domestic territory of the United States and also the reinforcements which can be obtained from dependable allies.
>
> The thesis of this book is that a foreign policy consists of bringing into balance, with a comfortable surplus of power in reserve, the nation's commitment and the nation's power.[12]

Lippmann goes on to say that in the period from 1823 to 1898 the commitment of the United States was the defense of the Western Hemisphere against penetration by European powers. This commitment was explicitly formulated in the Monroe Doctrine and had been balanced by a power to enforce it. The power, to be sure, was not that of United States armed forces (which were insignificant compared to those of the militarized European states) but that of a "dependable ally," namely Great Britain, who, for reasons of her own, was also committed to prevent the conquest of any portion of the Western Hemisphere by a continental power.

After the war with Spain in 1898, the commitments of the United States spread far beyond the limits of the Western Hemisphere. In fact, the occupation of the Philippines (begun the very next year) brought the United States all the way across the Pacific, and as a result the United States became committed to resist the expansion of the Japanese Empire. However, the task of matching the commitment with power to back it was neglected.

In view of his definition of foreign policy, Lippmann is led to the conclusion that in the first half of the twentieth century the United States "had no foreign policy." This lack came about, Lippmann argues, because the U.S. foreign policy of the nineteenth century (based on a commitment limited to the Western Hemisphere) had been so successful. When events are running smoothly, we are usually unconscious of them. During the nineteenth century Great Britain's mastery of the oceans was absolute, and it was the British navy that made the penetration of the Western Hemisphere by continental powers unfeasible. However, just because the *de facto* alliance between Great Britain and the United States was so effective, it escaped the attention of the American people. They came to believe that the safety of the United States was guaranteed by the mere existence of the two oceans or, perhaps, by the moral superiority of Americans and of the American political system. Consequently, when the commitments exceeded the power required to back them, the discrepancy was not recognized.

True, voices were raised now and then, calling attention to the new role assumed by the United States in world politics and urging the expansion of military and naval forces in order to "bring into balance" the power of the United States with its new "obligations"[13] For the most part, however, these voices were submerged in the prevailing isolationist mood.

Isolationism, Lippmann points out, was rooted in part in a desire simply to save money, but also to a considerable extent in moralistic and ideological conceptions. For the most part, Americans considered themselves different from Europeans. They conceived their origin as a nation to be a breaking away from

Europe with its despotic governments, its militarism, its power struggles. This image of America is understandable in the light of the events of the nineteenth century during which Americans were absorbed with the conquest of the continent and with building the industrial, agricultural, and commercial basis of their own prosperity. In reality, however, Americans were living on borrowed time, in Lippmann's estimation. When confronted with the facts of world politics, they found themselves perilously unprepared to cope with them.

The facts of world politics are conceived by Lippmann in the realist mode. The actors of world history are states, and their actions are dominated by pressures to extend their power and influence. The first danger to the United States was the emergence of Germany as a *naval* power. Lippmann notes that the emergence of Germany as the strongest *military* power on the continent was not a danger to the United States. The United States had no commitments in Europe; consequently there was no justifiable reason for becoming alarmed at Germany's victory over Denmark (1864), over Austria (1866), or even over France (1870). When, however, Germany challenged Britain's mastery of the seas by starting to build a strong navy, the situation became very different. This event coincided approximately with the enlargment of the United States "commitment" in the Pacific. Lippmann makes much of the incident in the Spanish-American War when Germany sent a fleet to the Pacific to "watch" Admiral Dewey. Two days before the Battle of Manila Bay John Hay sent a telegram from London, saying of Germany, *"Voilà l'ennemi."*[14]

The danger from Germany as a naval power was in the loss of security of American lines of communication across the oceans. Britain was still a "dependable ally" but no longer in supreme command of the seas. America's own naval strength had not kept pace with events because of the "lack of a foreign policy," i.e., the lack of understanding of geopolitics. Nevertheless an intuitive appreciation of the danger did finally force America's intervention in World War I. Lippmann goes to some lengths to refute the prevalent ideological interpretations of that intervention (including the official ones). Not a defense of democracy, not a thirst for justice, not a sense of outrage against the sinking of commercial ships by submarines, but geopolitical considerations forced the United States into World War I. The United States could not allow a "hostile" power (Germany) to command the Atlantic.

World War I found the United States "unprepared"; but since Germany was already virtually exhausted at the time of United States intervention, victory was assured by sheer preponderance of materiel and the possibility of delivering it, thanks to England's success in antisubmarine warfare.

After victory, still no U.S. foreign policy emerged. Pacifist and isolationist sentiments prevailed. The Versailles Treaty was not ratified because, in Lippmann's opinion, instead of explaining it to the American people in terms of the facts of world politics, Wilson persisted in his moralistic stance. The failure of matching power to commitments finally led to the disaster of Pearl Harbor. Lippmann concludes with an outline of what he considers to be a realistic foreign policy for the United States and an implicit hope that America will draw proper conclusions from the lessons of history.

In his recommendation Lippmann departs from pure *realpolitik* in two ways. First, the alliances to be concluded by the United States are conceived by him not on an *ad hoc* basis, say for the purpose of waging a particular war, but on a quasi-permanent basis for the duration of the foreseeable future. Second, an ideological component, absent in the pure realist conception, is partially admitted. These two modifications are related. The permanent alliance envisaged by Lippmann—the Atlantic Community—was to be anchored in the combined military might of Britain and the United States. Its function was to turn the Atlantic Ocean into a *Mare Nostrum* (as the Romans called the Mediterranean). This alliance is viewed by Lippmann as a "natural" one, since it would be based on a historically continuous concordance of interests of the two nations, and, moreover, cemented by the common language and the common origin of political institutions. Thus the permanence of the alliance was to have an ideological basis.

Then, what about Russia and China, who in 1943 were America's allies? The last chapters of *U.S. Foreign Policy, Shield of the Republic* are devoted to this question. Coming back to the fundamental assumption that not ideological affinity but common interests determine the alignments of power, Lippmann sees the collaboration between the United States and the Soviet Union in World War II as a vindication of this principle. Except for a few months in 1917 (when it appeared that Russia could develop into a parliamentary democracy), the United States and Russia (both czarist and Soviet) were ideologically poles apart. Yet at no time in history did the interests of the two states clash. Indeed, Russia was "sympathetic" to the colonies during the War of Independence and to the Union cause in the Civil War. Similarly, the United States declared itself against the "dismemberment of Russia" when Russia was impotent after her defeat by Germany in 1918. This mutual support was a natural consequence of global politics. The United States and Russia had common enemies: Germany in Europe and Japan in Asia. (To push the analysis further, we would have to recognize that in the 1770s and 1860s the common antagonist of the United States and of Russia was England, America's "natural" ally. But Lippmann understandably passes over this point.) From the point of view of geopolitics, the concordance of interests between Russia and the United States was a consequence of their geographical positions. Each is placed in the rear of the other's "natural enemy." (Again, one might interpose the observation that on a spherical surface who is behind whom is not altogether clear. But this point Lippmann also passes over.)

World War II is seen by Lippmann as the final phase of Japanese and German imperialist ambitions. He foresees (1943) the defeat of both.

> . . . Germany will never again be able to make a bid for the mastery of Europe and of the transatlantic region of American security. . . . Japan will never again be able to seek an empire over China and the Indies.[15]

And he asks the obvious question: "Will the Russian-American alliance endure after the threat to both has been eliminated?" His answer illuminates the events that are central to the subject of our present discussion.

> . . . the question in Europe is whether Russia will seek to extend her power westward into Europe in such a way that it threatens the security of the Atlantic states. The question in the Pacific is

whether as nearest neighbors by land, sea, and air, the United States and Russia will move towards rivalry or towards a common ground of understanding. The two questions are inseparable because, as the Russian statesmen have so often insisted, peace is indivisible. We should therefore be lacking in candor and realism if we did not face the fact that the crucial question of the epoch that we are now entering is the relationship between Russia and that Atlantic Community in which Britain and the United States are the leading military powers.[16]

With the defeat of Japan, the same question is raised with regard to China. It will take some time before China emerges as a world power. The United States has assisted in initiating this process by opposing the dismemberment and the colonial domination of China. In Lippmann's expectation:

Victory in this war will fulfill that commitment at least to the point of giving China a free chance to make herself a great power, and probably also to the point of our rendering China active assistance in making herself a great power.[17]

However:

We cannot know now what a great Chinese power in this region of the world portends, and we cannot afford to freeze our ideas about a situation which will only gradually unfold itself. All we can do is to act on the assumption that the conditions which for a half a century have made the integrity and security of China a vital interest of the United States will, as China becomes a great power, make the security of the United States a vital interest of China.[18]

Finally, Lippmann realizes that the Atlantic Community, Russia, and China are only half the world. There is also another half: India, Australasia, the Moslem countries. (Africa is not mentioned, but possibly would have been if Lippmann were reminded of it.) Of this other half, Lippmann says:

If stabilization of at least half the world is impossible in our time, then it follows that only by participating in the organization of sufficient lawful power can we hope to hold the impending and unpredictable changes within peaceable channels.[19]

Apparently Lippmann sees global politics in concentric circles, as it were. At the center is the United States and its "commitments." Immediately adjoining is Great Britain, and possibly renascent France to be admitted into a partnership with the

United States and Great Britain. It is hoped that Russia will cooperate in what Lippmann calls the "nuclear alliance." (The later ominous meaning of this phrase was not yet imagined in 1943.) All power is to be concentrated in this "nuclear alliance" (if it persists and is used in a way to insure the subsequent "peaceful" development of the rest of the world).

We see then, in Lippmann's conception, an amalgam of the Clausewitzian "community of states" and the older idea of empire. Lippmann expects the "community" of competing states to mature into a world community of cooperating states. The key to this process is the recognition of the common interests of the most powerful states, namely the protection of their security against encroachments by "expansionist" states. As a result of this recognition, the "nuclear" states together with "cooperating" Russia and China are expected to exercise a collective monopoly of power to ensure world peace.

The idea is not a new one. It was embodied in the concept of the Pax Romana, later in the Pax Britannica. Pax Americana is the latest version.

As it turned out, the Russians had their own ideas about "world peace," and China's ascendancy to the status of a great power took place not under American auspices. Neither Russia nor China chose to "cooperate" with the "nuclear alliance." How to enforce the Pax Americana under these conditions has become the chief, better said, the exclusive, preoccupation of U.S. policy makers.

Unlike the American Revolution, the Russian Revolution of 1917 took place in the midst of war in which Russia was defeated. The war was a principal issue of the revolution: the masses were urged by the Bolsheviks to turn against the provisional government because it had committed itself to the continuation of the war. Thus the "crime" conception of war also became deeply imbedded in the ideology which was to become the state ideology of the U.S.S.R. However, as in the United States, the ideology allowed a clear distinction between just and unjust wars. A "just" war in the Soviet view is one waged against an aggressor. A war may be "unjust" on both sides, as, for example, wars for possessions, power, or prestige waged by capitalist states against each other. Or a war may be just on one side and unjust on the other, as, for example, a war between a capitalist and a socialist state (since the latter cannot, almost by definition, be an aggressor), or a civil war fought in defense of a social revolution, or a war of national liberation. However, in the Soviet view, a war cannot be "just" on both sides.[20] In this view, therefore, the nineteenth century (Clausewitzian) conception of war is ideologically rejected as categorically as it is in the traditional American view.

Thus there are certain similarities between the ideological conceptions of war prevalent in the U.S. and in the U.S.S.R., at least in the popular conceptions. In both, war is rejected as a *normal* phase in international relations.

There is a crucial difference, however, between the experiences of Russians and Americans in the practice of international relations. Until quite recently the American ideological conception of war as an intervention to preserve peace was undisturbed and even reinforced by participation in World War II. In contrast, the Soviet ideological conception of war as a product of capitalism was found from the very start to be inadequate as a guide to foreign policy. To begin with, when proletarian revolutions, imminently expected as a consequence of the chaos engendered by World War I, failed to occur in Europe, the Soviets faced an immediate, pressing problem of averting a war against the newborn socialist state by the capitalist powers. This called for a "genuine" foreign policy of considerable intricacy, a sort of foreign policy for which the United States saw no pressing need in the period of its relative isolation. Two courses offered themselves in the pursuit of this dominant national goal. One was to follow the implications of the Communist conception of international relations, namely that capitalism is both necessary and sufficient for the occurrence of wars; that to eliminate the danger of war against the Soviet Union one needed to hasten or facilitate proletarian revolutions. The other course was suggested by the old idea that to prevent concerted action one should attempt to divide potential allies.

The first course required the creation of techniques not hitherto utilized in international relations, for example, the exertion of political influence on the populations of capitalist countries

over the heads of their governments. The second course required
the application of old techniques of diplomatic virtuosity in the
arena of "classical" international relations. The Soviet leaders
chose both courses. The function of the first approach was entrusted to the Communist International, that of the second to
the *Narkomindel* (the Soviet foreign office).

Needless to say, the two courses were at cross-purposes. The
Communist International was supposed to be a center directing
a world Communist movement aimed at overthrowing *all* capitalist governments. It was impossible to preserve the fiction that
the Communist International was a "private body" which "happened" to have its headquarters in Moscow. In the eyes of the
"capitalist governments" the International was a creature of the
Kremlin. In consequence of events within the Soviet Union, this
evaluation of the Communist International became increasingly
accurate and finally exact. However, even if this were not the
case, it would be next to impossible for the "capitalists" to separate in their own minds the aims of the International and those
of the only Communist state; and that is what matters. Under
the circumstances it was extremely difficult for any nation to
engage in a rapprochement with the Soviet Union, which is just
what the second course of "conventional" foreign relations demanded. At the same time, the aims of the second course inter-
fered with those of the first. When occasionally the Soviet Union
did succeed in establishing relatively cordial relations with a
capitalist state, this served to weaken the world Communist
movement.

As an example of the first dilemma, we can take the attempts
of the Soviet Union to "normalize" its relations with Great Britain in the 1920s. Normalization was vital for Russia's economic
recovery, which could be accomplished only by establishing
trade relations, which, in turn, depended on the resumption of
diplomatic relations. The existence of the Communist International impeded the reestablishment of diplomatic relations between the Soviet Union and the major powers, partly because of
the traditional conception of international relations and the attendant protocols: nurturing movements dedicated to overthrowing legitimate governments in the other states of a "community of states" was simply not done. One could wage war and

still be a member in good standing in the "community," but one could not promote revolutions. Finally, after herculean diplomatic efforts, the able and astute Soviet Commissar for Foreign Affairs, George Chicherin, succeeded (1924) in obtaining recognition of the Soviet Union by Great Britain. The success was short-lived, however. The alleged discovery of the so-called Zinoviev Letter[21] led to a break. The letter was most likely a forgery, but the existence and activities of the Comintern made it not at all incredible. Not until 1931 were diplomatic relations and some trade agreements reestablished between Britain and the U.S.S.R.

Because of the stronger ideological orientation of American foreign policy, the establishment of diplomatic relations with the United States was even more difficult. When this did come about in 1933, it is interesting to note that the activities of the Comintern were a major issue dealt with. In a formal note, the then Foreign Commissar Maxim Litvinov assured Roosevelt that the Soviet government would

> . . . refrain and . . . restrain all persons in government service and all organizations of the Government or under direct or indirect control . . . from any act overt or covert liable in any way whatsoever to injure the tranquility, prosperity, order or security of any part of the United States, its territories or possessions . . . Not to permit the formation or residence on its (Soviet) territory of any organization or group . . . which has as its aim the overthrow or the preparation for the overthrow . . . of the political or social order of the whole or any part of the United States.[22]

It is difficult to reconcile at least the last part of this pledge with the "residence" of the Comintern on the territory of the U.S.S.R. In the political sphere, however, when something needs to be done, definitions or redefinitions of terms never fail to do service in reconciling exigencies with principles. The fact of the matter was that the Soviet Union had become a "state" and *had* to be admitted into the "community of states" regardless of what others thought of its ideology or its moral stature. It remains true, however, that the Comintern made this process rather difficult.

As an example of how the actions of the Soviet state hindered the world Communist movement, we can take any of the drastic

changes in the "line" which had to be automatically and instan-
taneously echoed by the Communist parties throughout the
world. (We are speaking now of the period before 1948.) That
the Comintern, at least after 1927, became a mere appendage of
Soviet foreign policy was self-evident. In fact, it was implicitly
admitted by the Communists themselves, who rationalized this
role by the dictum that the first duty of any Communist is to
defend the interests of the "only socialist state." Stalin put it
bluntly:

> He is a revolutionary who without reservation, unconditionally,
> openly . . . is ready to protect and defend the U.S.S.R. . . . He
> who thinks to defend the world revolutionary movement apart and
> against the U.S.S.R. is going against the revolution and will cer-
> tainly slide into the camp of the enemies of the revolution.[23]

Given this formula, it would seem that the activities of the
Comintern and of the Narkomindel were perfectly coordinated;
but this is only a consequence of the verbal formula. The *practical* aim of the Comintern was to direct and to nurture the world
Communist movement. Its success depended certainly on
whether the movement could attract to its ranks workers, peasants, and intellectuals who had not been in the movement. To
these, the coincidence of interests between the Soviet state (that
behaved more and more like a "normal" state with "normal"
ambitions) and a world revolutionary movement was by no
means obvious. In fact, it is questionable whether a "world revolutionary movement" to which continual references were made
in the stylized rhetoric of the Comintern ever existed. There
were, of course, the Communist parties whose rank and file, we
may assume, took the verbiage seriously. However, except for a
short period in China (1924–1927) when the Communists were
the activist kernel of the Kuomintang, these parties for the most
part declined in significance in the period between the two
world wars. There were revolutionary struggles: for example,
the Civil War in Spain, the movement of national liberation in
India, etc.; at times Communists participated in these movements, but at other times (depending on what the current "line"
happened to be) they played a sectarian, disruptive role. On the
whole, the attempts of the Communists to become the elite of
all revolutionary and labor movements (Lenin's prescription,
which succeeded in Russia) failed on the world scale.

One of Marx's most valuable insights is that ideology grows out of "praxis," which in the Communist conception means predominantly experience in struggle. Soviet experience in the field of international relations has been marked by successes (as well as failures) in diplomacy but largely by failures in the proselytizing of ideology. It is not surprising therefore that the ideological campaign has been progressively relegated to ritual, and that foreign policy has been progressively oriented toward conventional techniques.

It is tempting to attribute this development to the personality and the *modus operandi* of Joseph Stalin whose word, after 1928, became law for all the faithful. Indeed Stalin represented the epitome of the Machiavellian conception of politics. His "achievement" in capturing absolute power over almost 200,000,000 subjects, including an absolute power of life and death, was probably unequaled in history. He was once quoted as saying that of all the pleasures the most intense in his experience had been that of carefully preparing the destruction of an enemy and, having brought it about, going to bed. Clearly ideology had no room in the mind of such a man, except as an instrument for accumulating power. The power of rulers derives from the power of the realm over which they rule, and in their minds the two become identified. Without question Stalin wanted power for Russia, which was also *his* power. The abandonment of ideology in favor of pure power politics was thus entirely in keeping with Stalin's character.

One must be wary, however, in attributing a historical process to the influence of one man, no matter how powerful he may be. Stalin's power resided not in his person but in the support he received from his henchmen, from the army, and from his subjects. People are always *selected* into positions of power. In another country or in another period, all of Stalin's genius for intrigue, manipulation, seduction, and betrayal would have availed him nothing. It is much more reasonable to assume that Russia turned to power politics because that is where Russia scored successes. One need not be a mystic to attribute psychological processes to states as well as to individuals. Both states and individuals are complex systems. The former are composed of individuals, groups, and their interrelations just as the latter are composed of neural cells and their interconnections.

And so, if we examine the foreign policy of the U.S.S.R., we see that throughout its history it becomes more and more state-oriented and progressively less ideologically oriented. Nevertheless the ideological *conception* of foreign policy is by no means dead in Russia any more than it is in America. It persists tenaciously in the popular mind, and it cannot be neglected in any serious examination of Soviet-American relations, because the power of rulers depends in the last analysis on the willingness of the ruled to be led.

The Russian conceives of the Soviet Union as a socialist state. He also believes it to be a democratic state. By socialist "democracy" the Russian means policies undertaken *by the state* that aim to promote the general welfare of the population. His conception of general welfare is quite concrete and actually not very different from that of the average American. It involves primarily living standards in the fundamental sense: plentiful and varied food, comfortable housing, attractive clothes, furniture, vacations, medical care, educational opportunities, etc. He believes, on the whole correctly, that these blessings accrue as a result of progressive increase of productive capacity, and that the greatest obstacle to securing these standards is war. War destroys wealth, and preparations for war prevent social wealth from being accumulated. The average Russian believes that his government, being democratic, that is, concerned with the welfare of the people, strives toward eliminating the necessity of channeling production into armaments, and that a disarmed and peaceful world in which nations with diverse social or political systems can coexist, freed from the threat of war, is the overriding goal of Soviet foreign policy.

The idea that the Soviet Union has ever waged or would ever wage an "aggressive" war seems utterly absurd to the average Russian. Russia, in his estimation, needs nothing from others. She asks only to be left alone in order to pursue the charted historical course—the building of communism, a realization of the ideal epitomized by the slogan "From each according to his ability, to each according to his needs."

Likewise, the Russian dismisses the idea that the Soviet Union might attempt to use its armed might in order to impose its social and political system on other countries. In support, he can quote appropriate chapter and verse from the speeches and writings of whatever leader can be appropriately quoted at the moment. Lenin, of course, having been canonized forever, is always quotable, and there are numerous passages in Lenin's works to support the Russian's conception of Soviet foreign policy.

We have, then, *two* Soviet perceptions of foreign policy. One is the citizen's, nurtured by the official definitions of Soviet national goals; the other is derived from usual diplomilitary practice. The two perceptions are not as incompatible as they might seem, because the tasks of Soviet foreign policy, at least until 1939, *were* those of defense in the literal not merely euphemistic meaning of this word. Until 1934 the policy was of necessity isolationist. From 1934 to 1938 it centered on an attempt to engage the Western powers in a collective security pact against Nazi Germany, also a purely defensive goal. When the attempt failed,[24] Stalin tried to ward off the inevitable assault by a "nonaggression pact" with Hitler.

From 1939 to 1941 Stalin restored the borders of the old Russian Empire. From 1941 to 1945 the "policy" was simply a fight for survival. From 1945 to 1948 Stalin acquired a "sphere of influence" in Eastern Europe.

On the face of it, then, the Russian's conception of Soviet foreign policy as a purely defensive one seems to correspond to facts until 1939. After that an excellent case could be constructed for describing it in purely realist terms. This was, in fact, done by Adam Ulam in his large and, in a way, illuminating book *Expansion and Co-existence.*

The title of the book suggests a double-barreled Soviet strategy. When opportunities for expansion come along, Soviet leaders seize them. When no such opportunities are on hand, or when the U.S.S.R. itself is threatened, Soviet leaders appeal to the civilized West's better nature and to world public opinion by playing up the peaceful coexistence theme.

This interpretation of Soviet foreign policy is at times juxtaposed to the images of the alarmists on the one hand and those of the wishful thinkers on the other. The alarmists are those who see in the very existence of the Soviet Union an unrelieved and immediate threat to the rest of the world. In 1945 the alarmists expected the triumphal march of the Red Army to continue to the Atlantic Ocean, and they still think that the only thing that stopped the Russians was the fear of the atomic bomb. When Russia "got the bomb," the alarmists saw the main danger presented by the U.S.S.R. to the United States in the form of a Pearl Harbor-type nuclear surprise attack. Some of them advocated a "preventive strike" by the United States to forestall it. The wishful thinkers are those whose attention is riveted on the coexistence theme of Soviet diplomacy. They see signs of "mellowing" or "reform" in every instance of a softened tone in Soviet diplomacy or rhetoric. They either relegate whatever expansionist tendencies Soviet policy may have had to "Stalinism" or deny it altogether.

In the course of his analysis, Ulam dismisses both the alarmists' fears and the wishful thinkers' hopes. In his view, Soviet leaders are ruthless and astute. Their ruthlessness warrants no expectation of genuinely cordial relations based on mutual trust and long-term cooperation between the Soviet Union and the West. On the other hand, the astuteness of the Soviet leaders permits a rational approach to U.S.-U.S.S.R. relations. Soviet leaders can be "trusted" not to jeopardize the security of the Soviet Union, not to plunge into adventures, not to cast challenges that cannot be backed, nor to accept challenges that cannot be met. Evidence for this characterization of Soviet leaders and this interpretation of their foreign policy is plentiful. Nor is it surprising in view of Stalin's complete domination of both the leadership and the foreign policy for fully one half of the half century. Stalin was ruthless, astute, and cautious. His ruthlessness was convincingly demonstrated in the character of his rule; his astuteness and caution were evident in his diplomacy. The implication seems clear: where Stalin had absolute power, he was a paranoid, homicidal despot; where he was confronted with countervailing force, he could be reasonable and accommodating.

Ulam projects this pattern on the entire conduct of Soviet foreign policy, in particular the period of the great "thaw" immediately after Stalin's death which was marked by a softening in Soviet diplomatic style and by "peace offensives."

"Was this policy 'sincere'?" Ulam asks. He answers that:

> . . . Soviet leaders' ideology was extremely helpful in allowing
> them to justify to themselves as well as to their followers those
> drastic shifts and improvisations which led their opponents,
> flustered and furious, to protest Russian 'insincerity,' attempts to
> 'lull the free world to sleep,' etc. To such accusations the answer
> was and is invariably that the 'objective historical circumstances
> have changed' and indeed are always changing, and with them the
> appropriate policies. In less dialectical terms one may say that the
> Soviet posture at the end of 1955 reflected the belief that *both*
> the dangers to the Soviet system and the opportunities for expan-
> sion of Communist-Soviet power were now greatly diminished.
> Hence a policy of *detente* was logically indicated, since it neither
> incurred undue risks to the U.S.S.R. and her satellites nor meant
> passing up any spectacular opportunities.[25]

The realist interpretation of Soviet foreign policy by Western
analysts has a built-in feature that is absent in the traditional
Clausewitzian conception. The U.S.S.R. is, in the Western realists' view, not a state like other states, for it has at its disposal
not only the traditional methods of extending its power and
influence (diplomacy and armed might) but also an ideology
which finds a response in populations outside of the ideological
conception in Western analyses of Soviet foreign policy. The
Soviet Union is seen to make use of the susceptibility of populations to Communist ideology, when it can, in pursuing its goals
as a state. In this way the expansionist model is immensely
strengthened, for the expansion of *communism* tends to be
identified with that of Soviet power. In careful analyses, such as
Ulam's, this identification cannot always be explicit because the
events of the last decades have undermined its basis. But a tacit
identification, which has been axiomatic in American perceptions of Soviet policy when world communism was a monolithic
force, persists and makes the thesis of expansionism incontrovertible. The "objective historical circumstances" argument helps
make it so, for it is an argument that points to the adjustability
of Soviet foreign policy. The policy adjusts itself to "objective
circumstances." To what purpose? one might ask. The realist's
answer is ready: in order to pursue more effectively the one and
only goal of foreign policy—power.

Ulam's analysis of Soviet foreign policy is, perhaps, representative of the most sophisticated perception of that policy within the limits imposed by the framework of thought in which works of this sort are conceived. Needless to say, to point out the limits is not to belittle either the importance or the worth of the work. Everyone is limited by a framework of thought, and it usually takes someone working outside the framework to recognize its limits. Ulam's framework is circumscribed, first, by the range of concepts that characterize the realist approach to international relations and, second, by the acceptance of the broad goals of U.S. foreign policy, at least that of "containing communism." The first restriction leads him to neglect (not altogether but by and large) the systemic self-generating components of Soviet-American relations; the second leads him to select those aspects of Soviet policy that corroborate his main thesis: the primary motivation of Soviet foreign policy appears to be a relentless aggressive struggle; coexistence is stressed only when opportunities for expansion are absent; *mutatis mutandis,* the U.S. policy of containment appears implicitly as one of self-defense.

To balance the picture, one ought to look for a comparably sophisticated analysis of U.S. foreign policy by a Soviet writer. However, because of the ideological restrictions on Soviet writers, such a search is not likely to be fruitful. This is not to say that the Soviet *perceptions* of U.S. policy are necessarily more distorted than the prevalent American perceptions of Soviet policy, only that *formulations* of Soviet perceptions must adhere strictly not only to official dogma in their broad outlines but also to whatever the official assessment of the international situation happens to be at a given moment. The latter is likely to change frequently and without notice. Although the role assigned by Soviet ideologues to the United States as the champion of imperalism has remained constant since 1945, the assessment of the threat to the socialist bloc and to world peace has fluctuated. The lot of a Soviet scholar who finds himself out of phase with these fluctuations is not an enviable one.

Nor is it easy to infer true Soviet perceptions of U.S. policy from the fluctuating assessment of threat, since the fluctuations may be simply symptoms of some internal process in Soviet politics. A case in point is H. S. Dinerstein's[26] account of the Soviet assessment (from 1953 to 1957) of the danger of war against the U.S.S.R. and of its probable course. Dinerstein notes that, with the accession of Malenkov following Stalin's death in 1953, the dominant theme in Soviet pronouncements was that the Soviet Union possessed an adequate deterrent against attack by the United States. In 1954, the tone changed. Editorials began to appear denouncing "complacency" and calling for the reestablishment of the priority of heavy industry (further buildup of the war machine), sharpened vigilance, etc. In 1955, immediately after Malenkov was ousted, alarmist outbursts subsided. A quiescent period followed, lasting until the beginning of 1957, at which time the "war plans of the imperialists" again came into prominence.

By the use of subtle content analysis and by juxtaposing it with promotions and demotions in the Soviet hierarchy ("Kremlinology"), Dinerstein shows that the fluctuations reflected first a power struggle between the Malenkov and Khrushchev factions, later Khrushchev's consolidation of his own position.[27] Nevertheless a simpler interpretation ought not to be dismissed. It may well be that the fluctuations reflected first an attempt to use the opportunity of Stalin's death to end the cold war; then a reaction to the failure of the attempt, signaled by John Foster Dulles' bellicose pronouncements (cf. p. 148), and to the U.S. decision to rearm Germany; then a second attempt to come to terms with the West (following the end of the first Indo-China war and the Geneva and Bandung Conferences of 1955); finally a reaction to the Middle East–Hungarian–Polish crises in the fall of 1956.

Whatever be the background of the oscillations in the Soviet public assessment of Soviet-American relations, the editorials and anniversary speeches fall far short of the sort of analysis from which a basic, theoretically anchored Soviet view of U.S. foreign policy can be inferred. Perhaps such a view does not exist, not even one that might be expected to emerge from Lenin's theory of imperialism. It seems as if Stalinist terror had eviscerated theoretic thought in the Soviet Union in all areas touching upon politics or history, having reduced all discussions of these matters to pious citations of texts, intellectual genuflections, and snarls.

In search of a Marxist analysis of U.S. foreign policy in Soviet writings, one finds detailed studies of the economic relations between the United States and Western Europe. A. V. Kirsanov, for example, presents a wealth of factual material (taken largely from Western sources) on volumes of military aid, trade balances, export of capital, etc.[28] However, the coupling between the data and "Marxist theory" is extremely loose, being confined largely to iterations of well-worn phrases, "the crisis of capitalism" (which has been presumably going on since Lenin wrote about it), "the sharpening of internal contradictions within the imperialist camp," etc.

In order to remain serviceable, a theory must be applied to specific data with the expectation that, in the process of application, the theory may be modified or even refuted, or that even a corroboration of the theory may lead to an insight that will present the theory in an entirely new light. A chronic, probably deeply internalized inhibition against challenging established dogmas precludes the developement of such a theory in the Soviet Union. In officialese, the established dogma is called "the unshakable tenets of Marxism-Leninism." However, the imposed framework of thought is much narrower than the theoretical framework of Marxist analysis. For, even *within* this framework, an analysis of the economic underpinnings of the clash of interests between the United States and the Soviet Union might reveal that the Leninist model of imperialism is applicable to both sides, each seeking to establish economic hegemony in a given region. Such a conclusion would be incompatible not with Marxist theory but with the *official* dogma, according to which Soviet foreign policy has always been and remains a purely defensive one. Actually, as we shall argue in later chapters, impressive (though not conclusive) evidence *can* be marshaled in support of this contention. Marxist analysis, however, penetrates beyond the conventional concepts of policies. Just as in mathematical physics the metaphysical categories of "cause" and "effect" lose their theoretical significance, so in Marxist analysis "offensive" and "defensive" policies are not particularly helpful concepts.

A Marxist analysis, unencumbered by a compulsion to vindicate in every instance the policy of the Soviet Union, could conceivably uncover the economic underpinnings of Soviet policy, in, say, Eastern Europe. That this policy was in part a "defense" of Eastern Europe against American economic penetration and ultimate domination is apparent. The question is what the analysis would uncover with regard to the relations between Soviet and Eastern European economies; whether, for example, at least some elements of what in other instances is recognized as economic exploitation, backed by political domination, would not *also* become apparent. Similar conjectures can be made with regard to Soviet intentions in Manchuria at the close of World War II (cf. p. 77), as Chinese Marxists may very well point out.

In short, a *complete* Marxist analysis of Soviet-American relations is not to be found in Soviet sources. To find a penetrating critique of American foreign policy, we must turn to other sources.

Critical analyses of U.S. foreign policy are, of course, many and varied. In searching for an analysis of U.S. policy that could serve as a counterpart of Ulam's study, the writings based on realist conceptions should be dismissed. These are essentially pleas for a "more realistic" U.S. policy in response to the challenge presented by the "Communist threat"—postwar extensions of Walter Lippmann's recommendations. They parallel rather than balance Ulam's outlook.

A proper antithesis to the realist conception of international relations is the systemic one. In this conception, the tenets of the realists' approach are not necessarily denied, but the question is put in another way. Not "how do states act in pursuit of their interests?" but rather "what is the genesis of the forces that underlie the compulsions interpreted as 'national interests'?" is the central question of the systemic approach.

As one would expect, answers to this question, related to the behavior of the United States in the world arena, reflect the special interests or areas of competence of the writers who offer them. There are psychological answers related, for example, to mechanisms of projection[29]; sociological ones related to the role of power elites[30]; Richardsonian studies, where the point of departure is the autonomous dynamics of the arms race or, more generally, the self-catalytic escalation of tension.[31]

Analyses tracing the roots of U.S. policies, domestic and foreign, to economic factors are well represented in American scholarship. Among historians, Charles A. Beard[32] has emphasized the close relation of politics to economics. William Appleman Williams traced the economic roots of American imperialism in the nineteenth century.[33] Lloyd C. Gardner examined the economic aspects of U.S. diplomacy from the start of the New Deal to the cold war.[34] More recently, Gabriel Kolko published two studies with a distinctly Marxist flavor, one covering the last two years of World War II,[35] the other the economic position of the U.S. vis-à-vis the developing countries.[36] I have chosen these as examples of the sort of analysis of U.S. foreign policy that might complement Ulam's "realist" analysis of Soviet foreign policy.

Kolko notes the increasing dependence of the United States on imports of critical raw materials. Thus, of the total consumed from 1930 to 1960, the percent of annual imports rose: for iron ore from 5 to 32; for bauxite from 64 to 98; for lead from 8 to 35; etc. By 1956, the United States imported at least 80 percent of thirty-nine necessary commodities. Many of these commodities come from developing countries and the security of these supplies depends, in the minds of U.S. political leaders, on the "political stability" of the regions from which they come. Kolko writes:

> America's ability to procure at will such materials as it needs and at a price it can afford is one of the keystones of its economic power in this century. The stakes are vast, and its capacity to keep intact something like the existing integrated but unequal relations between the poor, weak nations and the United States is vital to the future of its mastery of the international economy.[37]

At the same time, while United States' share in world *production* of some major agricultural products has been falling, its share in world *exports* of these products has risen, in some cases (wheat, oats, corn, rice) manyfold.

There emerges a clear picture of both increasing dependence on and increasing domination over world trade. According to Kolko, continued economic impotence of the Third World directly benefits the industrialized countries, particularly the United States.

The United States especially gears its investments [in poor countries] to increasing the output of exportable minerals and agricultural commodities, instead of balanced economic development. . . . [S]uch investments hardly scratch the living standards of the local peasantry or make possible the large increases in agricultural output that are a precondition of a sustained industrial expansion. Indeed the total flow of . . . capital to the developing areas . . . has only increased the output of resources needed in the Western world, and the flight of local capital to safe Western banks has partially offset even this form of capital flux.[38]

Behind the United States policy of forceful prevention of certain political changes is, in Kolko's estimation, the necessity of preserving the economic impotence of the Third World. It is worth noting that in this book dealing with *The Roots of American Foreign Policy* the role of the Soviet Union is completely ignored. The only mention of Russia is in connection with the fact that over one-half of the known world reserves of manganese are in Russia and China. One is reminded of Laplace's answer to Napoleon, who asked the mathematician what role the Creator played in his theory of celestial mechanics. "Sire," Laplace is said to have replied, "I had no need of that hypothesis."

In *The Politics of War*, Kolko discussed the origins of the cold war in more direct political terms.

His analysis of U.S. foreign policy that crystallized at the turning point in World War II (1943) revolves around three major themes: (1) the disintegration of prewar social systems with the concomitant growth of revolutionary movements all over the world; (2) the emergence of the Soviet Union as a great power; and (3) the decline of the British Empire. These themes are examined against the background of the principal peace aim of the United States: "to create a world economic order according to its own desires."

The Marxist bent in Kolko's thesis is revealed in the emphasis on economic determinants of politics and in the equal weight assigned to Soviet-American and British-American relations. (In Marxist terminology, the latter revolve around "contradictions within the imperialist camp.")

The elimination of Britain's power in large areas of the world, and the American entry into the wake, carried with it the enormous

. . . responsibilities which unavoidably befell those who wished global profit, and that new burden was as much a by-product of an American desire for world economic expansion as it was a response to the emergence of the Left everywhere, much less the growth of Russian power.[39]

Further:

There was nothing qualitatively unique about this goal or the tools that the United States employed, for the reliance on the state to attain the domestic and international objectives of private American business interests, or to advance a broader "national interest" on behalf of an allegedly new internationalism which scarcely concealed the imperial intent behind it . . .[40]

In summary, the Clausewitzian and the systemic views serve to complement each other in illuminating Soviet and American foreign policies. A realist analysis of Soviet foreign policy, such as Ulam's, brings out characteristics that the Soviet state shares with any other Great Power, characteristics that tend to be ignored or suppressed in the official Soviet definitions of Soviet foreign policy as well as in ideological views hostile to the Soviet Union. On the other hand, systemic analysis goes far deeper than traditional theories of international relations. It serves both to shatter ideologically nurtured moralistic illusions and to undermine the acceptance of the implicit identification of "national interests" with the security and aspirations of ordinary people.

CHAPTER 5

The Bargain

War, which has been endemic in Europe throughout her history, has on occasions exploded to pandemic proportions; for example, in the Thirty Years' War, in the Napoleonic Wars, and in the two World Wars. Each of these explosions was followed by attempts to organize some sort of *modus vivendi*. Such were the Treaty of Westphalia (1648), the Congress of Vienna (1815), and the Versailles Peace Conference (1919).

These conferences were understandably dominated by the "victors" or, at times, by the most domineering or the most astute diplomats representing the interests of the victors, for example, Metternich in 1815, Clemenceau in 1919. Nevertheless all parties involved were represented, because the *modus vivendi* to be instated affected all; the vanquished, as well as the victors, were expected to continue as members in the "community of states" and so to share in the power to be divided among them.

The conclusion of World War II led to no comparable multilateral peace conference. The setting up of a new "community of states" was relegated to the United Nations, formally a representative body but within which *all* power was to be concentrated in what was then thought to emerge as the Big Five: The United States, Great Britain, the U.S.S.R., France, and China. The latter two of the projected Big Five being at the time *hors de combat*, the Big Three undertook the distribution of power among their respective empires.

During the war the Big Three had been personified by the three war lords, Franklin D. Roosevelt, Winston S. Churchill, and Joseph V. Stalin. The three met in Teheran in November 1943 and again in Yalta early in 1945. In 1943 there was still much fighting to be done, and so military problems dominated the discussions. The Yalta conference, on the other hand, took place when the end of fighting in Europe was in sight. Here emerged the political problems foreshadowing the cold war.

Once the German armies disintegrated, the Western and the Soviet armies would be facing each other. While a commander facing a hostile army has at his disposal certain standard operating procedures, he has no such guidelines when facing a "friendly" army. The commanders of both armies may have received orders to occupy the same territory; obviously they cannot both occupy it. Occupation means setting up an authority; and since the authority set up by the military is absolute, there cannot be two such authorities. Therefore the orders given to commanders of allied armies coming in contact must be coordinated in advance, from above.

Part of the intent of the Conferences of the Big Three was to effect such coordination. The Big Three agreed to partition Germany and Austria into zones to be occupied respectively by Soviet, American, British, and French forces. As for the other territories in Eastern and Western Europe, their being cleared of German forces was seen as a "liberation" rather than an occupation. It was taken for granted that the states conquered or destroyed by Hilter's armies would be reestablished, and whichever foreign troops remained on their territories while military operations were still going on would leave soon after the termination of hostilities. The political problem arose from this prospect. Plainly put, the question was who was going to run the liberated countries. Each of The Three had different ideas on the subject.

The clearest ideas were those of Stalin. In order to understand how he thought, it is necessary, I believe, to dismiss any preconceived notion that Stalin was a "Communist." One could, of course, insist that Stalin was a Communist "by definition," something in the manner of Rodrigo Borgia being a Christian by virtue of being Pope. Such a definition, however, would serve no useful purpose.

To be sure, it is possible to trace the transformation from the apostles to the Renaissance popes and a parallel one from the early Marxists to Stalin. There is, for example, a resemblance between the roles of Paul and of Lenin: both laid foundations for a future world organization charged with proselytizing an ideology. Now, organization and exercise of power and the maintenance of faith in an ideal are psychologically antithetical. The former demands preoccupation with and sensitivity to external events, for example, evading threats posed by enemies, seizing opportunities, manipulating allies, etc., while the latter demands sustained contemplation and introspection, especially when the faith derives from intellectual conviction rather than from a childlike belief. The intellectual believer must constantly bring interpretations of events in line with his faith, must resolve contradictions, and so on; in short, he must live a complex inner life. The antithesis between involvement with power and devotion to a faith does not prevent the two from being occasionally combined in single, as a rule, unusually gifted individuals. There is evidence that they were so combined in Paul and in Lenin. Lenin's energies, like Paul's, were about equally divided between building a political machine, ultimately to become an instrument of absolute power, and working out a system of belief. Passionately committed, as he was, to the materialist (to his way of thinking the "scientific") mode of thought, Lenin was compelled to construct an intellectually defensible support for his system. Thus, even though the exigencies of the political moment often required him to twist and turn, to resort to casuistic arguments, and the like, still there is a thread of intellectual consistency in his "theory" and his policies.

Not a trace of either faith or intellectual integrity remained in Stalin. His contributions to political theory were negligible. Nor do we have any evidence of an inner struggle between the demands of power and a devotion to an ideal such as was manifested in Lenin's intellectual gyrations. Organization, usurpation, and extension of power (his own and the state's) were Stalin's only discernible preoccupations after his rise to eminence in the Communist hierarchy; and his unparalleled success in this enterprise enabled him to demolish the very foundations of "Leninism" while cynically avowing unshakable loyalty to Lenin's cause.

Thus, although Lenin's political program made necessary the welding of the Communist party into a rigidly disciplined body, Lenin still (sincerely, it seems) professed a faith in spontaneous political activity of the masses, at least of the "working class." Such an activity was no more possible under Stalin's rule than under Nicholas I.[1] Stalin's bureaucracy and secret police were monstrous exaggerations of their czarist counterparts. He resuscitated a crude nationalism that later degenerated into blatant chauvinism. Whereas in 1904 Marxists wrote that the victory of Japan checked Russian imperialist expansion in Asia, Stalin, declaring war against an already defeated Japan in August 1945, called on the nation to avenge the earlier humiliation and to erase the blot on "Russia's honor."[2]

Among historic figures whom Stalin admired there were no revolutionaries except canonized Lenin. He admired only potentates: Czar Ivan the Terrible,[3] Czar Peter the Great, and military leaders: General Kutuzov (of 1812) and General Suvorov. It is noteworthy that the latter was sent by Catherine II to crush a large and, at first, miraculously successful peasant revolt.

After Hitler's triumph over France, Molotov congratulated the German ambassador "on the success of German arms."[4] Hitler was then Stalin's colleague. Later Stalin showed considerable and probably sincere respect for Churchill and Roosevelt. At that time *they* were his colleagues. I do not believe that this respect was inspired simply by fear of the awesome power that at least America possessed (although the possession of power was to Stalin a necessary prerequisite to according respect). The respect in this case was rather akin to that felt by one tycoon or one monarch for another.

The victories over the Germans in World War II gave Stalin the wherewithal to play the global power game, and he came to Teheran and to Yalta to bargain.

Stalin's objectives were strictly limited: to restore and to consolidate the power of the Russian Empire, which meant, in effect, his personal power. He knew what he wanted and was prepared to pay for it within reason; he knew the value of the Red Army to the Western allies and he wanted to be paid for it. He promised to attack Japan three months after the fall of Germany. (He kept that promise to the day.) In return he asked for certain commercial concessions in Manchuria, and for certain portions of Japanese territory (some of it wrested from Russia in the Russo-Japanese War). As additional payment for his sphere of influence in China, Stalin promised to help Chiang-Kai-shek deal with the Chinese Communists.

The most important of Stalin's demands was a "sphere of influence" in Europe, specifically a reverse *cordon sanitaire*,[5] that is, governments "friendly" to the U.S.S.R. in the countries along the western borders of the Soviet Union. Afterward Stalin made some further demands such as for bases on Turkish territory, for a protectorate over Italian colonies, etc., but these were minor, possibly intended to concede in later bargaining in return for other concessions. The reverse *cordon sanitaire*, however, was not negotiable. It was to be Russia's Maginot Line.

Stalin thought in classical diplomilitary terms. A "won" war was for him an occasion to defray some of the cost and an opportunity to strengthen his position in the international power game. This is the way Bismarck thought in 1871. This is the way Clemenceau thought in 1919.

In all this horse trading, any more than in Stalin's personality, there is nothing that would make one think of Stalin as a Communist. Stalin did not bargain on behalf of "the toiling masses" of Poland or Manchuria. He bargained about the position of the Russo-Polish border and for shares of stock in the Eastern Chinese Railway. To be sure, one might point out that while bargaining with the imperialists Stalin had to speak their language, as Lenin did when he was bargaining with the Germans in 1918. Lenin, however, went to great lengths to explain or rationalize what he did in terms of the Communist theory of history and revolution. Everything he did had to be made consistent with the theory at least on the verbal level. Stalin saw no need for this. He was autocrat of all Russia. Populations did not exist for him except to the extent that they represented a labor or a military force. Granted, the Bolsheviks also manipulated the masses in their drive for power, but they were convinced that their own aspirations were those of the masses. In short, the Bolsheviks were dedicated people. Their ruthlessness and callousness stemmed in large measure from their fanatical dedication to what they believed to be the aspirations of the working

class. Stalin resembled a Bolshevik no more than Al Capone resembled Robespierre.

Churchill thought in categories similar to Stalin's, that is also
predominantly in nineteenth century categories of international
relations. Naturally, he was not obsessed with his personal power, having achieved his position by methods different from Stalin's and being accustomed to the idea of having to relinquish it
with a change in political weather. Churchill's involvement was
with the British Empire. At the close of World War II he still
thought that the prestige of the Empire could be restored, or at
least partially salvaged. Churchill also thought in terms of traditional British policy on the continent, that is in terms of the
continental "balance of power." In this conception states have
certain rights to be respected. In order to secure these rights to
the several states, the power ambitions of other states must be
"contained." Just what the limits of the "rights" of the U.S.S.R.
were to be in the new Europe that was to emerge from World
War II seems not to have been settled in Churchill's mind. He
seems to have been in accord with Stalin's idea that the geographical boundaries of Russia would have to be restored to
those of the old empire, except for Poland and Finland whose
national independence were a foregone conclusion. Churchill
seems also to have reconciled himself to the idea that the old
cordon sanitaire was not to be restored, which meant that the
U.S.S.R. had a "right" to expect "friendly" governments on its
western frontier. However, Churchill seemed to have been extremely apprehensive of a *cordon sanitaire in reverse,* that is, a
string of states in active alliance with Russia, probably under
Communist dictatorships.

In Churchill's estimation, the states of southeastern Europe
(the Balkans) were more important than Poland since they lay
on the way to the Suez Canal, and so on Britain's lifeline. This
basis was reflected in Churchill's position on the military
strategy of the war in Europe. Churchill opposed the establishment of a Second Front in France and recommended instead an
allied invasion of the Balkans, clearly intended to head off the
advance of the Red Army.

In effect, what Churchill wanted, it seems, was an Eastern
Europe that was Western-oriented but with governments that

would pose no military threat to the Soviet Union. But it was not easy for him to take a consistent stand on this matter. Sitting in London were the so-called London Poles who, when they became the Polish government-in-exile, considered themselves to be at war both with Germany and with the U.S.S.R. Their feelings on this matter were entirely understandable. Seventeen days after Hitler's armies entered Poland from the west, Stalin's armies entered from the east to finish off what remained of the defenders of that country. Shortly afterward Molotov, the Soviet foreign minister, explained how events disclosed the rottenness of the Polish state. "A short blow at Poland from the German army, followed by one from the Red Army was enough to reduce to nothing this monster child of the Treaty of Versailles."[6]

To the London Poles' way of thinking, there was only one way to erase this humiliation and that was to restore Poland's 1939 frontiers. Therein was the rub. For Poland's 1939 frontiers were themselves results of conquest and symbolized *Russia's* humiliation, which Stalin wanted erased. Stalin's position was greatly strengthened by the fact that, at the Versailles Peace Conference, Lord Curzon, a British statesman, had proposed a Russian-Polish border roughly along the lines of ethnic division (assuming that the Ukranians and the Byelorussians "belong" to Russia). In 1920 the Poles had attacked Russia, then embroiled in a civil war, and pushed the frontier eastward, incorporating large non-Polish populations into Poland. Stalin, in asking the restoration of the Curzon Line, was only asking what was rightfully "his" and besides had been acknowledged as Russia's by a British statesman. Churchill, therefore, was in no position to oppose the Curzon Line.

When The Three were conferring in Yalta, the Red Army had already penetrated into Poland. Clearly some sort of government had to be formed in order to administer the areas cleared of Germans. These areas became the Red Army's rear. Communication and supplies flowed through them to the front, and so the preservation of order in those areas was essential to the operation of the Red Army. Accordingly, the so-called Lublin Committee was formed (of Poles who had escaped from the Germans into the Soviet Union). Naturally these were people who would cooperate fully with the Russians, at least during the time that their country was being cleared of Germans. The question now was what the status of the Lublin Committee would be when the war was over.

Churchill's hope was that the Polish London government in exile would become the government of liberated Poland. Nevertheless he realized quite clearly that this would be impossible unless these London Poles showed some evidence of "friendliness" or, at least, of absence of "hostility" toward the Soviet Union. The question of the Russian-Polish border was a key issue here; and it is precisely on this question that the London Poles remained adamant. Churchill was exasperated by their attitude—not, as we shall see, because of any sympathy on his part for the Soviet Union or its territorial claims, but because he appreciated the power relations emerging in Europe as the Red Army was advancing westward. The London Poles had nothing with which to back their arguments except the conviction that justice was on their side and that therefore the power of the Western allies would be behind them. While they thought in these absolute terms, Churchill was calculating *how much* power the Allies could exert on Stalin and on what issues. He knew that the territorial claim of the London Poles was the weakest conceivable issue on which the West could take a stand.

Churchill tried to make the London Poles understand that by insisting on prewar frontiers they were destroying their chances of becoming, or even participating in, the postwar Polish government. If the frontier question was not settled, he warned them, the Russians would build up a rival government and gradually take over authority in Poland.

It appears, therefore, that, even though the border question could have been easily settled, the question of the organization of the Polish government loomed as an insuperable obstacle to agreement between Stalin and the Allies on Poland.

Roosevelt brought with him what remained of the traditional American view that the United States entered World War I and World War II in order to curb aggression and to prevent despotic oppression of nations. Roosevelt thought less in traditional diplomilitary categories than did either Stalin or Churchill. He still thought in Wilsonian categories, that is, of a restoration of a peaceful world order. It was clear to him that this was possible only with the cooperation of the Soviet Union. We do not know whether his hope of continuing cooperation with the Soviet Union persisted to the end of his days. We do know, however, that much of his thinking about the postwar world was dominated by this idea.

Like Churchill, Roosevelt had a problem with "his" Poles. These were not a paper government claiming legitimacy but a real political force, a large sector of the American electorate of Polish and other East European descent. The sentiments of these people were strongly anti-Russian and anti-Communist, and Roosevelt, who understood the facts of political life and death more clearly than Wilson, had to take these sentiments into account. The character of the future Polish government was therefore of concern to him, quite aside from the role that Poland was to play in a future "balance of power" in Europe.

The main result of the Yalta Conference was an "agreement" on Poland. Her eastern border was to be the Curzon Line. As compensation for the lost territories, Poland was to receive a slice of Germany. As Churchill put it, Poland was to be "moved westward." As for her government, it was to be a "broadly representative and democratic one."

After the war, two opinions concerning this "agreement" became widely current in the United States. One was that Roosevelt sold the Poles down the river and with them the American national interests in Europe. The other was that Stalin double-crossed the West and reneged on his promise to allow a "democratic" Poland. The two opinions (often held by the same people) are not compatible. For if the Poles were betrayed in Yalta, then Stalin did not break any "agreement." If, on the other hand, Stalin reneged on his promise, then a promise to allow a "democratic Poland" must have been extracted from him at Yalta, and so the Poles were not betrayed *there*. As for the Poles being betrayed afterward, it is clear that the only way they could have been saved from Russian domination was by getting the Soviet army out of Poland. To be sure, this course of action *was* advocated. What does not often occur to its proponents is that this very advocacy may have been responsible for the Sovietization of Poland.

It is quite possible that Stalin did not think he was deceiving anyone when he agreed to a "broadly representative democratic government" in Poland. As I have suggested in all seriousness, Stalin was not a Communist. Stalin's policy in Eastern Europe was directed at securing Russia's western borders against future attacks and, as it turned out, toward an economic exploitation of the region in connection with compensating Russia's vast losses. His goal was the establishment of "friendly" governments on Russia's borders. Granted it can be argued that Communist governments would be *ipso facto* "friendly governments." In fact, however, Stalin seems to have been actually uneasy about the existence of Communist states outside the U.S.S.R. Given Stalin's mentality, it is easy to see the reasons for this. Stalin related to others in one of two ways: either they were to be absolutely subservient to him, or they were opponents against whom he played a game of strategy. He thought of himself as a master of this game. In a way he was. He was in fact most at ease with opponents. A henchman could always turn out to be a traitor, and in his mind most of them did. He knew where he stood with an opponent. He did not conceive of "allies" in any sense except as a temporary expedient. For this reason, the existence of Communists outside the Soviet Union must have been a constant threat to him. Even though the Communist parties outside Russia (except possibly the Chinese) were, during Stalin's life, almost completely subservient to Moscow, Stalin could never be sure of their blind obedience. On several occasions he acted to curtail Communist movements abroad. He supported Chiang Kai-shek even after the latter started to massacre the Communists; he restrained the Communists of Western Europe from making a bid for power after World War II; he had the entire Central Committee of the Polish Communist party murdered; he is said to have ordered the "liquidation" of the Greek revolutionary movement; etc.[7]

It then stands to reason that Stalin would have preferred conservative governments to Communist ones in at least some countries of Eastern Europe. (As evidence, Stalin toyed with the idea of preserving monarchy in Romania.) All he wanted was for these governments to play ball with the Soviet Union in international relations and in the matter of economic concessions. It is even possible that he somehow sensed that Communists would eventually discover the truth about him, namely that he was a traitor to the Communist cause.

If the Western Allies had accepted the principle of strictly delineated "spheres of influence," which was the essence of Stalin's demand after the defeat of Germany, a general peace treaty might have been signed by the Allies and their erstwhile enemies. Whether this would have prevented the cold war and the nuclear arms race no one can say. All we know is that the sphere of influence principle was categorically rejected by the United States; that, in the years following, the coalition governments of Poland, Czechoslovakia, Romania, Hungary, and Bulgaria gave way to one-party dictatorships; that a nuclear arms race did develop; that the German issue remained unsolved; that the United States announced an enlarged "Monroe Doctrine" encompassing the whole world; and that this doctrine has remained to this day the guideline of its foreign policy.

CHAPTER 6

The First Confrontation

Of the three men planning to reorganize the postwar world at Teheran and Yalta, one was soon to die and another was soon to lose his office. Did it occur to any of The Three to wonder whether the "agreements" would be binding on their successors? Or did they take it for granted that the agreements were made by powers that outlive their rulers? If so, then they must have realized that there were not three powers but only two. It was the mighty juggernauts of the Soviet Union and of the United States that crushed Germany and Japan. Whatever tribute one chooses to pay to Britain's valor and steadfastness when she fought alone, the fact remains that the Axis would probably have been beaten without Britain but most likely not without either the United States or the Soviet Union. It would then have to be The Two who would reorganize the world. And if the scales of power were tipped one way or another, there was nothing to put on the scales to restore the balance.

As the end of World War II was approaching, it seemed to those who faced the problem of charting the course of future foreign policy that much would depend on the outcome of the first confrontation between the two real victors. For reasons mentioned in Chapter 4, information of what went on in the minds of Soviet rulers is scanty. On the American side, information of this sort is plentiful. Several of the principal actors picture the confrontation as that between the determination of

American leaders to restore a "democratic Europe" outside the borders of the U.S.S.R. and Stalin's adamant insistence on extending the power of the Soviet Union westward.

Herbert Feis, for example,[1] begins his account by showing that the Western Allies repulsed all the overtures of the Germans toward arranging a separate armistice on the Western Front even though it may have been advantageous for the Allies to do so, since it would have enabled the Germans to hold off the Russians until the Allies could occupy more of German territory and so be in a better postwar bargaining position vis-à-vis the Russians. The Allies proved their "good faith," as Feis puts it, by adhering strictly to the agreement of demanding unconditional surrender to all the Allies simultaneously.

Feis goes on to show that the Russians were sharply suspicious of the Allies' intentions to the very last day of the war. The simultaneous and unconditional surrender of the Germans did not allay the Russians' suspicions. According to Feis, it was repeated confrontations with these suspicions, nurtured by a fixed idea of an implacable hostility of the "capitalists" that forced the hardening of U.S. policy toward the U.S.S.R. Even then, Feis points out, the change of American attitudes lagged behind that of the British.

> As Soviet egotism and transgression became increasingly apparent, British and American authorities began to diverge in their ideas of how best to deal with the emerging situation. While the assault on Germany was in its last phase, Churchill and his colleagues reverted to the ways in which Britain had constrained or confined Russia in the past. They urged that the armies on the western front be directed to secure positions as far into the center of Europe as possible, and along as many enclosing edges of Europe as possible, and then kept in place, in full strength. They thought that, with Anglo-American diplomacy thus supported, the Soviet rulers should be confronted with a choice between moderation and coercion.
>
> But Truman and his colleagues were not so excited about the rifts in the coalition, or so sure about their depth or import. They regarded disputes about the time-beaten boundaries and alliances between nations in the center of Europe more calmly. When had all the countries of the European complex ever been in stable accord on these questions? Should the United States, too, like so many other countries in the past, be led into elevating minor conflicts over complicated equities into causes of crises? Was it not saner to show patience and friendliness?[2]

Nevertheless, Feis says a little later:

> . . . During all these weeks, while resisting British pleas, the
> American officials, civil and military, were wondering whether
> they ought not show a changed mien toward the Soviet govern-
> ment, and perhaps seek release from the agreements with it into
> which they had entered. They were verging toward somber second
> thoughts—called in more solemn later days an "agonizing reap-
> praisal."[3]

In a later book,[4] Feis reiterates the thesis that Truman was
at first determined to continue Roosevelt's policy of cooperation
with the Soviet Union but that his attempt was frustrated by
Soviet intransigence on the political fate of Eastern Europe,
which led to the abandonment of the policy of cooperation and
the pronouncement of the so-called Truman Doctrine and the
launching of the Marshall Plan in 1947.

The clash between United States fair-mindedness and Soviet
obstinacy may be taken to be the basis of the "official" United
States explanation of the first confrontation between The Two.
But, of course, views sharply dissenting from this "official" interpretation are also plentiful in American accounts of the origins of the cold war. Many of these appeared in print consider-
ably later, against the background of the painful consequences
of the cold war, such as the nuclear arms race, American involvement in counterinsurgency, etc. H. Stuart Hughes[5] calls
these dissenting accounts "revisionist history," which I take to
mean reconstructions of events with the intent to show that earlier perceptions and interpretations of those events had been
mistaken.

In his own recollections, Hughes tells of the opposition of "a
small group of [his] friends and associates [whose assumptions]
differed both from the conventional cold-war stance that was
then emerging and from the revisionist view that has recently
become so widespread."[6]

The opposition (which Hughes attributes also to men of such
diverse views as Henry L. Stimson, Henry A. Wallace, and
George F. Kennan) "pushed the spheres of influence line," that
is, presumably for a more "symmetrical" view of U.S. and Soviet
interests, bolstered perhaps by the adage that "good fences make
good neighbors." The failure of the opposition was reflected in
the refusal of the United States leaders to accept the partition

of Europe, preferring to "declare" the cold war simultaneously with the Soviet Union, as it were.

> It may sound paradoxical [writes Hughes] to have believed that a de facto partition of Europe would have facilitated rather than hindered the building of bridges from one side to the other. But that was what eventually proved true. In the crucial year 1946–1947 the Russians were treating this partition as the legitimate consequence of their military victories and the indispensable guarantee of their national security; the Americans were speaking of it as abnormal and immoral. Such at least was their public rhetoric; in actuality our government was to accept piece by piece over the years a situation it had originally rejected in toto. The proof came a decade later, in the autumn of 1956, when the United States failed to go to the aid of the anti-Communist insurrection in Hungary. And the result was what my friends and I had predicted: once the Russians knew that the Americans would not step over the line into what they had always considered their own sphere of influence, a thaw in the cold war, the beginnings of liberalization in Eastern Europe, and the inauguration of East-West cultural contacts finally became possible.[7]

In contrasting his view of the origins of the cold war with those of the "revisionists," Hughes presumably refers to the tendency of the latter to fix more blame on the United States than is warranted in a "realist" conception of international relations. Of course, it is impossible to measure the "amount of blame" or to fix a base line of comparison. Many of the revisionist accounts, with their heavy emphasis on aggressive thrusts by the United States, may well have been intended (consciously or otherwise) to counteract the self-righteousness that enveloped American public opinion with regard to the cold war in the early years.

Gar Alperovitz's account of the first confrontation is an example of the revisionist reconstruction of events in the spring and summer of 1945.[8] Alperovitz's thesis is that the direction of U.S. foreign policy was set by the conviction entertained by Harry S. Truman and some of his advisers that a monopoly of atomic weapons conferred upon the United States the power to shape the postwar world order in accordance with its own precepts. The factual evidence offered by Alperovitz provides impressive support of this view. Whether the events retold by him constitute the "key to the cold war" is not, of course, a meaningful question. There is no way of "isolating the causes" of large-scale historical events. However, the events surrounding the first appearance of atomic weapons on the stage of history were sufficiently dramatic to deserve careful scrutiny. I believe they are of importance in evaluating the *perceptions* of U.S.-Soviet relations, and that is primarily our subject of concern. We turn to an interpretation of the initial Soviet-American confrontation based on Alperovitz's account.

Roosevelt died on April 12, 1945. Upon assuming office Harry S. Truman was told about The Bomb, of which he evidently had no prior knowledge. According to Alperovitz the events from April to August 1945 indicate that Truman and his advisers regarded the bomb as a gift from Providence that made it possible for the United States to avoid the morass into which it was being drawn: the interminable negotiations, the bargaining and bickering, the bluffs and threats, the seizing of opportunities, and the prudent retreats—in short, the headaches of "mature" diplomacy. Now that the United States held the ultimate weapon, there was no need to negotiate with Stalin, Molotov ("The Iron Behind"), and their ilk. The United States held a Royal Flush and could raise on any bid.

This interpretation gains credence against the background of the traditional attitudes of the United States in world affairs. To be sure, the United States had never had the sort of monopoly of power that now the atomic bomb presumably conferred upon it. However, the traditional American outlook in world affairs has been such that its behavior in the months after Germany's surrender was just of the sort to be expected. One would expect that the United States would use its suddenly acquired, seemingly absolute power not so much to flaunt and brandish, or to intimidate with, as to free itself from the necessity of learning to play the power game according to the rules. In the eyes of people like Truman, an excellent specimen of the Average American, America always possessed Absolute Right. Now she attained Absolute Might. This might was not going to be abused. Like Superman, America would use it only in the interest of peace and justice. Those who were for peace and justice would have nothing to fear from America. Others would soon find out how far they might and might not go.

According to Alperovitz, the rejection of the Yalta agreement by Truman was categorical, deliberate, and immediate. Naturally a nation state seldom reneges on agreements explicitly. This happens only in connection with the launching of a war, as, for example, when Germany, about to invade Belgium, declared that the treaty guaranteeing Belgium's neutrality was no more than a scrap of paper, or when Stalin denounced the nonaggression pacts with Finland in 1939 and with Japan in 1945 while preparing to attack them. The usual maneuver is to interpret the agreement so as to make it appear that the other side violated it and that consequently it is no longer in force.

As has been said, the Yalta agreement provided ample opportunity for alternative interpretations. Specifically, in the case of Poland, it provided, on the one hand, that the future Polish government would be "friendly" to the Soviet Union and, on the other, that it would be "reorganized" to include a number of Western-oriented leaders. The question now became what is a "friendly" government and, above all, who is to judge whether a government is "friendly"? Is the proper judge in this matter the state toward which the government is to be "friendly," or other presumably more impartial parties? There was also the question as to what constituted a "broad representation" and a "democratic character" and, above all, by what standards these criteria were to be established. Soviet leaders maintained that the Yalta agreement was kept to the letter on their part, since some of the London Poles actually were included in the Warsaw government (which the Lublin Committee became), and several political parties were functioning in Poland. Americans were not satisfied because the agreed upon "free elections" were not held.

Quite aside from the Polish issue, however, Alperovitz shows that Truman's idea of "cooperating" with Russia was very different from Roosevelt's. Truman took pride in his bluntness and made ample use of it in the weeks immediately after Roosevelt's death. Alperovitz refers to the policy of those first weeks (until May 1945) as the strategy of Immediate Showdown.

The end of military operations in Europe, Roosevelt's death, and Truman's own inclinations led to the crystallization of that policy. Indeed, during Roosevelt's lifetime, all those who for ideological reasons had misgivings about or were repelled by the notion of cooperating with Communist Russia, but had been restrained while Russia's military contribution was still essential in Europe and while Roosevelt was still alive, now felt both constraints removed.

There was yet another constraint on the "tough line" which vanished in the spring of 1945; that was the need for Soviet cooperation in the war against Japan. As said in the previous chapter, both at the Teheran meeting of The Three and at Yalta, the Allies secured from Stalin a firm commitment to declare war against Japan two or three months after the defeat of Germany. By the spring of 1945, however, Japan was rapidly collapsing. Her navy gone, she could be completely blockaded and literally starved into submission. Now the makers of American strategy were looking around for a way of *preventing* Russia's entry into the Asian war.

With all constraints gone, the hard liners had a free hand. The advice now given to the new President, who had practically no experience in foreign affairs, converged on getting tough with the Russians. As noted, Truman's response was immediate and positive. There were several expressions of satisfaction on the part of the hard liners with how things were going. Acting secretary Joseph Grew said on one occasion:

> He [Truman] won't stand for any pussyfooting in our foreign policy, all of which warms my heart. You can imagine what a joy it is to deal with a man like that.[9]

Grew was convinced that "a future war with Soviet Russia is as certain as anything in this world can be certain. It may come within a very few years."[10]

As for Harry S. Truman, it is not difficult to surmise his attitude from his earlier remarks on the occasion of the outbreak of the war between Russia and Germany:

> If we see that Germany is winning the war, we ought to help Russia and if Russia is winning we ought to help Germany.[11]

What a man said on one occasion is not conclusive evidence about his frame of mind on other occasions. In the war years, when it seemed that the United States and the Soviet Union depended on cooperation for their survival, Truman's attitudes may well have undergone a change. It is noted, however, that when circumstances permit a man to return to a previous outlook with a feeling that he was right all along, he does so easily and with a sense of relief.

The policy of immediate showdown was revealed in Truman's meeting with Molotov on April 23. Truman's stand during that meeting was based on the assumption that there was nothing now that the Soviet Union could do militarily that was of any use to the United States and that, consequently, the United States had no further use for the Russians. The Russians, on the other hand, needed the assistance of the United States in the way of credits for reconstruction. Consequently the United States was in a position to state its demands once and for all. The Russians could take it or leave it.

Explicitly Truman said to Molotov that, although the Yalta agreement was subject to different interpretations, the American interpretation would have to be accepted by the Soviet Union. Molotov replied that, in his opinion, the difficulties could be ironed out. Truman replied "sharply" that the agreement arrived at in Yalta with regard to Poland would have to be carried out by the Soviet Union. This involved, in the American view, the complete reorganization of the Warsaw government. Molotov tried to explain that the Soviet Union had not broken the agreement. Truman said that American cooperation would not continue on the basis of a one-way street.

"I have never been talked to like that in my life," Molotov declared.

"Carry out your agreements and you won't get talked to like that,"[12] Truman responded.

That was laying it on the line. One cannot help but interpret this sort of "diplomacy" in the light of American historical experience. In 1919 the American plan for the "reorganization of the world" had been rejected, partly because of the intransigence of European statesmen, partly because the American public was not ready to accept the idea of continuing to be involved in world affairs. Now another such opportunity to "reorganize the world" was presenting itself. *This* time the isolationists had no voice to shout with. It seems that both Europe and the isolationists had learned their lesson: the world *needed* America, and America would see to it that the world was properly organized, in accordance with American percepts. As in

1919, America wanted nothing for herself—no territories, no colonies. On the contrary, America wanted to give, to continue giving as she had been giving so generously, intervening on the side of justice.

In the American view of the post-war world, American security that was now clearly seen to be bound up with European security, depended on the existence of "democratic" governments, established by "free elections," and preferably supporting economic systems based on "free enterprise." The only obstacle to this arrangement for a peaceful world was Russia, committed to an "authoritarian" form of government which she was now installing in the countries overrun by her armies. Experience with Germany had taught the world that the "appeasement" of dictatorships led to war. Dictatorships are by their nature expansionist, and yielding to their demands only serves to convince them that they can make more demands. Therefore firm resistance is the only stand one can make vis-à-vis a dictatorship. *None* of the Russians' demands are in the last analysis legitimate since they are motivated solely by their insatiable appetite for expansion and domination. It is therefore useless to try to engage them in a give-and-take negotiation. However, dictators understand the language of force. The United States could now use this language with perfect justification and impunity.

There was one man in Truman's cabinet who opposed the policy of immediate showdown. This was Secretary of War Henry L. Stimson. His opposition was on tactical grounds. He believed that the time for the showdown had not yet come. At the conclusion of fighting in Europe *the* trump card was not yet firmly in the hands of the President.

It should be stressed at the outset that it was *not* Stimson's intention to threaten the Russians with an atomic attack if they did not accede to American demands. This way of regarding atomic weapons was to come later. Stimson thought of the atomic bomb as a "trump" in the same way that American economic potential was a trump. His idea was to offer Russia joint control of atomic weapons, that is to offer to admit them to "atomic partnership" with the United States in the reorganization of Europe. That this was neither James Byrnes's nor Harry Truman's conception will presently be made apparent.[13] Nevertheless Stimson was able to convince Truman that the showdown must wait until the atomic bomb was a reality.

Thereupon Truman reversed his policy. Harry Hopkins, Roosevelt's erstwhile personal adviser and an advocate of cooperation with the Soviet Union, was sent on a mission to Moscow to make amends for Truman's initial blustering tone. The decision to stop all lend-lease to the U.S.S.R. immediately after Germany's surrender (to the extent of recalling ships already at sea) was modified at least to permit the delivery of the materials already en route. The Polish issue was played down. The idea was to stall. The hope was that the atomic bomb would be "demonstrated" before the meeting of The Three in Potsdam and so, to insure the possession of *all* the trump cards in American hands, could be revealed.

The reversal was bewildering to those who could not surmise the motives behind it. Churchill was especially disturbed by the delays of the Potsdam Conference insisted upon by Truman. In Churchill's mind, this meeting should occur as *early* as possible, before American troops started to be withdrawn from Europe. Indeed, Churchill wanted to use the presence of American troops in what was to be the Soviet-occupied zone of Germany as a bargaining point. In short, Churchill thought it was in the interest of the West to settle all political questions as soon as possible. He was apparently reconciled to the "spheres of influence" interpretation of the Yalta agreement as the basis for discussion, hoping to get as much as could be gotten starting from there. He therefore was exasperated by the delays of the Potsdam Conference. Assuming at one time that the delays were instigated by Stalin, he wired to the latter, protesting the postponements, to which Stalin truthfully replied that it was not he but President Truman who insisted on them.[14]   Truman and Byrnes were waiting for two events, first the test explosion of the atomic bomb in New Mexico, second the atomic bombing of a Japanese city. The first event would put their own minds at rest by the knowledge that they really were in possession of the fantastic weapon. The second event would demonstrate to the world—primarily, of course, to the Russians—what this weapon could do.

It should be noted at this time that some of the leading scien-

tists involved in the development of the bomb attempted to dis-
suade first Roosevelt, then Truman, from actually using it on
people. They recommended a demonstration similar to the New
Mexico test explosion which the Japanese would be invited to
witness. The demonstration, they argued, would be used as an
ultimatum to the Japanese in the demand for unconditional surrender. This proposal was never seriously considered. As Truman himself has stated, there was no "decision" to use the
atomic bomb on the Japanese. It was simply *assumed* that it
would be used. Against the arguments of people like Albert Ein-
stein and Leo Szilard was the psychological consideration that a
"harmless" demonstration might fail to impress the Japanese,
even if they accepted the invitation to see it. If so, the total
impact of the weapon would be lost. No, the weapon had to be
demonstrated "in combat."

Note the use of the word "combat" in this context, an example of the extended meaning this word was to assume thereafter.
This meaning can be surmised from the formal definition of
"military target," later to appear in the U.S. Air Force Manual:

> Any person, thing, idea [*sic*], entity or location selected for de-
> struction, inactivation, or rendering non-usable with weapons
> which will reduce or destroy the will or ability of the enemy to
> resist.[15]

And so, in Alperovitz's view, Truman and Byrnes hoped that
the Potsdam Conference would take place after the atomic
bomb had been demonstrated "in combat." This was not to be.
The test explosion coincided with the start of the Conference.
When Truman was informed of the complete success of the test,
his mind was made up. There would be *no* concessions to the
Russians. However, neither was the final showdown to take
place at the Conference. It would take place in a few days, after
the bomb was exploded in Japan. It was, therefore, pointless to
continue the Conference, and Truman insisted on winding it up
without further haggling about the future of Eastern Europe.
The last traces of whatever advantages could be gained from
Russia's entry into the war against Japan were also lost. In short,
as far as Truman was concerned there was nothing more to talk
about.

Feis also notes the effect on Truman of the news from New Mexico:

> To that alert observer [Churchill] Truman had seemed to be a changed person, maintaining his stand against the Russians in a more emphatic and decisive manner. . . .
> Some of the President's attendant staff had the same impression of new gusto and greater firmness.[16]

Nevertheless Feis discounts the idea that the possession of the bomb made a major difference in the aims or in the conduct of American foreign policy. He goes on:

> But also, [the change] is not detectable in the dull monochrome tone of the American minutes of the conference. Nor can I discern that any change in mood or attitude or judgment lasted through the following days of the conference. Certainty that we would be able to defeat the Soviet Union in war did not cause Truman or his advisors, military or civilian, to be more demanding. It apparently did not lead them to anticipate that the Russians would be more yielding after the great destructive power of the weapon was proved in use against Japan.[17]

The official apology for the slaughter of civilians in Hiroshima and Nagasaki is that it served to shorten the war, often with the implication that the bombings actually *saved* lives, both American and Japanese, that would have been lost in an invasion of Japan. The "humanitarian" motive need not be taken seriously in view of the powerful political incentive to end the war before the Russians had the chance to be in on the kill and so demand a share of the spoils.[18] From Alperovitz's account, however, one gets the impression that, aside from this political motive, an important, perhaps predominant, reason for using the atomic bomb as a terror weapon was the necessity to demonstrate to the Russians who was going to do the organizing of the postwar world, and who was being given the opportunity to do the cooperating. Russia could cooperate, it turned out in subsequent confrontations, if she stayed within her old borders, approximately those of the old empire (minus Finland and Poland), and abandoned any ideas about exercising any "influence" outside of those borders. If she behaved, she could share in the benefits of America's largesse. This was the aim of atomic diplomacy.

As already noted, Alperovitz describes two versions of this

diplomacy, Stimson's on the one hand and Truman's and Byrnes' on the other. Stimson wanted to use the atomic bomb as a carrot—as an inducement to the Russians to cooperate with the United States in return for some joint or international control of atomic weapons. Truman, and especially Byrnes whose views Truman accepted throughout, intended to use the bomb as a stick. The stick conception prevailed.

After the Potsdam Conference there was no longer any question of "sharing atomic secrets" or establishing any scheme of controlling atomic weapons. "As far as I was concerned, this was not a matter for discussion," wrote Truman in his *Memoirs*.[19] The tone of American diplomacy made it apparent that if "cooperation" between the United States and the Soviet Union was to be resumed it would be strictly on terms dictated by the United States.

According to Alexander Werth,[20] there was a "soft faction" in Stalin's entourage, people who hoped for solid aid from the United States, for more openness in Soviet life, and for resuming contacts with the West. Whether that faction would have prevailed if Truman refrained from trying to intimidate Stalin, we shall never know. Possibly the "objective situation" would have dictated a different course regardless of Stalin's constitutional inability to trust anyone. For it would have been incomparably easier to rebuild ravaged Russia with American aid and credits than by putting the squeeze on the "liberated" people of Eastern Europe. It is also possible, however, that Stalin was relieved by Truman's intransigence. "Cooperation" had never been Stalin's forte. Now he could say, not without some justification, that the United States was determined to see to it that the Soviet Union got *nothing* for its colossal sacrifices. He could now revert to his customary (and, in his view, successful) autocratic policies. The satellites would have to become "blood donors" to Russia's devastated economy. This could be accomplished only by strict totalitarian controls. Also the Russians would have to be insulated from ideas that could stimulate consumer appetites. Therefore an iron curtain had to be lowered across Europe. This was Stalin's answer to atomic diplomacy.

CHAPTER 7

Perceptions of the Cold War

"Cold war" is a catch-all phrase that subsumes the entire course of Soviet-American relations since 1945. To the extent that these relations have a central theme, comprise some "whole" that hangs together, so to say, the phrase serves a purpose. However, the image conveyed by the phrase tends to remain constant (because the phrase remains the same) while the events, processes, attitudes, and policies subsumed under it keep changing. It is easy to lose sight of the complex, changing reality behind the simple, constant label.

The purpose of analysis is to examine events and processes behind the labels so as to get a better understanding of what, if anything, we are talking about.

A process can be analyzed on the level of events and on the level of perceptions. The former analysis is an inquiry into what happened, the latter into how what happened was perceived or interpreted by specific individuals or groups. Analyses carried out in the natural sciences are usually confined to the level of events, and rightly so, if we are convinced that the events in the nonhuman world have an ultimate objective reality independent of our perceptions. Analyses of human affairs, however, cannot be confined to the level of events. In any process involving human affairs, perceptions and interpretations of events by human beings are *themselves* events, sometimes of prime importance to the process. Moreover, we cannot examine all events, and so must select from among them those to be included in our analysis; and our selection will depend in large measure on our own perceptions and interpretations. If we wish to be objective, we must be aware of these perceptions and of their sources. Finally, the way we select the events to be described may influence the further course of the process. If we are not indifferent to what course will ensue, we have a certain responsibility in making our selection. For this reason, too, we must be aware of our perceptions and their sources. We shall approach our analysis of the cold war in this spirit.

We shall be primarily concerned with the way the cold war was, or is, perceived by the military, by the makers of foreign policy, and by the populations at large.

Clearly all of these perceptions and their effects are interrelated. Military policies must have influenced diplomacy and vice versa. Public opinion and moods must have reflected trends in policy and may have been in greater or lesser measure among the factors influencing the trends. The task of tracing all of these influences and interdependencies (what is now fashionable to call "systems analysis") is far beyond the scope of this book. Here we can only sketch the outlines of American and Soviet perceptions.

The perceptions most clearly derived from *realpolitik* were those of Stalin. We may, perhaps, assume that they were the only ones that prevailed in the conduct of Soviet foreign policy at the close of World War II and in the crucial early phase of the cold war. As we have seen, Stalin's vision of postwar Europe was a simple one. The countries of Eastern Europe occupied by Soviet armies were to be incorporated in the Soviet "sphere of interest." Stalin assumed also that the United States and Britain would take a free hand in countries occupied by their armies, and there is ample evidence that he was willing to accept this arrangement as reflecting the true power relations of the time.[1]

If this is so, then several notions prevalent in the United States about the origins of the cold war lack foundation. One of these notions held that it was Stalin's intention to "take over" all of Europe and that he was deterred from doing so first by the American monopoly of the atomic bomb and later by the economic restoration and rearmament of Europe under American auspices. Another notion was that Eastern Europe was "sold down the river" at Yalta, the implication being that the Soviets might have been expelled from the region by a combination of resolute diplomatic and military moves after, or even during, the war. Finally there was a widespread notion that Stalin reneged on his promise at Yalta to allow a democratic, "widely representative" government in Poland.

As to the first, if should be noted that, prior to an aggression by a modern state, evidence of such an intention is always on hand: demonstrable military preparations, advance justification of attack or intervention, provocations calculated to provide an excuse, etc. Thus Mussolini's attack on Ethiopia, Hitler's attack on Poland, Stalin's attack on Finland, Japan's thrust into Indonesia— all of these moves were highly predictable events, advertised well in advance by word and deed. Of such symptoms there was no trace in 1945–1948 with regard to an impending Soviet aggression in Europe.

The notion that Stalin could have been kept out of Eastern Europe was equally unfounded. To attempt it would have meant to continue the war in Europe after Germany's collapse. While this course may have been on occasions advocated by one or two U.S. senators, it could not be seriously considered in the political climate at the close of World War II. Nor is it likely that frank threats based on the U.S. monopoly of the atomic bomb would have been enough to scare Stalin into withdrawing from Eastern Europe. As will be shown below (cf. p. 103), the appearance of the bomb made no dent in the Stalinist military doctrine, reinforced as it was by the outcome of World War II. Stalin fully expected to be able to parry any military thrust into Eastern Europe, bomb or no bomb.

Whether Stalin reneged on his promise to allow a "widely representative" government in Poland depends on the meaning ascribed to this phrase.

I offer an interpretation of the affair that exonerates Stalin of "duplicity" without adding an inch to his moral stature. Stalin simply had no conception of what his partners at Yalta meant by the term "representative government" when he promised to allow such governments to be established in the countries of Eastern Europe. I venture to say that very few among those who exercise political power really examine what a genuinely representative or democratic government involves; nor are the meanings of these terms easy to define. Like beauty, they are usually "so" only in the eyes of the beholder. To the Westerner, the criteria of "democratic government" are satisfied, at least in theory, if certain election procedures are adhered to, meaning the procedures prevailing in Western nations. In the Soviet Union there is an equally strong conviction that a crucial criterion of "democratic government" is the representation of all different social strata in government bodies. A Russian will proudly quote statistics showing that the Supreme Soviet is composed of members of "the working class," representatives from collective farms, intellectuals of all calibers, and, not the least, women. "How many women are members of Congress in the U.S.A.?" he will ask after having quoted the impressive Soviet figure. Actually, his conception is not much different from that of a New York mayor who, in appointing various commissions, is careful to include the requisite proportions of Jews, Italians, Irish, Blacks, etc.

Now, in the West, these indices of "wide representation" and "democracy" are considered to be mere trappings. In challenging the genuineness of Soviet "democracy" we insist on probing the political realities behind the trappings. But so does the Russian when he challenges American conceptions of democracy. And if we go along with him and examine our own political realities, shall we find much of the democracy with which we glibly identify the political image of the United States?

So, when Stalin agreed to allow a "widely representative government" in Poland and in the other states of Eastern Europe, he may well have had in mind the same sort of "representation" that characterizes the Soviet government, even going further in allowing several "political parties." (To this day there are three formally organized "political parties" in Poland with representatives in the Seym.)

In other countries of Eastern Europe, the initial "wide representation" was even more evident. For example, in Hungary, according to a U.S. State Department report, power was exercised by "a coalition government headed by a conservative general [which] includes representatives of the five principle parties

of the center and the left. . . . There has been no attempt to
. . . substitute a purely leftist regime for the present coalition
government." Colonel Kimon Georgiev, heading the "Father-
land Front" government of Bulgaria, installed in October 1944,
was described by a State Department representative as a "true
conservative." The new premier of Romania, Groza, was a prosperous landowner and industrialist with an anti-Communist record.[2]

It may well have been the case, as United States leaders insisted, that all of these coalition governments were only facades
erected in preparation of Communist take-overs. At the same
time, in view of the events described in Chapter 6, it is no less
reasonable to suppose that the Sovietization of Eastern Europe
(completed by 1948) was a consequence of Stalin's reaction to
the policy of immediate showdown. Truman's demands regarding the "reorganization" of East European governments were a
far cry from Churchill's "formula" whereby the U.S.S.R. was to
be allotted "50 percent influence in Hungary, 75 in Bulgaria,
and 90 percent in Romania," whatever these figures were
meant to represent.[3] Stalin may have well become convinced
that it was the intention of the United States to despoil the
U.S.S.R. of the fruits of its victory, essentially to eliminate it
from European affairs and put it in the same vulnerable position
in which it had been in 1939. In the logic of power politics,
lowering the iron curtain could just as well be interpreted as
an act of self-defense.

Thereupon the postwar period was transformed into a prewar
period, particularly in the minds of the military, whose business
anywhere is to plan military operations in times of "peace" as
well as to execute them in times of war.

The principle problem faced by the U.S. military at the start
of the cold war was the fact that the forces available to Russia
were much superior to whatever Western Europe could muster
in the immediate future, while American manpower and materiel had to be delivered across an ocean. The tactical situation,
seen in terms of conventional forces, definitely favored the Russians. Only one factor—an overwhelming one as it seemed
then—tipped the scales in favor of the United States: the bomb.
If the American monopoly of the bomb could be maintained,

Russian military advantage could be effectively canceled. Thus, it appeared to the U.S. military at the beginning of the cold war that the superiority of American arms depended crucially on that new devastating weapon. And since the military considers it axiomatic that the security of a nation stands or falls with the superiority of its armed forces and with the readiness to use them, it followed that the security of America hinged on the bomb and on its inclusion in the plans for the next war. The task of the U.S. military was clear: to build up an arsenal of atomic weapons and the means to deliver them, and to work out a plan for using them when and if the time arrived. This was done. The first tangible result was the Strategic Air Command.

It is important to note the meaning of the word "strategic" in this context. In common usage the term "strategy" denotes a more or less long-term plan of contingent actions. In military language, "strategic" is often used in contradistinction to "tactical." Tactical considerations are those related to the conduct of a battle; strategic ones are those related to a plan of campaign or to the conduct of a whole war. Now, in World War II, these terms came to denote specific Air Force operations. Tactical bombing usually denoted bombing in support of ground troops, that is bombing assisting specific tactical tasks. Strategic bombing, on the other hand, came to mean operations calculated to have long-term effects, specifically attacks on the industrial installations of the enemy and, as it soon developed, on civilian populations. The meaning of the Strategic Air Command is to be understood in these terms. Strategic atomic bombing was to be directed against industrial installations and against the populations of the enemy. The immediate task of the Strategic Air Command was to plan such bombing, that is, primarily to draw up priorities and schedules for dropping atomic bombs on Soviet cities. The idea was that this constant threat of devastation might deter the Russians from attacking Western Europe. In the event that it did not, it was surmised that the destruction of Soviet industrial capacity and the decimation of its population would win the war for the United States. Of course, plans for conventional military operations were also made. These, however, were conceived as primarily holding operations pending the atomic strike.

The problem faced by the Soviet military at the onset of the cold war was that of preparing an appropriate response to an attack by the United States. Work on the atomic bomb must have begun immediately. However, a strategic theory to guide the use of the weapon was apparently not worked out until years later. Such a theory would have required a basic revision of military doctrine, which during Stalin's time was impossible to undertake, since any substantive suggestions stood in danger of being branded heresies with well-known consequences for the authors.

Stalin had spoken *ex cathedra* on the factors determining the outcome of a war. These he called the "permanent operating factors": size, equipment, and training of the armed forces; industrial capacity; morale of the population. Other conditions—for example, the acquisition of a new weapon or the achievement of tactical surprise—were classed as "transitory factors" having no bearing on the outcome of a war.

Clearly this doctrine reflected Russia's experience in World War II in which the initial successes of the Germans (attributed to tactical surprise) were eventually dissipated. The numerical superiority of the Russians (in later phases also superiority in equipment) and, of course, their phenomenal fervor and tenacity decided the final outcome. The "permanent factors" doctrine also seems relevant to the outcome of World War I on the Western Front, where the initial German successes achieved by a rapid march across the unfortified Belgian frontier were not sufficient and were eventually dissipated in a war of attrition.

Declaring the "permanent operating factors" to be an "immutable law of war" was in keeping with the habit of Marxist-Leninist ideologues of claiming a monopoly on discovering "immutable laws" of social phenomena. However, a more clearly pragmatic underpinning is also discernible in the doctrine. It was necessary to preserve the faith in the invincibility of the Soviet Union. Thus, in 1947, a Soviet historian depicted in a public lecture a hypothetical war initiated by the United States against the Soviet Union, presumably by an atomic attack. The immediate response, said the historian, would be the occupation of Western Europe by Soviet armies. In this way the bombings of Moscow and Leningrad would accomplish nothing.

An ocean would separate the United States from occupied Europe. The latter would present no problem because the workers would be on the side of the Soviets. (In 1947 this was not an unrealistic assumption.) In the ensuing stalemate, the "permanent operating factors" would eventually decide the issue.[4]

This scenario may have made sense before the advent of intercontinental missiles. By 1953, however, ICBMs were on the technological horizon, and Stalin was dead. Almost imperceptibly a debate developed among Soviet strategists, beginning with cautious jibes at the "immutability" of Stalinist doctrine. Characteristically, the arguments used by the revisionists (or the "radicals," as the American military Sovietologist, R. L. Garthoff, calls them) were of the same sort that were used by the Soviet scientists, artists, and writers in their pleas for ventilation of the intellectual climate. Military science, it was argued, had been stagnating in the stifling atmosphere of Stalinist dogma. The time had come to remove the impediments to its vigorous growth.

After Malenkov's removal, the attacks on dogmatism became bolder and more intense. Thus *Voyennaya Mysl*[5] *(Military Thought)* editorialized in March 1955 as follows:

> Instead of taking the statements of authorities as starting propositions for the expansion and elaboration of military theory, many research people have limited themselves to mere logic chopping, to commentary on well-known statements and to endless production of quotations. As a result of this, views once expressed by great theoreticians or important men of affairs are converted into dogma and these research works acquire a Talmudic character and actually delay further progress in military science. . . .
>
> The necessity to elaborate strategic theory thoroughly in modern conditions is perfectly obvious, since the circle of persons concerned with strategic leadership is becoming ever larger. These persons, certainly, should have a comprehensive knowledge of theory for the preparation and conduct of war. . . .[6]

In the ensuing debate, the revisionists emerged victorious. By 1962 one could read:

> . . . the initial phase of a present day nuclear missile war will obviously be the main and decisive period that will predetermine the development and outcome of the entire war.[7]

The erstwhile "transitory" initial phase was promoted to a decisive phase. Actually the importance of the surprise attack was stressed already in 1955 when the idea of the preemptive strike was first put forward.

> The duty of the Soviet armed forces is not to permit an enemy surprise attack . . . and, in the event of an attempt . . . to deal the enemy counterblows or even preemptive surprise blows. . . .[8]

Thus, in the minds of the Soviet military, the perception of the cold war evolved from one calling for preparedness to wage a protracted defensive war (a repetition of 1709, 1812, and 1941) to a mirror image of the American military perception, that of a balance of terror.

U.S. strategists have made much of this development and it has become a major theme of most American writings on Soviet military strategy. It is stressed also by Garthoff.[9] The military policy implications of the development were obvious. If the Soviet strategists have come around to recognizing the importance of a "preemptive strike," the task of American strategy is to devise means of preempting the preemption. More will be said on this matter in Chapter 10.

As we have seen (cf. Chapter 6), to Harry Truman, to his then Secretary of State (James Byrnes), and to his closest advisers, the origin of the cold war appeared in stark simplicity. At the close of World War II Russia had the choice to cooperate with the United States in reorganizing the world or not. "Cooperation" meant going along with the U.S. plans of reorganizing Europe.

Specifically, the United States demanded a reorganization of the Warsaw government, the former Lublin Committee. The issue of the Hungarian, the Bulgarian, and the Romanian governments also arose, though in less acute form.[10]

It appeared already in the ill-fated foreign ministers meeting in London (October 1945) that Russia would refuse to "cooperate." The Americans concluded that the Russians' aim was to consolidate their power in Eastern Europe without considering the national interests of the United States, and eventually to use the expanded power base in Eastern Europe as a springboard from which to attack "free" Europe or, at any rate, to intimidate it into submitting to a "Communist take-over."

American policy makers acted on those assumptions.

The clearest formulation of the "Containment Policy," as the United States cold war strategy came to be called, is seen in an article by "X," later identified as George Kennan.[11]

The Soviet leaders behave as they do, writes Mr. X, because they are guided by a fixed ideology and have been conditioned by their long experience in wielding absolute power. He traces the transformation of Marxian theory of history into the Leninist doctrine of revolution—the seizure of political power by a highly disciplined group and the establishment of absolute rule by this elite, rationalized as a dictatorship of the proletariat.

The original aim of this group (the Bolsheviks) was to destroy capitalism, which they saw as the source of all social ills, and to build a Communist society. Having successfully seized power in Russia, ruined and disorganized by a disastrous war, the Bolsheviks were immediately faced with enormous problems for which they were not prepared either theoretically or practically. Marxian theory dealt only with the collapse of the capitalist system; it had little or nothing concrete to say about how a socialist society was to be built, least of all in a backward country.

Lacking a positive practical program, inexperienced in the art of politics, faced with sullen opposition, particularly of the peasantry who had their own ideas about the aims of the revolution, and determined to stay in power at all costs, the Bolsheviks acted in the only way they knew how—by establishing a police state.

Absolute rule requires a doctrine of infallibility; the myth of infallibility is maintained by the exercise of absolute power. Mr. X goes on to describe the well-known methods and effects of Stalin's reign of terror. The doctrine of infallibility also put its stamp on the conduct of Soviet foreign policy. Since the ideological tenets were unassailable, it was impossible for the Soviet leaders to give any serious thought to cooperation with the Western world. The governments of other states were, in Soviet eyes, nothing but instruments by which the capitalists maintained their rule. Since, according to the infallible doctrine, this rule was bound to be overthrown, and since the historical mission of the Communists was to hasten its collapse, any "sincere" cooperation with "the capitalists" was out of the question. At most, the Soviet government can on occasions set its signature to a document. But this ". . . is to be regarded as a tactical maneuver permissible in dealing with the enemy (who is without honor) and should be taken in the spirit of *caveat emptor.* Basically, the antagonism remains. It is postulated. And from it flow many of the phenomena which we find disturbing in the Kremlin's conduct of foreign policy, the wary suspiciousness, and the basic unfriendliness of purpose."

Given this interpretation of the mentality and the methods of the Soviet rulers (for which, incidentally, there was certainly considerable evidence), the implications for Soviet-American relations seem obvious to Mr. X.

First, it seems to him clear that the United States cannot expect in the foreseeable future to enjoy political intimacy with the Soviet regime. It must continue to regard the Soviet Union as a rival, not a partner, in the political area.

Second, the United States must take due cognizance of the differences as well as the similarities between the Soviet rulers and individual aggressive leaders like Napoleon or Hitler. A fundamental tenet in Communist ideology is that history is on the side of communism. Consequently the Communist leaders are not driven by compulsions to stake everything on sudden thrusts. Above all else, the continued existence of the only center of Communist power, the Soviet Union, cannot be endangered. Therefore the Soviet leaders are responsive to the logic of power. They are quite ready to retreat if strategic calculations indicate that a retreat or a redirection of effort is warranted by an existing disposition of power.

> . . . under the compulsion of no time table, the Kremlin does not get panicky under the necessity for such retreat. Its political action is a fluid stream which moves constantly, wherever it is permitted to move, toward a given goal. Its main concern is to make sure that it has filled every nook and cranny available to it in the basin of world power. But if it finds unassailable barriers in its path, it accepts these philosophically and accommodates itself to them. The main thing is that there should always be pressure, unceasing constant pressure toward the desired goal.

In this view, the Communists' *responsiveness* to pressure makes it possible for the United States on its part to apply constant, unceasing pressure. The first function of the containment policy is to hold the line against Soviet communism. It is not the only function, however. Mr. X goes on to say that eventually the unrelenting counterpressure will increase enormously the strains under which Soviet policy must operate. The mass of the Soviet people are disillusioned, skeptical, and no longer accessible as they once were to the magical attraction that Soviet power still radiates to its followers abroad. The United States thus has it in its power ". . . to promote tendencies which must eventually find their outlet in either the break-up or the gradual mellowing of Soviet power."

Mr. X ends on a note of confidence:

> In the light of these circumstances, the thoughtful observer of Russian-American relations will find no cause for complaint in the Kremlin's challenge to American society. He will rather experience a certain gratitude to a Providence which, by providing the American people with this implacable challenge, has made their entire security as a nation dependent on their pulling themselves together and accepting the responsibilities of moral and political leadership that history plainly intended them to bear.

It appears from Mr. X's article that Communists' intentions can be most reliably inferred not so much from what Communists *do* as from they *are*. This basic assumption was stated more explicitly in a book by Fred Schwartz. Dr. Schwartz ably summarizes his thesis in the first two sentences: "The thesis of this book is very simple. It is that Communists are Communists."[12]

He goes on to describe the tenets of Communist ideology and to draw conclusions about both Communist intentions and the future course of history if the Communists are allowed to act on those intentions. In contrast to Mr. X's article, which is addressed to intellectuals, Dr. Schwartz's book is written in "Reader's Digest style," lively, chatty, interspersed with anecdotes, aimed, like the *Reader's Digest,* at the seventh grade level of literacy.

Dr. Schwartz's first anecdote is about a mental patient in Australia who was convinced that the Americans were trying to poison him. Dr. Schwartz gives a vivid picture of a paranoiac, apparently normal in all respects but obsessed by a fixed idea that cannot be removed by logical argument, reassuring persuasion, or any known form of treatment. Eventually the man killed two American officers. Dr. Schwartz draws a parallel.

> The Communists believe that they are at war with us. This conviction will never be changed in the slightest degree by any action of the Free World. If, tomorrow, the leaders of the Free Nations were to accede to every demand made by the Communist leaders, if they were to neutralize every Strategic Air Command base, if they were to grant the demands on Germany, if they were to neutralize Formosa, if they were to recognize Red China and admit it to the United Nations, if the United States were to withdraw every serviceman and weapon within the borders of continental United States, the Communists would merely believe that they had won massive victories in the class war. A step toward our final conquest and destruction would have been taken. We must either recognize this and defend against it, or ignore it and be destroyed. We have no other choice.[13]

The perceptions of the cold war reflected in Mr. X's article and in Dr. Schwartz's book, with their characteristic emphasis on Soviet perfidy, were very widely spread (although by no means universal) in the American popular mind for almost two decades. The reasons for this compulsive preoccupation of people with Russia are not as apparent as in the perceptions of the military and of the Administration. As has been said, the job of the military is to prepare for and to wage war. At the close of World War II, Russia was the only potential enemy to be seriously considered. The Administration formulates and executes foreign policy. Russia's "refusal to cooperate" was evident (at least to the Administration) from actual confrontations with Russia's political moves in Eastern Europe. Truman, Acheson, Forrestal, Marshall, Mr. X, all of them actually met and talked with Russian diplomats and functionaries, and their conclusions were based on direct experience or, at least, on their not unreasonable interpretations of their experiences. On the other hand, an overwhelming majority of Americans never met a Soviet Russian, nor even a card-carrying Communist. To be sure, they were exposed to persistent reiterations in the mass media of views on the cold war identical to those of Mr. X and Dr. Schwartz. However, a thoughtful examination of mass behavior suggests that the success of propaganda is not assured by its massiveness per se. Propaganda succeeds if it finds a response in the mass mind; and this response occurs if there is a psychic need to accept the perceptions suggested by the propaganda.

The Soviet government enjoyed a monopoly on propaganda almost from the time the Communists siezed power. Yet they were never able to win the peasantry and had to resort to terror in carrying out the collectivization program. Oppositely, before the Revolution the Bolsheviks were a tiny minority. Yet their propaganda succeeded in mobilizing enough support to deliver power into their hands. Clearly, there must have been something in the Bolshevik propaganda that found an immediate response in the masses. In 1917 there was a sharply felt need among the Russian masses to withdraw from a disastrous war. Only the Bolsheviks and their then closest political allies exploited that need. Moreover, in times of stress or despair there is a well-known need to single out an enemy on whom the disasters can be blamed. The Bolsheviks also provided a target—the bourgeoisie.

In Russia, a social enemy had been part of the actual life experience of the masses. The peasant knew oppression by the landlord, the worker knew it from the boss or the straw boss. The soldier knew the officer. Each could relate his misfortunes to the power exercised daily by specific persons or authorities over his life. We know from history, however, that the Enemy named by demagogic propaganda need not be related to any actual experience. For example, the Jew, who was made the incarnation of evil in Nazi propaganda, was not related to any concrete experiences of most Germans. Yet the Jew was wholeheartedly welcomed as the much needed Enemy.

If we try to delve deeper in our analysis, we cannot avoid making certain conjectures about mass psychology. These conjectures may be reasonable, but it is well to keep in mind that they remain mere conjectures. Thus the answer to the question why the Germans embraced Nazi leadership so eagerly is not so clear as in the case of Russians' acceptance of Bolshevik leadership in 1917. Certainly the privations of the Germans, even in the midst of the Great Depression, were not comparable to those of the Russians after Russia's collapse. We conjecture that the Germans suffered psychic privations of comparable magnitude. Some plausible sources of these privations have been suggested, such as "wounded national pride," a "national inferiority complex," trauma stemming from the authoritarian structure of the German family, and the like.

At the moment we are interested in the question why Americans at the close of World War II so readily accepted the devil image of communism. Whether or not this image was a faithful reflection of the "true nature of communism," the fact remains that communism was no more related to most Americans' actual concrete experiences than "international Jewry" was to that of the Germans. Nor did the Americans suffer physical privations as the Russians did in 1917, or even the presumed psychic privations of the Germans in 1933. The Americans did not lose a war, nor did they suffer the aftermaths of a destructive war. On the contrary, they won a most decisive victory in their history and, moreover, at a comparatively negligible cost. What then were the disasters for which communism was to be blamed?

I think the answer is again to be sought in the Americans' conception of their role in world affairs, outlined in Chapter 4. Americans by and large had accepted the responsibility "that history plainly intended them to bear," as Mr. X put it. Reluctantly but with a sense of mission, America turned away from its normal, peaceful pursuits to help extinguish conflagrations started by ruthless adventurers and would-be enslavers of humanity. And if there was some question about the wisdom of such intervention in 1917, clearly there was no choice in 1941. America was treacherously attacked, even as the emissaries of the perfidious power were pretending to keep negotiations going. The attack was a catalyst that triggered a crystallization of a national purpose. Mr. X in his closing paragraph thanks Providence for providing the American people with an "implacable challenge" in the face of which they must "pull themselves together." It seems to me that many Americans, unconsciously perhaps, thanked the same Providence for Pearl Harbor in the same spirit.

The situation was not new. Enthusiasm engendered by the outbreak of a war was a common phenomenon throughout the age of nationalism. Some psychologists attribute this enthusiasm to the release of aggressive urges, a feeling of relief that a repressed drive to destroy and to kill need not be repressed any longer. Without questioning the extent of validity of this explanation, I venture to offer another, less morbid one. People have an urge to engage in exciting collective activity. Capitalist society provides few outlets for this urge. Especially in the United States, the home of an extreme individualistic ideology, community life has become progressively impoverished, and a sense of national purpose was chronically lacking. World War II provided this sense. Moreover, throughout the war there was no occasion for this sense of total commitment to sour, as happened to European nations toward the end of World War I. What few defeats America suffered occurred in the first months of the war. From June 1942, the war was a crescendo of triumph for the United States. In short, World War II was for most Americans an experience of rich fulfillment.

And then the war ended. What was to fill the void? How could the sense of purpose which, once experienced, becomes a need, be maintained? The sense of purpose had centered around the overriding necessity to crush a ruthless, savage enemy. The war destroyed the enemy. To maintain the sense of national purpose, a new enemy was needed. Mr. X's Providence again stepped in and provided one.

There was another factor that contributed mightily to the anti-Communist neurosis. Communism was discovered as a surefire election campaign issue.

In the United States, politics is generally considered to be a calling no different from any other profession or business. A decision to become a lawyer or a real estate operator or "to go into politics" is a choice of a career, and in every career there are certain visible criteria of success. Further, it is held self-evident that a normal man becomes preoccupied with advancing himself in his chosen calling. A tenet of American ideology is that the sum total of such strivings contributes to the vitality and prosperity of society and that, therefore, in "climbing the ladder of success" a man is discharging a social responsibility.

As in every other profession, success in politics involves certain skills which have become identified with the techniques of getting elected and reelected. What is called "statesmanship," that is, the actual practice of politics *in office,* is typically considered to be simply one of the factors contributing to political promotion. In the pragmatic outlook that dominates American ideology, tangible criteria of success are typically preferred to controversial ones. No one can dispute a politician's victory at the polls; the quality of his statesmanship is a matter of opinion.

Many American politicians readily saw the superb political leverage offered by the issue of communism. Already in 1946, Richard M. Nixon staked his campaign against Jerry Vorhees (for a seat in the House of Representatives) on the freshly discovered issue. The fact that the House of Representatives plays little or no part in the formulation of foreign policy made no difference in the efficacy of the campaign. The issue of communism was becoming a "gut issue," highly valued by politicians. That is, it was an issue that aroused passions and fears and enabled a politician to avoid substantive analysis and so to spare the electorate the trouble of thinking. Communism was an issue that enabled politicians to destroy political rivals by the simple expedient of labeling them Communist sympathizers.

After his victory over Vorhees, Mr. Nixon repeated the performance in 1948 in the campaign against Helen Douglas for the United States Senate. Here, too, he was victorious. The key to political success revealed by Adolf Hitler, namely the discovery of a single, simple gut issue and a refusal to be deflected from it, worked admirably. Years later, when someone recalled Nixon's tactics, particularly against Mrs. Douglas who had been highly respected for her ability and integrity, Nixon is said to have expressed dismay that his accusations were taken "personally." The implication was that politics was a game one played to win and that the strategems used in it should be taken in a proper spirit of sportsmanship. I do not know whether the story is authentic, but it is certainly in keeping with the tradition of American politics. The Communist issue was only a new trick of the trade, and, as frequently happens, the effectiveness of the trick is greatest when used for the first time.

The value of the Communist issue was not lost on the politicians. It soon became *the* issue in political campaigns for whatever office, however minor. The initiative in this offensive was taken by the Republicans. The Democrats, because of their ties

with Roosevelt's New Deal, had already in the 1930s been accused of promoting "creeping socialism." It was a simple matter
now to extend the label to "communism." Thereby a disbalance
of power was introduced into U.S. politics. In the old days,
when the most common ammunition in election campaigns was
a charge of corruption, or a lapse in personal morals, the accusa-
tion could be easily matched with an identical one directed at
the accusers. "Communism," however, was not a label that
could be as easily stuck by a Democrat on a Republican. The
Republicans had always been staunch defenders of the "American way" against the inroads of "socialism" and moreover had
never dealt with the Russians. There was only one course of
self-defense open to the Democrats—to prove themselves as
good anti-Communists as the Republicans, or better. The political battles were joined on the issue of who was more
anti-Communist.

The infusion of the Communist issue into political life fanned
the·hysteria. The hysteria kept the Communist issue in focus.
The exploits of Joseph McCarthy are well-known and need not
be retold here. His targets being mostly political figures, the
damage to morale and self-respect resulting from McCarthy's
broadsides was confined at first to those circles. Not so with the
spread of McCarthyism through communities. Everywhere,
self-appointed guardians of Americanism appeared, probing into
every aspect of community life, cross-examining and firing
teachers, purging libraries, censoring school books. Typically the
victims of the anti-Communist crusade reacted with a standard
response: a profession of loyalty, which was axiomatically
equated to staunch anticommunism.

There were some dramatic recantations. In contrast to the
meaning of this ceremony in the Soviet Union, where it was
usually the terminal act before liquidation, repentent American
Communists were richly rewarded. They became key figures in
the espionage trials, which deserve special attention and will be
discussed below.

Not everyone was silenced or cowed. Some prominent intellectuals voiced their disgust with the antics of the witch hunters.
Archibald MacLeish, for example, satirized the hysteria in a
quotation from an imagined article written in the 1980s about
life in America in the late forties:

Never in the history of the world was one people as completely dominated, intellectually and morally, by another as the people of the United States by the people of Russia in the four years from 1946 through 1949. American domestic politics were conducted under a kind of upside-down Russian veto: no man could be elected to public office unless he was on record as detesting the Russians, and no proposal could be enacted, from a peace plan at one end to a military budget at the other, unless it could be demonstrated that the Russians wouldn't like it. American education was Russian education backward: ignorance of Communism was the principal educational objective recognized by politicians and the general press, and the first qualification demanded of a teacher was that he should not be a Communist himself, should not have met persons who might have been Communists, and should never have read books which could tell him what Communism was.[14]

The tenor of MacLeish's subsequent remarks is characteristic of what constituted dissent in the early years of the cold war. Those who criticized, bemoaned, or ridiculed primitive, compulsive anticommunism contended almost unanimously that the United States was throwing away the opportunity to exercise positive leadership in the postwar world. MacLeish made nebulous allusions to the Revolution of the Individual, which, according to him, the United States had started in the eighteenth century and should be carrying to completion. Generally, whether they waxed poetic or were urging aid to impoverished countries, the spokesmen of liberal humanism saw the increasingly paranoid behavior of America vis-à-vis Russia and internal dissenters as an aberration, a failure to grasp the true meaning of America's mission and to fulfill it. There was hardly any doubt in those years that America did have a mission and that the world would certainly accept America's leadership, if only U.S. leaders showed some understanding of the true meaning of the challenge to the United States and refused to be intimidated by the threat. That there *was* a threat to democracy, or to the "free institutions of the Western World," or simply "to America" was widely accepted as self-evident. Even MacLeish says, almost in passing, that "we had no choice in the face of Russian threats of force and Russian conspiracies of fraud but to arm ourselves and to resist." His complaint is that resistance to the Russians became an end in itself, and that this has had disastrous effects on the quality of life in America and on American morale, and has deflected America from her world mission. The popular self-image of America as a fundamentally peaceful and benevolent giant was not yet shaken in those early postwar years.

Anti-Communist hysteria reached a peak of intensity in the early 1950s following a rapid succession of headline events: the Berlin blockade, the victory of the Communists in the Chinese civil war, the explosion of the first Soviet atomic bomb, and the outbreak of the Korean War. The Berlin blockade appeared as a direct challenge to the Western Allies in Europe. The victory of the Chinese Communists appeared as a direct armed assault by the Communists on the Free World. The explosion of the Soviet bomb appeared as evidence of the efficiency of Soviet espionage.

The Republican political machine, preparing to make its bid for power in 1952, fully exploited the opportunities. Twenty Years of Treason was to be the theme in the coming presidential campaign. The Democrats were made to appear as appeasers of communism, repeating the fatal blunders of England and France in dealing with Hitler. They had sold Eastern Europe into Communist slavery, it was said. They "lost China." They tied the hands of General MacArthur and "snatched defeat from victory" in Korea. Their "liberalism" incapacitated them in dealing with the enemy within, and so the Administration became infiltrated with Soviet agents, spies, and saboteurs.

The Democrats invariably responded to these attacks by proving that they were *not* "soft on communism." The McCarran Acts of 1952, for example, authorized the establishment of an elaborate "security system" for purging government institutions of people suspected of leftist tendencies. The Act provided also for an American counterpart of the Iron Curtain, in the form of restrictions of contacts with the Soviet Union and Eastern Europe. Procedures of applying for visas were drawn up that barred any person from a non-Communist country from visiting the United States unless he swore to have no Communist affiliations. The oath was necessary in any case but not sufficient for obtaining a visa; in practice visas were granted or denied at the discretion of the State Department. Similar restrictions were imposed on the travels of Americans abroad. Passports were denied to individuals if their travels were considered to be "inimical" to the interests of the United States.

The Attorney General prepared and widely circulated a list of "subversive organizations." The list was used as a guide in screening employees both in the government and in private institutions.

Congressional committees toured universities and held facsimilies of public trials, but without defense procedures. The only right granted to the "witness," as the *de facto* defendant was called, was that of refusing to answer questions on the grounds of self-incrimination. Refusal could only be total and had to be accompanied by an explicit appeal to the Fifth Amendment of the Constitution. In practice, such an appeal was tantamount to an admission of "guilt." In most cases, dismissal from academic positions followed automatically. The requirement of answering either all questions or none left no choice for many of the "witnesses." For, once they answered any of the questions, they were compelled under threat of contempt charges to answer all of them. Invariably, such questions were commands to reveal the activities or views of others. Considering the purposes to which such "evidence" was likely to be put (and usually was), the "witness" had to choose between implicit self-accusation ("taking the Fifth") or acting as a finger man for the investigating committee.

Labor unions conducted extensive purges on their own initiative. In the 1930s, when the Congress of Industrial Organizations revitalized the American labor movement by extending unionism from crafts to entire industries, Communists played an active part in the organizing campaigns. Many remained in positions of leadership at the local level. It is unlikely that many of them retained Communist party affiliation, if only because the Communist party in the U.S. had dwindled to insignificant size during and after the war. Now, in the struggle for power that always goes on in all organizations, the purge mentality gave a decisive advantage to those who carried no Communist stigma, and especially to those who loudly denounced communism.

The most spectacular events in the Era of Purges were the espionage trials, particularly those of Alger Hiss, Julius and Ethel Rosenberg, and Morton Sobell. Evidence of espionage being insufficient in the Hiss case, he was convicted of perjury instead. He was given a five-year prison sentence. The Rosenberg's were convicted of having given "atomic secrets" to the

Russians. Since the alleged espionage occurred in wartime (albeit for an "Ally"), this was a capital offense. The Rosenbergs were executed in 1953. "Atomic secrets" were not involved in the charge against Sobell, but he was tried together with the Rosenbergs and sentenced to thirty years in prison with a recommendation that a parole be refused.

A heated controversy on the question of guilt of these persons ensued, remindful of the turmoils attending former celebrated trials in times of intense preoccupation with "internal enemies," for example, the Dreyfus affair in France (1898), and the Mooney-Billings and Sacco-Vanzetti cases in the United States (1916, 1920). The espionage trials have a very special relevance to the theme of this book because they reveal a key factor in the American popular perception of the cold war. The trials provided an explanation of how it happened that the very foundation on which the military security of America and of the "Free World" depended collapsed.

In Chapter 6 it was pointed out that the *monopoly* of the bomb provided the impetus for a United States policy toward Russia. In the popular conception, the bomb won the war against Japan. The administration's rationalization of the use of the weapon ("to end the war") reinforced this feeling. When the war indeed ended a few days after the bombings of Hiroshima and Nagasaki, the bomb became imbedded in the popular mind as "the ultimate weapon," conferring on its possessor powers enjoyed by the heroes of wish-fulfillment fantasies. It seemed as if Providence put this terrible weapon into the hands of people who would use their power wisely and justly. Providence, moreover, as it is conceived by Americans, is on the side not only of the just but also of the strong, those who are "able to help themselves." The bomb, the crowning achievement of American "know-how," was one more conclusive proof of America's qualification as an arbiter and the enforcer of justice in world affairs.

The secrecy surrounding the production of the atomic bomb, and the popular image of the scientist as a sorcerer who discovers "secret formulas," led to the notion of "the secret of the atomic bomb." American security hinged on the exclusive possession of the "secret." If the Rosenbergs, then, had betrayed the secret to the Russians, they betrayed America and the Free World.

The comments of Judge Kaufmann in passing sentence on the Rosenbergs faithfully reflect the popular perception:

> I consider your crime worse than murder. Plain deliberate contemplated murder is dwarfed in magnitude by comparison with the crime you have committed. In commiting the act of murder, the criminal kills only the victim. The immediate family is brought to grief and when justice is meted out, the chapter is closed. But in your case, I believe your conduct of putting into the hands of the Russians the A-bomb years before our best scientists predicted Russia would perfect the bomb has already caused, in my opinion, the Communist aggression in Korea, with the resultant casualties exceeding fifty thousand and who knows but that millions more of innocent people may pay the price of your treason. Indeed, by your betrayal you undoubtedly have altered the course of history to the disadvantage of our country. No one can say that we don't live in a constant state of tension. We have evidence of your treachery all around us every day—for the civilian defense activities throughout the nation are aimed at preparing us for an atom bomb attack.
>
> I . . . assume that the basic Marxist goal of world revolution and the destruction of capitalism was well-known to the defendants, if in fact not subscribed by them, when they passed what they knew was this nation's most deadly and closely guarded secret to the Soviet agents.
>
> . . . In the light of the circumstances, I feel that I must pass such a sentence upon the principals in this diabolical conspiracy to destroy a God-fearing nation, which will demonstrate with finality that this nation's security must remain inviolate, that traffic in military secrets, whether promoted by slavish devotion to a foreign ideology or by a desire for money, must cease.[15]

In summary, by the early fifties the American people perceived themselves to be locked in mortal combat with a diabolical enemy who threatened the very existence of their nation. This image was easy to conjure up, because the Americans had recently dealt with just such an enemy embodied in Nazi Germany and Imperial Japan. They had rejected the disastrous appeasement policy that encouraged Hitler and the Japanese militarists to pursue their conquests. (Already in 1937 Roosevelt had called for a "quarantine" against aggressors.) Now America was determined to hold the beast at bay. Eventually the beast would be driven back to his lair or, if he cared to attack the Free World, he would meet the fate of Hilter, Mussolini, and Tojo. *Then* there would be nothing to obstruct the fulfillment of the American Mission.

The popular perception of the cold war in the Soviet Union is sometimes pictured as a symmetric counterpart of the American. Although many analogies can be drawn, the mirror-image model is not accurate. The Soviet mood was rooted in quite different collective experiences and, of course, developed in a very different political climate.

Already in the interwar period, and especially in the 1930s, a self-image crystallized in the Soviet people the core of which was a heroism of a new kind. Traditional nationalist heroism, a notion spawned by the Napoleonic wars, has always been military. In modern society there has been hardly any other channel for the expression of feelings of identity with a nation. Economic pursuits in the countries of developing capitalism were motivated by private gain. Artistic expression, beginning with the romantic era at the start of the nineteenth century, became increasingly more individualistic and exclusive. The military was the only clear focus of national unity where the self could be submerged. There is ample evidence that the need to submerge the self—to become a part of "something bigger than one-self"—is as powerful in human nature as the need for self-assertion.

Communist ideology, as it developed in the Soviet Union, created a channel for identifying with the nation, hence with the state, in other than military contexts. It promoted a heroics of work, especially of construction, that gave rise to an entirely new form of patriotism. The feelings engendered by this version of patriotism were continuously stimulated and nurtured in the schools, in the mass media, through ceremonials, by the system of social rewards, etc. Thus the Soviet peoples saw themselves as a peace-loving nation, wholly immersed in the task of "building a better life," asking only to be let alone.

If this self-image needed any reinforcing, the events of World War II certainly supplied it. No less than twenty million Soviet citizens died as a result of that war. Their economy was ruined, their land and their cities devastated. But victory had been won, a dearly bought and richly deserved victory.

There is no doubt that the average Russian was keenly aware of the disproportionate amounts of effort expended on the war by the Soviet Union and by the Western Allies. When after Pearl Harbor the United States finally entered the war as a full belligerent, there was an understandable sharp rise in Soviet morale. Hopes were centered on the opening of a "second front" to drain off at least a portion of the German flood. No second front developed either immediately nor in the summer of 1942 (the summer of the most severe Soviet defeats), nor in 1943, when the Germans in Russia were already in retreat. Instead, the Allies engaged in peripheral operations: in Africa, which not only failed to relieve pressure on Russia but actually served to increase it, because the invasion of North Africa was a clear signal to the Germans that no second front was forthcoming in Europe for quite some time. Consequently, when the Allies "tipped their hand," the Germans were able to transfer forces from *west* to *east*. Churchill reports Stalin's estimate of twenty-seven German divisions so transferred.[16]

Opposition to opening a second front in France came mainly from Churchill, not from the Americans; and in the years of mortal danger to the U.S.S.R. Churchill's views prevailed. The average Russian was not privy to the complex military and political considerations that led to the divergence between the British and American views. Nor could it be expected that the average Russian would have been impressed by these considerations if he did know about them. The average Russian knew only that he was dying by the millions, that his land was ravaged, and that, for all the fine words in the West about his magnificent heroism, no help was forthcoming to lessen the pressure of the relentless German military machine.

• Though during the fateful years of the war the average Russian was disappointed with the Western Allies, he was not bitter.[17] In the first place, he kept believing through 1942 and 1943 that the second front was imminent. Second, the alliance with the West touched off some old deep longings. The national patriotism of the average Russian had been remarkably free from chauvinism. That is, his deep love for his country was not coupled (as patriotism frequently is) with contempt or a patronizing attitude toward things foreign. On the contrary, Russians have always looked on the West with admiration. Historical memory played a part in this feeling. The Russian Social Democrats, from whom the Bolsheviks sprang, were the most Western-oriented of the Russian revolutionaries. The "builders of social-ism" emulated the West in their admiration and respect for technology if not for Western political ideas. Understandably this attraction toward the West became ambivalent as the no-tion of "capitalist encirclement" and of continued hostility toward the Soviet regime pervaded the Russian's consciousness. So, all the more intense did this attraction become when the West was now linked with the Soviet Union in a common strug-gle. Frederick C. Barghoorn gives a vivid description of this deep-seated friendliness of "the common people" of the Soviet Union toward "the American people" (together with the prob-lem it presented to the ruling elite in the immediate postwar years).[18]

I had similar impressions while serving in Alaska from 1942 to 1944 where I had continual and rather intimate contact with Russians, mostly youngish junior comissioned offcers from a wide range of backgrounds. In discussing the postwar world (a favor-ite topic), they all consistently returned to the same theme: the war had finally put an end to Russia's isolation; cooperation with America would continue. Incidentally, America interested the Russians far more than did Europe. America was bigger, stronger, richer; Americans were more open ("like the Rus-sians"), expansive, jovial, disdainful of stuffiness. Above all, they enthused, in the postwar period, Russians would be able to travel and see the world. How they pictured the unfolding of political developments was rarely discussed. What, it might be asked, would, in their eyes, happen to "capitalist encirclement"? Most likely the answer is that they gave no thought to future political problems any more than GIs did. They embraced the idea of "peaceful coexistence" instinctively, that is with their whole being. They had always wanted to think of "international relations" in this way (at least since the emergence of their new nonmilitary patrotism). It was especially comfortable to think this way during the war.

War has always appeared, and probably will for a long time to come, to the average Russian as a disaster. Most Americans may insist that they share this view of war, but the Russian knows much more at first hand what the hackneyed phrase actually means.

Did the average Russian expect any important internal political changes after the war? It seems so. There was considerable talk, as I remember, about how life would be when the Soviet Union was no longer threatened with destruction. The Russians' ideas about what "democracy" means to a Westerner were rather vague, but certainly not altogether devoid of understanding. On the whole, there was unbounded confidence that after victory things would work themselves out.

On such good-natured confidence in the future the impact of the cold war sparked more resignation than resentment in the Soviet public. It is not likely that the so-called "issues" of the early phase of the cold war interested the Russian. He did not care who sat in the Polish, Romanian, and Hungarian governments, nor who controlled Trieste. He did know that American lend-lease aid was stopped immediately and abruptly after Germany's surrender; that the American attitude toward the Soviet Union suddenly changed from admiration to hostility, and that the same change of attitude took place in the Soviet press toward the United States; and these developments were indeed puzzling. From disquiet to alarm to defensiveness are small steps.

There was no difficulty in demonstrating to the Soviet population that the United States had adopted aggressive designs. To begin with, American cold war oratory, generously quoted in the Soviet press, was not distinguished by reserve. It is difficult for a Soviet citizen to conceive that a prominent political or military personage would, in making public statements, be expressing his own personal views rather than those of the government. The Soviet press could, and did, have a field day merely quoting various American dignitaries on the subject of the Soviet Union and what the United States was going to do in order to bend the Russians to its will.

The typical reaction of the average Russian to this turn of events was a plaintive "Why?" Why was Russia, after having suffered so much and after having saved Europe from genocide and enslavement, now threatened with destruction by people with whom Russia had made common cause? "What have we ever done to you?" was a question frequently posed to Americans before contacts dwindled to practically zero. The usual answer, to the effect that the United States had no wish to threaten Russia, that, on the contrary, Russia was a threat to others, elicited nothing but incredulity on the part of the Russians.

In the meantime the Stalin political machine for its own internal purposes was making preparations to purge the country of Western sympathies that had been strengthened by the wartime alliance. As with other Soviet nationwide propaganda campaigns, this one was "total"; that is, its ramifications pervaded virtually all aspects of Soviet life. This purge, in the late forties, however, differed from that of the late thirties in an important respect of great significance for the development of the cold war. Although the earlier purge claimed vast numbers of innocent victims and was marked by the ferocity of punishments meted out, still the standard accusations against the victims were of crimes punished in all "civilized" countries— treason, sabotage, conspiracies to commit murder, etc. This postwar purge was far less bloody but it aroused even more ominous premonitions among the Western publics, particularly the intellectuals. For now accusations included charges not only of criminal acts but also of "alien ideas." Consequently, this purge exacted the heaviest toll among artists, writers, and scientists. The most publicized episode was the expulsion of geneticists from biological faculties and research centers, the so-called Lysenko affair.

Lysenko was a disciple of Michurin, a Russian "practical biologist" whose achievements paralleled those of Luther Burbank in the United States. Ignorance of biology was not an obstacle to him any more than ignorance of physics is an obstacle to an inventive mechanic. His contributions to agriculture were considerable and recognized, but he evidently aspired also to acclaim as a great scientist and, as those who knew him maintain, to power. The anti-Western purge gave him the long-awaited opportunity to become czar of Soviet biology. The aspiration was not unrealistic. Under Stalin, autocracy was extended from politics to all fields of activity. Every region and institution had its little Stalin, a watchdog to sniff out "treason." In the immediate postwar years the satrap system was being installed in the intellectual realm. In every field of thought there was one correct "ism" and a practically unlimited number of "subversive" "isms." The correct "ism" in philosophy, including the philosophy of science, was dialectical materialism; in politics it was Marxism-Leninism-Stalinism; in biology it was Darwinism (to the extent even of calling professors of biology professors of Darwinism). The late Ivan Pavlov became the supreme authority in psychology. The correct line in literature and the arts was socialist realism, and so forth.

Lysenko extended "Darwinism" to include "Michurinism." He aimed to relate himself to Michurin in the same way that Stalin related himself to Lenin, as the legitimate heir of a dynasty. Lysenko succeeded. In the summer of 1948, in a setup strongly reminiscent of the Moscow Trials of the previous decade, all of the leading Soviet biologists who had made outstanding contributions to genetics, a cutting edge of biological science, were accused of heresy. The label of "idealism" was affixed to genetics, a word that required every "right"-thinking Soviet intellectual to immunize himself by making the Marxist-Leninist-Stalinist equivalent of the sign of the cross. A defense on substantive issues was out of the question. At best, some of the accused tried to convince their tormentors that they too were loyal "Michurinists," that at least some of the ideas of genetics were not in contradiction with orthodox doctrines, that a collaboration between geneticists and Michurinists was possible, and the like. Nothing short of unconditional surrender was acceptable to the establishment.

> They want a discussion. But we shall not discuss with the Morganists [geneticists] (applause); we shall continue to expose them as adherents of an essentially false scientific trend, a pernicious and ideologically alien trend, brought to our country from foreign shores.[19]

Humiliating self-flagellations and tearful recantations followed, repeating the grim pattern of these orgies. The *razgrom*[20] was extended to other sciences. Physicists were castigated for

failing to bring the philosophical foundations of physics in line
with the dicta of dialectical materialism. "Reactionary" foundations of the theory of relativity were exposed.[21] Cybernetics was
proclaimed to be a pseudoscience. Mathematical logic and
mathematical statistics were condemned as excrescences of
"idealism," etc.

American reaction to exhibitions such as these strengthened
the position of those in U.S. intellectual circles who pictured the
Communists as a gang of monomaniacs intent on enslaving the
world both politically and spiritually. Their justified indignation
over the Soviet attack on science captured the attention of the
public as well as of the policy makers. It also made for good
newspaper copy, and wise-guy ridicule appeared as often as critical analyses. All this produced an important side effect, namely
the expectation that compulsions of orthodoxy had already
emasculated and would shortly destroy Soviet science. All the
more traumatic was the shock attending the appearance of the
Soviet atomic bomb, soon followed by the hydrogen bomb and
the space satellite. Before 1949 the conviction that the Russians
were "mad" in matters of modern science, and therefore no
match for U.S. technology, may have diluted Americans' fear of
the Soviet Union. As has been noted, the Soviet atomic bomb
initiated a spy hysteria (the Russians must have "stolen" it). Subsequent technological successes of the Russians demolished the
myth of their scientific backwardness, but the antiscientific raids
of the late forties had helped to fixate an image of a regime determined to eradicate the very roots of Western civilization.

So, the anti-Western campaign had on the whole contributed
to the polarization of The Two. It helped to fix the notion in the
public mind that the coming confrontation was, after all, between two incompatible philosophies of life and that it was
upon the outcome of this confrontation that future history
would be determined. Americans were reinforced in their belief
that they were now saddled with the responsibility of being the
only effective protectors of the "Free World." The Soviet elites,
spurred on by the frenzy of the witch hunt, saw themselves as
watchdogs, protecting the achievements of the Revolution
against diabolic schemes of subversion.

CHAPTER 8

The "Issues"

What would it take to "settle" the cold war?

People concerned with the resolution of conflicts tend to think in terms of "issues." A dispute between a seller and a buyer about the sales price of a house is a convincing example of a conflict over an issue. The conflict is resolvable if the highest price that the buyer is willing to pay exceeds the lowest price that the seller is willing to accept. Otherwise the outcome will be status quo (no sale). Arbitration and mediation boards, courts of domestic relations, and similar bodies are supposed to clarify the issues of certain kinds of conflict and so enable the parties to resolve them, if possible.

There are, however, conflicts that do not revolve around issues. A dog fight is a conflict of this sort: it ends only if one of the parties flees, or if some outsider stronger than both dogs takes drastic measures.

Views on whether the cold war is (or was) resolvable differ. Its origins are so described by some that it is easy to imagine how the cold war might have been prevented or settled in its early phases. One wonders what would have happened if Stalin had allowed the "reorganization" of Eastern European governments demanded by the United States, or if the United States had allowed the neutralization of Germany.

Others take a broader view of the "issues." Raymond Aron suggests that the real issue between communism and Western democracy is that the Communists are intent on destroying Western democracy, while Western democracy is intent on getting the Communists to abandon that goal.[1] Still others maintain or imply that there are really no specific issues that matter. In their view, so-called "issues" are merely symptoms of an underlying eternal power struggle between states or blocs of states; if the current issues were settled, others would arise in their place. Finally some relate the global conflict to man's aggressive urges. In this view, the states themselves are merely institutions through which man's aggressive and destructive urges can function.

None of these views can be convincingly supported by evidence. Contentions about the inherent aggressiveness of states or of men are too broad to serve as explanations of specific events; and it is idle to speculate about "what might have been." Might-have-beens are in the minds of men and only there. Ulam argues that the Sovietization of Eastern Europe was "inevitable" in view of the expansionist tendencies of the Soviet Union and the unavailability of a countervailing force in that region. Kolko argues with equal conviction that the Sovietization of Eastern Europe was a consequence of the global policy of the United States, whose leaders had a very definite war aim: to reestablish a (somewhat reformed) Old Order in the whole world. We cannot pit the one theory against the other, because history cannot be rerun, like an experiment, starting with different initial conditions.

There is, however, one "issue" of the cold war that permits us to probe somewhat deeper into the causes of the cold war, namely Germany. The Grand Alliance was forced on the United States and the Soviet Union because both found themselves on the same side in a struggle for survival, in the case of the Soviet Union in a literal sense, in the case of the United States in the sense suggested by Walter Lippmann (cf. pp. 54–55). As long as the German armies were fighting, neither the United States nor the Soviet Union had any choice but to continue *military* cooperation. When the tide of war turned, political considerations "surfaced," as it were. The dispute over Eastern European states appears as a classical dispute over a sphere of influence, at least from the Soviet side, those states being of the sort that were traditionally incorporated into a great power's sphere of influence. In the case of Germany, however, the situation was much more complex, for Germany herself had been a Great Power. The same was true of Japan. However, Japan was beyond the Soviet Union's reach and so was incorporated into the American sphere without a challenge. Germany *was* within the reach of the Soviet Union, and its fate was perceived by both sides to be the key to the reorganization of Europe.

The Three had agreed to divide Germany into four occupation zones. Since Germany was *the* enemy, unlike the "liberated" countries (among which even Austria was eventually included), there was no hurry about withdrawing troops. Consequently decisions about the ultimate fate of Germany were postponed until agreement could be reached on whether, when, and how to restore an independent German state.

The Soviet zone included Berlin geographically. But the Anglo-Americans could not agree to leave Berlin to the Russians. It was felt that the control of the capital would somehow give the Russians a leverage in the European power struggle. It was therefore decided to divide Berlin itself into four occupation zones like the rest of Germany.

The power of language in directing people's thoughts is truly remarkable. Berlin's economic importance had never matched its political importance as the capital of the German State. There was, however, no German State in 1945, and a future German State, if any, was to be shaped entirely by the victors. Nor did Berlin have a symbolic significance for the Germans as, say, Paris had for the French or Moscow for the Russians. Berlin had not been a nucleus around which the German nation evolved. Yet it was the capital. The army to capture it would view itself as the victor over Germany. There had been much ado about allowing French troops to be the first to enter Paris. In the same sense, control over the pile of rubble still called Berlin was symbolically identified with control of Germany. Thus it was decided that Berlin was to be administered by a joint Allied Commission.

The organization of world peace required an agreement on the political structure of Europe, particularly of Germany, once the strongest state in Europe. It was clear what each side wanted, but it was not at all clear how to bargain for it, nor even how to implement one's desires even if one could have one's way. At one time Henry Morgenthau, Secretary of Treasury under Roosevelt, proposed to deindustrialize Germany, to turn her into an agricultural country. Castration of sex criminals is sometimes contemplated on somewhat similar grounds. However, an impotent Germany did not fit in with the United States plans for a postwar Europe. The United States wanted a restoration of Germany as an industrial power, because Germany's industrial potential was vital for the stability and prosperity of non-Communist Europe, which, in turn, was to be a bulwark against communism (or what to the Americans was the same thing, Soviet domination). At the time, however, if the subsequent analysis of the situation by Western writers is to be accepted, a *remilitarization* of Germany was not yet a goal of United States policy. That was to come later.

Preventing the resurgence of Germany as a military power was a foremost goal of Soviet policy; but keeping Germany poor was not. Quite aside from the possibility of having a mighty Germany in the Soviet orbit, the prospect of an economically strong but neutral Germany must have been an attractive one to the Soviet Union. Traditionally, Germany's industry was seen as a natural complement to Russia's riches in agriculture and raw materials. The question was, could Germany be kept economically strong and at the same time militarily weak?

One might think that the prospect of an economically strong *Communist* Germany was even more alluring to the Soviet Union. After all, this was Lenin's foremost dream. This interpretation of Soviet aims in Germany was, and still is, considered to be self-evident in American government circles. Yet Ulam, after, one must assume, a thorough search for concrete evidence on this point, poses the question: "How far were the Soviets determined to make a bid for all of Germany?" And he answers: "Djilas recalls the statements by Stalin and the Soviet leaders made before the Bulgarians and the Yugoslavs in the spring of 1946, that all of Germany must be ours, that is, Soviet Communist." Djilas's complete statement reads, "I could never understand the statements by Stalin . . ." etc.[2] As a reflection of the trend in Soviet policy, Djilas quotes Stalin as saying: "The West

will make Western Germany their own, and we shall turn Eastern Germany into our own state."[3]

In fairness to Ulam, it must be pointed out that he quotes this
statement also. The first statement was made in 1946, the second
in 1948. On the whole, evidence favors the view that, whatever
notions Stalin may have toyed with at the close of the war, he
soon abandoned the idea of imposing a Communist regime on
Germany by force of arms. This restraint is attributed by Ulam
to Stalin's extreme caution in playing the power game. In my
opinion, another factor must be seriously examined, the one
mentioned earlier: Stalin nurtured a deep fear of Communists
whom he had the slightest reason to suspect of tendencies toward independence. A Communist Germany (or France or Italy)
may well have been a persistent specter in the nightmares of
Stalin as well as in those of Forrestal.[4]

Questions about Germany presented themselves to both sides
not *in vacuo* but in the medium of the continually intensifying
cold war. As the positions on Eastern Europe hardened, it became increasingly clear to both sides that an "agreement" on
Germany receded into the realm of the impossible. Each side
was therefore determined to consolidate what it already had.
The Western Allies had Western Germany. They proceeded to
restore its industrial might and to prepare to rebuild its military
machine. The Soviet Union had Eastern Germany. It was transformed into another Eastern European satellite.

Nowhere else is the Richardsonian process more evident than
in the escalation of the cold war over the fate of Germany. As in
an armament race, each side justified its moves as responses to
the moves of the other. Since the moves followed each other in
quick succession, each side could support its own justification by
ample and concrete evidence. The result of the escalation may
have been damaging to the aims of both sides (assuming, for the
moment, that both sides "wanted" to get on with a European
peace settlement), but neither could do anything to stop the
drift into a hopeless impasse. Attempts by one to break the impasse *automatically* elicited reactions by the other to plug up
the escape hatch. For example, in March 1952, the Soviet Union
proposed a unified neutral Germany with a *right to rearm* to the
extent necessary "to defend herself against attack." Ulam re-

marks that in the 1940s this proposal would have been eagerly
accepted by the Western Allies. Now, however, it was too late.
Plans for incorporating Western Germany into the Euro-
pean-American defense system were too far advanced. Now
Washington felt that the Russians were "not playing fair." Ulam
writes:

> Here American diplomacy has finally put together a plan for the
> defense of Europe and the construction of a sizeable army—in the
> process overcoming American neo-isolationism, British apprehen-
> sions, French suspicions, and German touchiness—only to find the
> wretched Russians with yet another beguiling plan. . . .[5]

The organization of the Federal Republic of Germany is pictured by Western apologists as an answer to the Berlin Blockade
(June 1948–March 1949). The Berlin Blockade is pictured by
Soviet writers as a response to the currency reforms introduced
by the Western Allies in Berlin which allegedly violated the
Potsdam agreement. The United States viewed the Berlin Blockade as a challenge to the American presence in Europe or, at
least, as a probing of the Americans' determination to stay. The
fall of West Berlin, it was argued, would have been a signal to
the Russians that the West would not fight. (The Russians had
not anticipated the air lift that kept Berlin supplied during the
blockade and obviated the necessity of challenging the
blockade by an armed thrust.) Eventually giving up Berlin
would have meant the withdrawl of American troops from
Germany which Americans felt would open the way to the
dreaded catastrophe of a Communist Europe. Therefore the Allies argued they had no choice but to stick it out and to emphasize their resolve by going ahead with the remilitarization of
West Germany. The Russians had concluded long before that
the United States was determined to remilitarize West Germany
and to use it as an outpost threatening the U.S.S.R. The Russians
viewed the Berlin Blockade as a demonstration of *their* resolve
to parry that threat.

If one is to believe the war aims of the Grand Alliance as
stated in solemn pronouncements—the prevention of future
wars—then the freezing of irreconcilable positions resulting from
the impasse over Germany took them away from this goal. A
plausible conclusion is that the leaders of both the United

States and the Soviet Union were powerless to prevent what actually happened. That is, forces must have been at work over which the policy makers had no control. Another possible conclusion is that the professed peace aims were not the real peace aims, that a continuation of conflict became a necessity to both sides.

It was once suggested, perhaps semiseriously, that the problem of West Berlin could be easily solved by simply *moving* the city into the Federal Republic, that is, building an exact replica of it. This would remove the thorn in the Soviet Union's side without abandoning the brave two million West Berliners to the mercy of the Communists. The new city could even be built on the border between the two Germanys, so that it could continue to discharge its function as a showcase of free enterprise in full view of the captives of communism. The total cost of this enterprise was estimated at five billion dollars, a trickle in the total costs of keeping the cold war going.

The inanity of this proposal is immediately apparent, but not on practical grounds. It appears absurd because it completely misses the real meaning of the struggle over Berlin. The struggle was not over the city (of no strategic importance), nor over the fate of the inhabitants (makers of foreign policies are not known to attach great weight to the fate of populations), nor over the role of Berlin as an escape route from Eastern Germany, nor as a showcase of capitalism. Each of these "issues" could have been resolved quickly and cheaply, given a serious intent to resolve them. The real object of the struggle was not about Berlin but about who was going to have his way about Berlin.

"War," to quote Clausewitz again, "is an act of violence intended to compel our opponent to fulfill our will."

This is also the opening sentence of Raymond Aron's work on global sociology.[6] If we couple this definition with Clausewitz's other celebrated definition, stated backwards: "Policy is the continuation of war by other means," we have the foundation of the so-called "realist" view of international relations. The imposition of one's will upon another is the exercise of power. The exercise of power, however, has other consequences besides the "fulfillment of our will," namely an increment or a decrement in the reservoir of power. It stands to reason that an unsuccessful attempt to exercise power (for example, a military or diplomatic defeat) may diminish the power of the user. Even a successful application of power may decrease this reservoir. It may happen in two ways: through excessive expenditure of resources (a Pyrrhic victory) or by stimulating a mobilization of resources and a stiffened resistance on the part of the opponent in anticipation of the next encounter. It follows that the costs of a victory must be weighed not only against the anticipated fruits but also against the long-run consequences, that is, a future redistribution of power. All of these considerations are entirely in accord with the Clausewitzian view and, in fact, constitute the core of the realists' conception of the uses of power.

If one wishes to apply these conceptions in a concrete situation, the question immediately arises how power is to be estimated. In a purely military confrontation, certain standards are generally accepted. One calculates the relative destructive potential or weapons systems, the strategic value of certain positions in terms of logistics, etc. However, in terms of Clausewitzian percepts, every military situation has a political component that must be taken into account. Moreover, this political component has grown immensely in importance since Clausewitz's time, because every act of a great power elicits repercussions not only among its own population and that of its opponent but also over the whole globe. Clausewitz never had to worry about what the Chinese, or the Egyptians, or the Thais would deduce from Prussia's military or diplomatic successes or reverses.

When we are faced with decision problems of great complexity and cannot escape the responsibility of making a decision, we tend to simplify our perception of the situation. We single out some one aspect of the problem that seems to us the most important and subordinate all considerations to an overriding goal. The overriding goal of the United States foreign policy after World War II became to "stop the spread of communism." With "communsism" the United States identified, first, Soviet expansion, later, all revolutionary movements in which Communists might participate. For the Soviet Union an overriding goal became to be recognized as a Great Power with a voice in world affairs. Neither state paused to consider what effect the pursuit of these goals would have on the ultimate goals supposedly served by the immediate ones, such as, in the case of the United States, a peaceful world allowing an orderly evolution toward a community of prosperous, democratic societies, and, in the case of the Soviet Union, the building of a Communist society in the U.S.S.R., or even, for that matter, the promotion of proletarian revolutions abroad.

Both the United States and the Soviet Union achieved their overriding goals in Europe. No country outside the Soviet orbit went "Communist" or stands in imminent danger of doing so. The Soviet Union became a great power with a voice in European affairs. Except for some defections, it has held on to its "sphere of influence." Both states achieved their goals by frustrating the thrusts of the other *in every instance* where this could be done without unduly incurring the risk of war. The intrinsic importance of each issue was of no consequence to either. The most important aim of each maneuver was simply to prevent the other from having his own way if this was possible.

To illustrate, the Russians refused to participate in the Marshall Plan and would not let Poland or Czechoslovakia do so either, *because* the plan was proposed by the United States. The United States refused to change the status of West Berlin *because* the Soviet Union insisted on it. The eminently reasonable Rapacki Plan[7] was rejected by the United States without any substantive analysis of its merits or defects because it was proposed by a Soviet satellite. Both the U.S.S.R. and the United States undermined the effectiveness of the United Nations as an organ of peace, the one by compulsive use of the veto in the Security Council, the other by deliberate provocations of the veto (introducing resolutions known in advance to be unacceptable to the Soviet Union).

Note that the justifications advanced by each side for its resistance to the moves of the other were not at all absurd. The Russians argued that the Marshall Plan was a design for an economic domination of Europe by the United States and for the reestablishment of a militarized Germany. And this turned out to be the case. The United States insisted that the apparently "mixed" regimes installed in Eastern Europe by the Soviet Union at the close of World War II were only facades covering up a complete Sovietization of the countries. It so turned out. In view of what actually happened, it can be argued that the fundamental goal of each of The Two was simply to frustrate the designs of the other. Therefore, both have succeeded and both have failed.

We may therefore conclude that the "issues" in terms of which the confrontation of The Two in Europe is usually described were only chimeras. An "issue" between two sovereign states is either a matter that can be resolved by compromise or one that precipitates a war. There was neither compromise nor a war. The so-called issues were apparently neither important enough to be settled nor important enough to fight about. What was important was the confrontation itself.

CHAPTER 9

The Issue

Whether the Americans reneged on the Yalta agreement by demanding a voice in Eastern European affairs or whether the Russians violated it by refusing to allow the "reorganization" of the Warsaw government, the fact remained that Soviet armies occupied most of Eastern Europe and the Americans had a free hand in Western Europe. The ghost of Clausewitz contemplating the situation would surmise that each power would thereupon consolidate its position and, having done so, would start developing schemes to expand its realm and to frustrate the attempts of the other to do the same.

There are those—neo-Clausewitzians—who still think in these terms. Like Clausewitz, they picture the ideal foreign policy as an amalgam of diplomacy and military strategy; or, as Walter Lippmann put it, as a matching of foreign commitments with sufficient military power to back it (cf. Chapter 4). In contemporary world politics, however, another factor must be taken into account, namely the populations.

To be sure, Clausewitz brought this new factor into his theory of war in the form of nationalism. In his scheme, though, "the people" were only an additional source of power of a state. Nationalism bolstered the morale of armies and so made them more effective instruments of politics. The goals of politics remained what they became when the "community of states" emerged after the religious wars of the sixteenth and seventeenth centuries. Each state sought to extend its influence and power at the expense of the influence and power of the other states. "Power" still meant administrative and military control of the realm, and "influence" meant the preemption of other states as allies.

Today populations are seen as having aspirations of their own. Whether these aspirations are correctly perceived or understood by policy makers is another matter. Somehow they must be included in the making of modern foreign policies and expressed in such a way as to make the espoused foreign policy appealing. In other words, an ideological component *must* enter the formulation of foreign policy no matter how "realistically" it is conceived. Each power must make it appear that the expansion of its influence and power would benefit populations presently outside its realm or sphere of influence, perhaps all of humanity—an idea entirely absent from the Clausewitzian conception of foreign policy. The new conception must allow (though it need not emphasize) an eschatological vision—a world order to supplant the classical "community of states."

The American conception of "freedom" and "democracy" is axiomatically equated with license for *expansion* of enterprises organized and managed with a view of earning profits. When the United States was young, such opportunities were indigenous on the North American continent, and in pursuit of them American "free enterprise" extended its realm from coast to coast; by the end of the nineteenth century, its conquest burst through the limits of the continental United States, and the foundations of an empire were laid.

In previous centuries, empire-building was territorial; and when two expanding empires collided, they waged war against each other. The American empire expanded in another way, namely by economic penetration. The global political events of the twentieth century uniquely provided some remarkable opportunities for this sort of growth. World War I was such an event. It led to a severe exhaustion of the principal imperial powers of Europe—England and France—who thereby became debtors of the United States. The United States emerged from World War I not only unscathed but with a tremendously increased potential for economic penetration. In fact, the United States was the first to discover that economic conquest can be undertaken not only by acquiring colonies but also by attaining an ever-increasing control over the economies of industrially developed countries.

World War II further exhausted Europe and led to the collapse of empires ruled from Europe—the British, the French, the Dutch, and the Belgian. Not only did the opportunities for economic expansion vastly increase for American profit-making enterprises, but also the United States found itself after World War II practically without rivals. Only one obstacle was seen to the economic conquest of the planet: the existence of regimes under which economic penetration by profit-making enterprises was precluded. The recognition of this political fact determined the direction of United States foreign policy and gave it its anti-Communist bias.

• Thus, the United States foreign policy has always stemmed from the goals of profit-making enterprises, principally market expansion. The Open Door Policy imposed on China was a demand for equal economic opportunities for United States commerce. The "defense of democracy" in World War I was a defense of a political system that was more permissive toward economic competition. However, only after World War II did this "national interest" of the United States reach the dimensions of an obsession. Then, simultaneously with the collapse of the old barriers (that is, the old empires), new forbidding barriers appeared in the shape of regimes that prohibited capitalist economic penetration in regions which they controlled.

Plainly speaking, then, the so-called "national interest" of the United States has been shaped to preserving and extending global capitalism, by which I mean here the maintenance of ubiquitous political conditions permissive to competitive private enterprise. Ordinarily American capitalists have felt that in free competition for the economic domination of the world they would always have an edge over others. For the most part their expectations were realized, especially where the old rivals had been exhausted in wars. Against competition from vigorous recovered rivals, for example, contemporary West Germany or Japan, the United States does not seem to be doing as well; but this latest development has not resulted in any discernible inclination by Americans to question or reexamine their perceptions of their "national interests."

Since the spread of Marxist ideas, "capitalism" has acquired a pejorative connotation among, probably, the majority of those who understand this word. In the United States, however, although the euphemism "free enterprise" is sometimes used as a disinfectant, "capitalism" is not considered a dirty word. On the contrary, the word is associated with steady economic expansion, and the latter with steady enrichment. Moreover, in American experience, economic expansion and the enrichment of people in business was not visibly associated with abject poverty of the working classes as it had been in England, the original home of industrial capitalism. In the minds of Americans, the growth of business enterprises is firmly linked with a constantly rising standard of living, and this association is projected onto the rest of the world. That is to say, Americans see economic penetration by the United States as mainly beneficial in the countries where it occurs. The economic recovery of Western Europe under the stimulus of the Marshall Plan is seen as evidence for this view. So, because the Marshall Plan helped put parts of a war-devastated world back on its feet, subsequent combinations of private business and government subsidies, such as the irrigation projects in Pakistan, fertilizer plants in India, and the like, became fixated as proper methods of "helping" underdeveloped areas.[1]

In summary, the real issue of the global conflict appears, from the point of view of the United States, as follows.

1. Economic development everywhere in the "Free World" along the lines of expanding free enterprise, technological progress, and a rise in the general standard of living is in the interest of the United States. Thus the United States is guided by enlightened self-interest. Benefits to the United States and to the rest of the world coincide.

2. The United States has not opposed, and at times has encouraged, the struggle of former colonial peoples for political independence, and stands ready to help the new nations in their economic development.

3. Prerequisites for steady economic development are certain social and political conditions. Of particular importance is a strong middle class, that is, business and professional people, skilled workers, farmers who own their land, etc. These strata insure social stability since their personal interests (career suc-

cess) coincide with those of a developing society. A country with a strong middle class is on the way to nationhood. The political corollary is, of course, a government permissive to free enterprise and sympathetic to the aspirations of the middle class.

4. To promote the above conditions and the economic development throughout the world, the United States is ready to give massive aid in the way of loans and capital investments. It is important that this aid include military assistance to regimes sympathetic to these goals of the United States in order to protect them from outside conquest and inside subversion.

5. From time to time it may become necessary to remove regimes inimical to the goals of the United States. Preferably this should be done by unobtrusive pressures so that the regime appears to have been removed by an orderly internal political process. On occasion, however, it may become necessary to engineer a putsch. In extreme cases, frank military intervention may be required.

Obstacles to this program are, by definition, forces inimical to the interests of the United States. These obstacles are, by extension, regimes that resist United States economic expansion. It makes no difference whether such regimes are actually installed by, or have the military, economic, or moral support of the big Communist powers, or whether they come into being spontaneously. Their existence on any grounds is an obstacle to the national goals of the United States. The coming into being of *new* regimes of this sort is a direct threat to the goals of the United States and therefore to its security. Consequently the United States should direct its total diplomatic and military effort to preventing the expansion of regions that are inaccessible to economic penetration by the United States.

This is the meaning of the Containment Policy, the Truman Doctrine, the Eisenhower Doctrine, the Doctrine of Massive Retaliation, and the "counterinsurgency" schemes. The political complexion of Eastern Europe, the fate of West Berlin, the fate of Germany, the containment of China, the support of some regimes and the overthrow of others in Latin America or in the Middle East, or wherever—all of these "issues" are subsidiary to the main one, the preservation and expansion of the American

Empire, by which I mean here a world where American economic penetration is either welcome or cannot be effectively resisted.

A denial of American imperialism is usually based on the contention, first, that at least since the Spanish-American war the United States has not engaged in military conquest of territories; second, that even economic domination by the United States does not constitute colonial exploitation. An examination of this argument would take us far afield. The nature of imperialism is not the subject of our discussion. The subject is U.S.-Soviet relations. In order to understand them, we must understand the prime mover of American policy and of its rationale. The prime mover has been the need of American capitalism to expand. This is not to say that the *avowed* aims of American foreign policy, such as to insure world political stability, continuing economic development, and peace, are mere window dressing. On the contrary, a politically stable world and its progressive "bourgeoisification" would be quite in accord with the primary goal of the United States, provided that the preponderance of United States economic might would continue. Nor are Americans deluding themselves and others when they assert that the sort of capitalist expansion they espouse is not predicated on ruthless plundering of underdeveloped countries, as was the expansion of European empires.

Therefore, *from a particular point of view,* the program embodied in the idea of Pax Americana can be defended both on practical and on humanitarian grounds. If only no resistance were offered to American economic penetration by the countries about to be penetrated (all such resistance being perceived almost exclusively as Communist-influenced), it would not be necessary for the United States to support oppressive regimes (when they are the only bulwarks against communism) or to devastate poor countries by counterinsurgency wars (the insurgents perceived to be invariably Communists). The whole world could come under a vast Marshall Plan. To be sure, United States enterprises, due to their superior management, would inevitably play a leading role in world economic affairs. But the world population would not suffer on that account any more than the American population suffers (that is, perceives itself as "suffering") under the economic rule of giant corporations. At any rate, the "rule" of the giant corporations, as it has been exercised in the United States, is far more humane than that of the totalitarian Communist states. On the whole, the corporations need not resort to police state methods. They permit local autonomy in community affairs, much more freedom of expression than the totalitarian regimes, etc. Given the opportunity, this benevolent rule could be extended over the entire globe, or at least over the portion of the globe not controlled by the Communists. If only the Communists stayed in their own world and did not try to extend their power or influence beyond it, the Pax Americana could become a reality. In due time the superiority of the free enterprise system over the Communist totalitarian would become apparent, and the latter would have either to give or to "mellow" into traditional liberalism.

Such would be a frank statement of the primary American goal.

It would be tempting to draw an analogous picture of the Soviet side, a vision of a peaceful and humane Communist world order, of the obstacles in the path of social revolutions, the strategies used in the overcoming of these obstacles, etc. However, there is no justification for drawing such a symmetrical picture. There is no Soviet analogue for the gradual economic penetration posed by the United States. Moreover the vision of a Communist world order in the foreseeable future was only a fleeting one at the close of World War I. Soon after that war it became clear that the capitalist world order would survive that shock and that the newly acquired economic power of the United States would more than offset the decline of the hitherto dominant imperialist powers, England and France. Thereafter the vision of a Communist world order became little more than an ideological prop for Stalin's internal policy. Thus there was no *practical* program for bringing the Communist world order into being.

There might have been such an analogue if the Communists had been willing to engage in conventional political activity, for example, by allying themselves with the European Socialist parties to capture political power by parliamentary means. This sort of activity, however, was precluded by Leninist ideology which demanded that the main political blows be directed against reformist socialism. When in the middle thirties attempts were made to forge such a grand alliance of the Left, it was too late. In short, while the American program of economic penetration was completely in accord with American political ideology (liberalism), there was no concrete program that could be geared to the supposed long-term goals of Communist ideology. Before World War II, the Soviet Union was not a Great Power. When it became a Great Power after World War II, it could not compete with the United States for the domination of the world. Only militarily was the Soviet Union a match for the United States. Its economic power was negligible. As for its ideological power, which in Lenin's time was thought to be its greatest asset, it was lost. In Europe the "toiling masses" became increasingly seduced by bourgeois and reformist ideologies. Elsewhere rival centers of Communist influence appeared (China, Yugoslavia) and eventually became a greater danger to the Soviet Union (in the perception of its leaders) than the perseverance of the Old Order.

Consequently Soviet policy cannot but appear to be a purely defensive one to the Soviet leaders, not merely in the sense of self-justification (in this sense all nations perceive their foreign policies as defensive) but in the sense of perceived available options. The Soviets lack the powerful instruments of economic penetration that are at the disposal of the United States. They are well aware of the limitations of imposing Soviet-type regimes by military force except possibly in small countries adjoining the U.S.S.R. For two generations they cherished the conviction that, if "history" with its "laws of development of human societies" is allowed to continue on its course, eventually the whole world will be "socialist." However, even this faith now provides scanty reassurance to the old-fashioned preoccupation with "national security" in view of recent developments in China. Still, deeply ingrained habits of thought persist; and the chief threat still appears to be the determination of the United States, the champion of capitalism, to prevent or even to reverse the "natural" course of history, especially the determination of the United States to fill the power vacuum left by the demise of the old colonial empires.

In the eyes of its leaders, the policy of the Soviet Union may appear, not unreasonably, to be a containment policy—containment of expanding United States power. This power, it must be remembered, is wielded primarily by economic weapons with only occasional resort to force. Nevertheless the potential of American economic expansion is backed by a ubiquitous military presence that exceeds in extent and visibility that of any empire in history.

From this point of view, the reverse *cordon sanitaire* in Europe, the support of Arab nationalism, and even the ill-fated attempt to provide Cuba with her own "nuclear deterrent" appear as defensive measures.

It is understandable that, in the minds of American leaders and of the American public, it is American policy that appears defensive and Soviet policy that appears aggressive. The reason is not alone the excusable desire to justify one's own case. There is also a deeper reason, mentioned earlier, that, to people who accept the "free enterprise" system as "natural," the aggressive features of the dynamics of that system do not appear as such. That the United States has acquired considerable control over the European economy is attributed to the greater efficiency of American management and technology. American economic domination of the Western Hemisphere, if perceived at all by the American public, is seen as a natural consequence of help extended by America to backward economies. As for Southeast Asia, American goals are seen as efforts to bring those countries to the "take off point," as Walter Rostow put it, from where they can continue the development on their own accord to evolve into prosperous democratic states. This is "nation building." The more drastic moves, such as the overthrow of "Communist-dominated" regimes and of military interventions, are seen as defenses against a Communist take over. And while it is realized, at least among the more enlightened, that the Soviet Union alone cannot possibly be the designer of all the obstacles in the path to Pax Americana, "expansionist communism" remains the catchall name for these obstacles.

Actually, aside from the vagueness of the term, the conception does capture a portion of historical truth. There *is* resistance to the process that, if not checked, would establish the United

States' economic empire in the vacuum left by the disintegrated colonial empires. Following the collapse of Western power in the underdeveloped world, this resistance increased both in extent and intensity. Invariably the resistance has been identified by American policy makers with "Communist expansion," and, since the latter was automatically assumed to be instigated by the Soviet Union, Soviet policy was always perceived as "expansionist." Whether a policy is expansionist or defensive depends, of course, on how one defines the "legitimate" area of control. At the close of World War II, the "legitimate" area of Communist rule was confined, in the minds of American policy makers, to the borders of the U.S.S.R. Consequently, the policies ✔ that appeared to the Soviet leaders as purely defensive, such as consolidating a clearly circumscribed sphere of influence, shielding it from "ideological erosion," and occasional spotty support of anti-Western resistance movements, became for Americans clear evidence of Soviet expansionism.

On closer examination, the bulk of contemporary revolutionary movements, from guerrilla operations to student protests, is not only uncoordinated with Soviet policy but actually antithetical to it. A failure to realize this political fact or, perhaps, a deliberate decision to ignore it, has been, in my opinion, largely responsible for the ominous character of Soviet-American relations.

The conflict over Europe came to a stalemate in 1949. Eastern Europe was by then Stalinized. The Americans showed by the Berlin airlift that they were not leaving Europe and instead proceeded with their plans to weld their half of the continent into a military bloc under the North Atlantic Treaty Organization. Thereafter, the remilitarization of Europe developed of its own accord. After a half-hearted resistance on the part of France was overcome, the remilitarization policy led to the inevitable result: West Germany became the strongest military power in Europe, to United States leaders "a staunch ally," to the Soviet leaders a denial of the primary goal for which Russia had bled, a revival of the old deadly threat. In assessing the meaning of this threat, Americans might ponder a hypothetical analogue: a fully remilitarized Japan, firmly allied with the Soviet Union.

After the course in Europe was set (with the establishment of NATO), the attention of the United States was turned to the Pacific. Chiang Kai-shek's power in China collapsed just at that time. A careful analysis of the forces that led to that outcome was made by Owen Lattimore.[2] It was ignored, and Lattimore became *persona non grata*. Already during the war General Joseph Stilwell, the commander of American forces in China and adviser to Chiang Kai-shek, saw the futility of backing Chiang and his clique as founder of a renascent China friendly to the U.S. Stilwell was not a political analyst. His task was a purely military one, and he argued for building up a Chinese land army imbued with a consciousness that they were fighting to rid their land of a foreign invader.[3] But Chiang was more afraid of the Chinese than of the Japanese. He wanted no "people's army." All he wanted was American materiel. Stilwell was dismissed.

When Chiang collapsed, the event was interpreted as a conquest of China by the Soviet Union. Dean Rusk, later Kennedy's and Johnson's Secretary of State, insisted that the "Peiping government" was not viable because "it was not Chinese."

The Korean War may or may not have been instigated by Moscow. It may have been one of the "opportunities" seized upon by Stalin to consolidate his empire. (It must be noted that North Korea, unlike China, was a Soviet satellite.) The war led to an initial defeat of United States forces by the Chinese. This was the first war since 1812 that did not end in an American victory. It initiated the anti-Soviet hysteria that dominated the 1950s.

The Korean War and its interpretation in terms of Soviet expansionism led to a change of American policy in Southeast Asia. In the late 1940s the United States viewed with equanimity, perhaps with satisfaction, the dissolution of European empires in India, Burma, and Indonesia. Before 1950 the French could expect little from the United States in the way of helping them reconquer Indo-China. Then the Korean War established Asia as a major battleground "against communism." By the time the French were beaten by the Viet Minh, the United States was underwriting three-quarters of France's war in Vietnam. In a way, therefore, the first Indo-Chinese war was another war the United States "failed" to win. True, American troops were not involved, but influential voices were raised in favor of intervention even to the extent of using atomic bombs to lift the siege of Dienbienphu. Military intervention was not undertaken at that time, but the psychological effect in some military and government circles was that of a "lost war." The idea was still prevalent at the time that any war resolutely undertaken by Americans could be won, so that a failure to undertake it was tantamount to a failure to win it.

It was about that time that the policy of massive retaliation was announced by John Foster Dulles, Secretary of State. The main idea of that policy was that "local response" to "Communist aggression" was not sufficient. Since the Communists were the aggressors, they could choose the time and place of aggression, and this gave them tactical advantage. Said Dulles:

> Local defense will always be important. But there is no local defense which alone will contain the mighty land power of the Communist World. Local defenses must be reinforced by the further deterrent of massive retaliatory power. . . . Otherwise, for example, a potential aggressor glutted with manpower, might be tempted to attack in confidence that resistance would be confined to manpower. . . .
>
> The way to deter aggression is for the free community to be willing and able to respond vigorously at places and means of its own choosing.[4]

At a later press conference, Dulles amplified his meaning:

> The question of circumstances under which you retaliate, where you retaliate, how quickly you retaliate, is a matter which has to be dealt with in the light of facts of each particular case. One thing I want to make clear beyond the possibility of doubt is that I don't believe you should tell the enemy in advance just where, how, and when you plan to retaliate. The whole essence of the program is that the action should be an action of our choosing and he is not to know in advance what it is, and that uncertainty on his part is a key to the success of the policy.[5]

The argument loses its force if either of its two tacit assumptions is invalidated; that is, either if the Kremlin is not really a "control center" of revolution, or if the United States does not in fact have a monopoly on the possession of the ultimate weapon. As it turned out, both assumptions were invalidated. "Aggressions" continued to occur. One was the appearance of a popularly supported government in Iran; another the election of a leftist government in Guatemala. Still another was the overthrow of a pro-Western government in Iraq. Clearly it was not practical to drop bombs on Moscow in response to each of these events, even when the United States had a clear superiority of nuclear weapons and means of delivery. Willy-nilly, then, the United States was forced to resort to "local responses." Mossadegh's government, and that of Arbenz, were overthrown by putsches engineered by the CIA. U.S. Marines were landed in Lebanon, ready to save freedom in Iraq; but President Eisenhower had second thoughts on this matter, and nothing came of it.

In the meantime the American nuclear monopoly was irretrievably lost. A consequence of "instantaneous massive retaliation" was now clearly seen to be "instantaneous massive counterretaliation." The policy was quietly abandoned. Or rather, it merged with another policy called "deterrence." The only thing that deterrence could clearly deter, or was ever claimed to deter, was an unprovoked attack on the United States or on Western Europe. On the Soviet side, the only thing *their* deterrence policy could clearly deter, or was ever claimed to deter, was an unprovoked attack on the Soviet Union or on the satellites, and (for a time) on China. Since a "nuclear exchange" of this sort could have no conceivable *political* aim, one could say that with the establishment of the nuclear balance of terror the Clausewitzian theory of international relations was abandoned. It proved much more viable, however, than such a conclusion would indicate, as will be shown. At any rate, the nuclear stalemate became a permanent fixture in Soviet-American relations.

CHAPTER 10

Strike One, Strike Two

The first Soviet atomic bomb, ending United States monopoly of the weapon, was exploded in July 1949. The first Soviet hydrogen bomb, ending United States monopoly of that weapon, was exploded in 1953. Still, throughout the 1950s the United States had a preponderance in the means of delivery—long-range bombers capable of making the round trip. Thus in 1954 John Foster Dulles could still believe that a threat of massive retaliation against the Soviet Union was a deterrent. At that time deterrence was conceived as the prevention of occurrence of events anywhere in the world that the U.S. interpreted as Communist aggression. Since such events kept occurring, it became apparent that either (1) the Kremlin had no control over the events or (2) the Soviet Union did not believe the threat. The former conclusion clashed with the established U.S. doctrine, namely that communism was a monolithic conspiracy promoted by an organization with a centrally directed global strategy of conquest and subversion. The latter conclusion was more comfortable, especially since the realization of Soviet retaliation potential finally dawned on the makers of U.S. foreign policy.

The full impact of this realization came with the launching of the first satellite (Sputnik) by the U.S.S.R. in 1957. A satellite is launched by a thrust with sufficient energy to put a projectile into orbit around the earth. This meant that the intercontinental ballistic missile became practical and that the threat of annihilation no longer depended on a formidable air force.

With each technological innovation, professional soldiers are faced with the problem of fitting the new devices into tactics and strategy. Recall that tactics relate to the conduct of a battle and strategy to the conduct of larger operations, including an entire war. Thus the introduction of the machine gun in the late nineteenth century brought with it certain tactical techniques of utilizing its entire power; and it also had an important effect on strategy. Being a comparatively stationary weapon, it greatly strengthened defense, especially coupled with barbed wire, land mines, and similar means of fortifying a whole front rather than isolated points. The machine gun neatly checkmated the cavalry and infantry charges by means of which battles were won in the eighteenth and nineteenth centuries. It turned World War I into a war of position.

On the other hand, the tank, being a mobile weapon, reintroduced the offensive thrust into battle and turned World War II into a war of movement. The airplane opened up new possibilities of attacking the enemy's rear, especially his industry and transport. It could also be used—and was so used—as a terror weapon to break the morale of the enemy's population.

What sort of changes could nuclear weapons be expected to introduce into the art of war? It should have become clear to a thoughtful military man that nothing in the way of new tactics could be expected. Tactics are learned from experience. (It took many battles in the two world wars—plus Ethiopia and Spain in between—to develop progressively more effective ways of using the tank and the airplane and of defending against them.) A nuclear war is not likely to be a protracted affair with many battles. Rather it is thought of as lasting only a few days; with the development of ICBMs, perhaps only a few hours. What nuclear war would mean in terms of strategy relating to the conduct of an entire war—owing to its short duration, nuclear war had to be envisaged in its entirety—now loomed large. It was not to be expected that in the course of such a war much could be learned from experience on which to base changes of strategy. The strategies had to be prepared in advance on the basis of theoretical considerations. These considerations had to do with geography, physics, meteorology, economics, and so on. The demand for people with the requisite expertise skyrocketed.[1]

Accordingly, in the United States, and it can be assumed likewise in the Soviet Union, research institutes were established whose primary purpose was to work out problems of conducting war in the nuclear age. The indispensability of science in the broadest sense to military strategy became firmly embedded in the minds of both the policy makers and the military. Before long the range of scientific disciplines geared to military projects was enlarged to include psychology and sociology. It was now important to know how people would behave during and after a nuclear attack, and what the problems were of reconstructing society following a nuclear war. Research contracts were distributed to universities. Seminars and conferences proliferated. In short, research relating to the conduct of up-to-date war became a way of life for a large group of scholars and scientists.

For many intellectuals this way of life provided considerable satisfaction. I made the observation earlier that World War II must have provided gratification to many Americans by creating a sense of community and singleness of purpose where little or none had existed before. In a large collective effort, an individual, although he may be but a cog in a wheel, can nevertheless feel important; for a cog in a wheel is, after all, important to the functioning of the machine. A similar novel feeling of being needed must have blossomed in many an intellect worker who became a member of the so-called "strategic community."

Gratification in work stems from two sources: mastery over the materials one works with (craftsmanship) and devotion to a common purpose. Industrialization has stunted the role of individual craftsmanship in working with things, but in the intellectual realm craftsmanship of sorts has been preserved, namely the ability to work with intricate ideas, to make subtle distinctions, to organize masses of data into a coherent picture, etc. Industrialization has also impaired the sense of community, previously provided by religion, by extended kinship systems, and by small, compact settlements. A sense of national purpose became a substitute, and the notion of defending the nation against an enemy the most effective catalyst in the crystallization of a common purpose.

The prospect of a nuclear war is not attractive. The prospect of *preventing* a nuclear war is. And so is the prospect of using threats as a substitute for war. This was an avenue of escape from the dilemma posed by the balance of terror. Without this escape hatch, it would be difficult for a person with a normal sense of belonging to the human race to participate in what the strategic community was doing.

In summary, the outlook that underlies the so-called theory of deterrence involves the following features:

1. No experience with actual nuclear war, nor much prospect that acquiring experience in such a way could be meaningful. This serves to keep the theory on an abstract level and so to preserve the sanity of its adherents.

2. Dedication to intellectual craftsmanship; sophistication.

3. A devotion to a newly found community, the strategic—or defense—community, entrusted with the tasks of defending the nation.

The concept of deterrence provides a rationale for the existence of nuclear arsenals and at the same time a palliative from the horrifying idea of a nuclear war. The fundamental axiom of the theory of deterrence is that each state knows that the other side has the capacity to wreak complete destruction upon one's own population. This knowledge inhibits the temptation to attack the other side. Moreover, granted the potential possessed by both sides for completely destroying the other, the ability to use nuclear blackmail to wring political concessions out of the world politics game is minimized; each threat can be matched with a counterthreat.

Clearly deterrence is the nuclear age version of the balance of power theory that had dominated the thinking of statesmen in the eighteenth and nineteenth centuries. However, differences must be kept in mind. The preservation of the balance of power was assumed to prevent wars by dimming the likelihood of victory. If war did occur, the equality of the two sides was theoretically to demonstrate the futility of continuing the war. Thus, the balance of power concept was thought of not only as a deterrent against war but also as a means of restoring the *status quo* should war occur. Nuclear deterrence can conceivably be expected to perform the preventive function, but certainly not the restoring function.

And so a deterrent strategy had to be directed *entirely* to the task of preventing nuclear war. If such a war did occur, the strategy would have to be considered an utter failure. A nuclear war between "balanced" opponents could not be expected to solve any political problems except, perhaps, via elimination of both sides and hence of the problems engendered by them. The Chinese seem to regard this possibility with some satisfaction.

Let us now see what a genuine deterrence strategy would involve.

Designers of nuclear strategies distinguish between "first strike" and "second strike" capabilities. A first strike capability is one that enables the initiator of a nuclear attack to wipe out the other's means of retaliating in kind. Conceivably this could be done by an attack so sudden and so massive that the other side finds itself "dead" before it has time to respond. Alternately, a first strike could be directed selectively, that is, only at the nuclear installations of the opponent. Thereby the opponent would not be totally destroyed, but he would find himself deprived of his "deterrent," hence at the mercy of the successful perpetrator of the first strike.

A second strike capability is one that enables the side that has "absorbed" a nuclear attack to respond effectively.

Now, each type of strike capability requires a different strategy of attack and defense. Clearly a first strike must be directed primarily at the opponent's launching sites in order to neutralize his response potential. Whatever destruction is rained on his cities could have the purpose of postponing his recovery. It can be argued on both pragmatic and humanitarian grounds that the opponent's industry and population may well be spared in the first strike. But *all* of the opponent's nuclear capability must be destroyed, just as *all* cancerous tissue must be removed if surgical intervention is to be effective.

The second strike, on the other hand, is not to be directed against the launching sites of the opponent. This is because after the opponent has launched his first strike (to which the second is the other's response) his launching sites are empty. The second strike ought to be directed at the cities of the opponent in order to serve as a deterrent against initiating the first strike.

So much for the attack strategies of the first and second strikes. Let us now look at the defense strategies.

If one wishes to preserve one's second strike capability, one ought to concentrate on defending one's *launching* sites, for those will be the objects of attack on the first strike. On the other hand, if one wishes to preserve first strike capability, then cities ought to be protected. For, if the first strike should, God forbid, be only a partial success, the opponent's second strike will be directed at one's cities.

It is easier to defend launching sites than cities. Launching sites are imbedded in deep silos that can be protected even against a nuclear attack (barring direct hits). Moreover, even if most of one's launching sites are destroyed, whatever remain represents a second strike capability. Cities, on the other hand, are almost impossible to defend against nuclear attack by intercontinental missiles. Therefore the preservation of a second strike capability is not only more palatable on moral grounds (it has clearly a defensive function) but also more feasible. Accordingly, the "moderates" among the nuclear strategists preferred the second strike nuclear policy. In their arguments they brought out still another consideration having to do with the extension of the meaning of "balance" in the phrase "balance of terror." The idea runs something as follows.

An important difference between first and second strikes is that the former must be delivered as a complete surprise, while the second strike by the attacked party should, of course, surprise no one. Consequently, preparation for a first strike requires a great deal of secrecy. Preparations for a second strike, on the other hand, not only do not require secrecy but, on the contrary, require sending loud and clear signals to the opponent. The opponent should *know* that one's launching sites have been made invulnerable so he can expect with *certainty* that, if he attacks, his whole country will be destroyed. In this way, it is assumed, communication between opponents, each committed to a second strike, has a stabilizing effect on the relations between them. In a second strike strategy, if each is certain about the intentions of the other, no strike ought to occur.

Since in the first strike strategy, preparations must be made in the greatest secrecy, consider now what can happen if, in spite of all precautions, information leaks out that the other is preparing a first strike. A second strike can conceivably *deter* a first strike attack, but only a first strike can *prevent* it in the sense of making it impossible rather than just unattractive. Therefore, if information leaks out about a preparation for a first strike, the other side, if it has first strike capability, will try to anticipate the first strike by a first strike of its own. This, in turn, induces the first side to anticipate the anticipation. The vicious cycle is closed, and a preventive first strike by one side or both becomes inevitable. Thus it is argued that, while a second strike strategy is a stabilizing one, a first strike strategy is a destabilizing one. If the object of the balance of terror is to prevent a nuclear war, each side ought to strick to a second strike strategy.

The argument, convincing as it sounds, has one serious drawback. A second strike strategy implies not only that the launching sites must be "hardened," that is, made invulnerable to nuclear attack, but also that cities must *not* be protected. For the stability of the balance of terror depends crucially on what each side believes about the other's true intentions. Leaving one's cities unprotected against nuclear attack amounts to a message to the opponent which says, "Look, I have not protected my cities. Therefore rest assured that I do not fear your *second* strike. It follows that I am not contemplating a first strike." On the other hand, if attempts are made to protect the cities (or their populations), this is likely to be interpreted as saying to the opponent, "I fear your *second* strike." Why should one be afraid of a second strike? Obviously because one is contemplating a first strike. As a result, the measures that can be most reasonably interpreted as *purely* defensive, such as the construction of bomb shelters, appear on second thought to be the most threatening. They are indicative of an intention to strike first. To be consistent, an argument in favor of a second strike strategy had to be coupled with an argument *against* civil defense!

Understandably, it was virtually impossible for the military establishment to oppose civil defense. The argument against it described above is not the sort that the public can readily understand, much less accept. Besides, the military had its own public relations problems. The traditional trappings by which military establishments of the past presented an attractive image (resplendent uniforms, parades, regimental codes, and the like) were never prominent in the United States, and efforts to introduce them into the mainstream of social life have largely failed. Only one theme remained on which to base the justification of the enormous budgets on which the United States military establishment fattened: insurance against destruction. As in all propaganda tasks, the military public relations officers stuck to tried and true methods—which in the U.S. have been further cinched by Madison Avenue techniques. The messages must be simple, related both to familiar experiences and the emotional involvements of people at whom they are aimed. Civil defense ideally answered the requirements of an advertising copy theme. Civil defense measures could be coupled to public works undertaken as protection against natural disasters, and to taking out insurance, both eminently sensible activities. Better still, the greatest virtue of civil defense as a public relations vehicle for the military is its community character. Everyone can be involved in civil defense, even little children. It is a ready-made focus for drives, campaigns, and community activities that give citizens a vivid sense of participating in the affairs of the nation.

As it turned out, though, the civil defense tactic backfired in the United States. The initial thrust of the campaign was to induce citizens to build their own home bomb shelters. Most Americans live in single-family dwellings, and home ownership is an important feature of the American way of life. The family bomb shelter fitted naturally into the average American's idea of security. In 1961, during one of the recurring Berlin crises (the East Germans had just erected the Berlin Wall), civil defense campaign posters, displayed in every post office, showed an unscathed street of a typical American town with people dousing the pavements with garden hoses, washing away the residue of radioactive dust. The idea was that, with one's own private shelter to provide protection against radioactive fallout, people could sit out the attack and its aftermath and emerge to resume a normal American life. Manufacturers were quick to seize the opportunity for selling prefabricated shelters, and merchants put survival kits on the market with which to equip the shelters. Discussions ensued about what to take to the shelter to while away the time; which parlor games, phonograph records, hobby gadgets. Then certain ethical problems were raised: what to do about neighbors who might insist on being admitted to the bomb shelters when it was not safe to open the door; for example, was it permissible to shoot them? And so on.

Out of this flurry of public attention it seems that the implications of nuclear war became too vivid, and the first energetic protests against the continued balance of terror made themselves felt in the spectrum of public opinion. What also stimulated the protests was the emphasis on radioactive fallout (necessary to make people cooperate with the bomb shelter program). Once sensitized to the dangers of fallout, the population began to pay attention to information sources other than those of the government and the military.[2] These other sources made it known that radioactive fallout was not confined to some future enemy bombing attack but was also a by-product of *testing* hydrogen bombs in the atmosphere. The fallout, mostly strontium 90, settled on grazing lands and so got into milk and eventually into the bones where it was stored. The most deleterious effects would be, of course, on children. Lively debates ensued concerning the extent of the dangers to the world population, including unborn generations, because absorbed radioactivity was known to affect genetic structures. Such facts as became available were marshaled to support one and the other sides of the debate. As was to be expected, differing emphases, interpretations, and extrapolations, and especially different priorities of values, served to sharpen the debate rather than to settle the issues. Beginning in the sixties it became clear that the military policy with which the United States initiated its rearmament—that is, a virtually open-ended drive for a complete preponderance over the Soviet Union, based on a nuclear arsenal sufficient to destroy all of humanity many times over—had to cope with mounting, at times organized, intense opposition.

CHAPTER 11

Coexistence

To understand an event, or a
sequence of events, means to fit it into a preconceived scheme
of thought or perception. It may be a scheme shared by many,
or it may be one's own private scheme. At one extreme are the
conceptual schemes of science, called theories; at the other, the
delusions of psychotics.

A physicist understands an observed event if he can deduce it
from a few general principles called physical laws. In his
deduction he must adhere to very strict procedures, usually
mathematical ones. Since practically all physicists accept the
same physical laws as given, and in their deductions adhere to
the same rules, their common understanding of the events with
which they are concerned as physicists is highly consistent. As a
matter of fact, a physicist can say that he has understood an
event only if he could have *predicted* it (by deduction) from the
conditions under which it was observed.

A paranoiac also "understands" events; and he exhibits
understanding by making the event appear to be a necessary
consequence of his assumptions. His "explanation," however,
does not imply that he could have predicted the event. It is an
ad hoc explanation, *made* to fit into his "theory." In fact, all
events observed by the paranoiac are fitted into his theory,
which thereupon becomes *unfalsifiable*. Unfalsifiable theories
are worthless in science, but they serve a purpose and are
tenaciously held by persons with certain psychic needs. For

example, if a paranoiac is convinced that foreign agents are watching him, and, while driving, sees the same car in his rear-view mirror for a length of time, he may conclude that he is being followed. If the car turns off, he may take this also as conclusive proof that he is being followed and that the car turned off to escape detection. Unlike the scientist, the psychotic does not put his "hypothesis" to a test, which would be something like this: "If the car remains behind me after the next three turns, I shall conclude that I am being followed; otherwise I shall dismiss the idea." *Whatever* happens is, for the paranoiac, a confirmation of his belief.

Historians and social scientists also try to fit observed events into conceptual schemes so as to understand them and explain them. Their schemes are not so idiosyncratic and bizarre as are the delusions of psychotics, but they are seldom put to tests as rigorous as are the theories of natural science. In particular, specific theoretical explanations of events that constitute international relations are seldom individualistic; they are usually shared by whole sectors of scholars in the field—what is meant by "schools of thought." What consistency of this sort amounts to is simply that individual scholars have in common a particular conceptual scheme to which they fit the events they study. No procedures have been developed so far by which the various schools of thought can be pitted against each other by empirical tests that would prove one right-er than the other.

Explanations strongly paralleling descriptions of paranoia pervade interpretations of the behavior of states, particularly of states that are perceived as enemies. That is how it has been with Soviet-American relations. In crude "devil image" schemes, such as that of Schwartz (cf. Chapter 7), or those drummed into the Soviet citizen by the monopolistic Soviet propaganda machine, *every* move of the perceived Enemy is interpreted as a strategem in the tightly knit plot to destroy "us." If the enemy threatens, this is prima facie evidence of his hostility; if he purports to seek an understanding or makes conciliatory gestures, this is an attempt to lull us into a sense of false security.

In more sophisticated analyses such vulgarizations are eschewed. All the same, fitting a nation's acts into a preconceived scheme is demanded by the very nature of the subject matter called "international relations." The realist view, in particular, pictures the goals of a state in terms of extending its power and influence in the face of obstacles posed by other states' attempts to do likewise. While this view contains "built-in" paranoid features, we must not on that account dismiss it as a delusion of international relations. War-waging states, conceived as actors, *do* exhibit paranoid behavior, and when two paranoiacs confront each other each may appear to be a realist; so also will the observer who describes the behavior of one from the point of view of the other.

Since the middle fifties, Soviet leaders called their foreign policy a policy of coexistence with capitalist states. Western analysts of international relations who are of the realist school interpret "coexistence" to be only one component in Soviet foreign policy, the other being "expansion." The two components are fitted into a single scheme by way of identifying each with an alternative strategy: whenever opportunities arise, the Soviet Union seeks to extend its power and influence; when conditions for expansion are unfavorable, it seeks a *modus vivendi*. The realists do not accuse the Soviet leaders of using the coexistence theme to delude their enemies. They view attempts to come to terms, to relax tensions, etc., as a necessary phase in the overall strategy of Soviet foreign policy. Under certain conditions, such attempts should be welcomed, in the realists' view—but, they warn, these overtures should not be taken as evidence of a "change of heart," or signs of "genuine good will," or anything of the sort. Such interpretations may be valid with regard to human relations, but they have no place in international politics, in the realists' estimation.

Soviet leaders, on their part, are equally careful to explain what they mean by coexistence: essentially it is the establishment of relations among Communist and non-Communist states which, in the first instance, will reduce the danger of war, and next will enable the two blocs to engage in mutually beneficial forms of cooperation, such as trade, cultural exchanges, etc. Coexistence does *not* mean (and this the Soviet leaders emphasize with great vehemence) the end of the ideological conflict between socialism and capitalism. It does not mean a "merging" either of social systems or of ideologies; least of all does it mean a relaxing on the part of the socialist societies of "vigilance" against the infiltration of alien ideas.

The Soviet policy of coexistence has been associated most closely with Nikita S. Khrushchev, who may be remembered for having introduced an element into diplomacy that had seldom been observed before nor is likely to be observed again in the foreseeable future. At the risk of sounding ridiculous, I shall name this element "sincerity," and now, having named it, I realize how much explaining I have to do.

Khrushchev conducted Russia's foreign policy personally and passionately. This itself does not make him unique, nor is it evidence of "sincerity" as the word is commonly understood in human relations. Hitler and Mussolini gave vent to passions in public, and no one would call them "sincere" on that account, even though at least the more savage of the two must have actually felt the passions that he spewed forth. These passions, however, were no more than outbursts of primitive animal rage. Khrushchev, in contrast, was a complex human being. His passions had a wide diapason. When I say he was "sincere" I mean that a whole gamut of human emotions, which he made no effort to conceal, was discernible in his style.

Is this important? I think so. Because *among* the emotions that seem to have moved Khrushchev to his extravagant public exhibitions of temper was one that pervaded the entire Soviet population since the end of World War II: a longing for peace, not just a detente, not just a breathing spell in preparation for the next round in the power struggle, but genuine, permanent peace of the kind pictured on UNICEF Christmas cards.

Is *this* facet of Khrushchev's psyche important? Did it, in fact, exist? I don't know. I offer my guess about Nikita's inner life as a hypothesis and submit that his behavior is consistent with it.

Khrushchev's career is typical of high-ranking Soviet functionaries of his age. A locksmith in his youth, he was a member of the Communist party since the revolution and rose in the party hierarchy in the usual way. His promotion to full membership in the Politbureau is said to have been in consequence of his effective (i.e., ruthless) organization of Stalinist terror in the Ukraine. He seemed in no way distinguishable from other figures of the Kremlin establishment until his emergence on the international scene, where he remained in the limelight in virtue of his frequent and extensive travels and his propensity for effusive and picturesque speech.

Who can know whether historians will treat Khrushchev as a personage (like Richelieu, Henry VIII, Lenin, or Stalin) or bury him in a footnote? It is my own opinion that he deserves to be remembered for having exercised uncommon imagination while being the head of a superstate—one, moreover, already rather notorious for heavy-handedness. The saying goes in the U.S.S.R. that Khrushchev was brought down for having indulged in "hare-brained schemes." This is all too credible. Improvisation by a man in his postion is a risky business. Khrushchev got carried away by his own robust ingenuousness. Incidents worth noting: At one time he thought the answer to all construction problems was prestressed concrete slabs. At another time, if he had his way, all Soviet farmers might have switched from wheat and rye to maize. His virgin land project was an expensive flop. The installation of ground-to-ground missile launching sites in Cuba might have cost the Soviet Union and the United States half (or all) their populations.

I am not defending Khrushchev's "hare-brained schemes." I am raising the question why a head of state with a fertile imagination is these days an anomaly—even a kook. Khrushchev was bold, volatile, expansive. Above all he was childlike in his enthusiasm. That he was for these reasons dangerous in our age indicates, sad to note, that the danger is inherent in the age, not in the exercise of imagination. Had Khrushchev not been a slave to habits of Soviet thought ingrained in the Stalin era, had he not had orthodox nonentities breathing down his neck, had he not had to deal with two enemies (United States and China) ready to exploit the slightest opening to score in the power game, who knows but that he might have repeated the feat of Peter the Great (another great dilletante, improviser, and frequent bungler), that is, clawed his way through a window to the West that Stalin had sealed.

There were two Khrushchevs. (There often are two personalities in any imaginative and "normal" character assigned to role playing of any kind; and so I do not mean in any way to suggest

a schizoid "split," which to most people implies disconnect-
edness and irresponsibility of one "personality" to the other.) K_1
tried to browbeat the United States into coexistence. He failed.
K_2 tried to speak in the language of the common Russian: let's
be friends and forget the whole silly business of "international
relations." He, too, failed. Nobody who was anybody (i.e., power
pedigreed) listened. Khrushchev was put down as an exhibition-
ist, as a plotter who outsmarted himself, as a boor, as a braggart,
and as a spoiled child. The American newspapers made a circus
of his complaint about not being allowed to visit Disneyland and
had a field day when he banged his shoe on the desk in a session
of the United Nations. His eruptions of enthusiasm were also
received with a mixture of sniggers and disdain. On one occasion he embraced an American pig; on another an American
pianist. It occurred to no one (at least, no one who "counted")
that these gestures (made on American soil), if generously responded to, may have led to a breakthrough in Soviet-American
relations. This was no ignoramus indiscrimination; on the contrary, it was sheer ebullient appreciation for different, but related, creative worth. But U.S. columnists and commentators could
play it for laughs. Or, if we want to ascribe these eruptions to
calculated symbolism by K_2, it can be said that in embracing the
pig (or was it a goose?) Khrushchev may have been expressing a
deep felt, boundless admiration for what might have made
American civilization great—the use of the New World's boun-
ties in the service of all mankind; that in embracing, in turn, the
American pianist (Van Cliburn) who had already become an idol
of Soviet audiences, he may have been expressing what the ordinary Russian fervently hopes for and has long been
denied—friendship across national boundaries, rooted in the admiration of the good and the beautiful, qualities of human experience that do not respect power politics and so, wantonly
and enduringly, lodge indiscriminately with friend and foe.

Some say Khrushchev's gestures were ploys. Others say they
may have been genuine enough but could hardly be of any
consequence to the relations between two Great Powers. These
relations, it is argued, are not determined by feelings of individuals, be they common citizens or rulers. I agree this is so,
now. But I want to know why this should continue to be so.

On the American side, the bid for coexistence found, as could be expected, a wide range of responses. There were, of course, the dire warnings about being lured by honeyed words while surely another Pearl Harbor in nuclear terms was being prepared. On the other hand, the self-defeating character of an unlimited nuclear arms race was becoming too obvious to be ignored even by the military think tanks. The portents did not escape the men of good will who, while supporting what they conceived to be the reasonable and constructive goals of U.S. policy, were not hypnotized by the image of omnipotent America having its way in world affairs by bullying the Soviet Union into submission. These people took the prognoses of the containment policy seriously. In their view, the proper stance (or "posture," to use the jargon then current) of the United States vis-à-vis the U.S.S.R. should be one of firmness but not malice. The Russians should be made to understand that their expansionist ambitions would be checkmated. At the same time, however, they should be made to feel that their legitimate needs for security were recognized. Above all, the door should always be held open.

In the minds of the moderates, the spread of communism was still indissolubly linked with Russia's expansionist drive; but, to their way of thinking, time was not on the side of communism (the Russians and many American alarmists insisted it was) but rather on the side of Western democracies. Their hope was buttressed by the economic recovery of Europe, which, powerfully stimulated by the Marshall Plan, was completed sooner than expected. The same pattern, it was maintained, could be established in the underdeveloped world to make it "immune" to communism. A detente with Russia could contain provisions against Soviet interference with this process. Finally, Russia herself, soon under the leadership of another generation that would surely be more pragmatically oriented, would, in consequence of her own rising living standards, gradually turn into a middle-class-type nation disposed to cooperate in the building of a prosperous peaceful world.

This was in sum American liberalism's conception of coexistence. Its realization called for persistent efforts "to improve communication with Russia." In particular, areas of cooperation had to be sought out. Joint scientific enterprises, and a cultural exchange program, were promising in that direction. Both ventures turned out to be moderately successful. The International Geophysical Year (which stretched to two years, 1957–1959) was an outstanding example of productive scientific cooperation. The cultural exchange program provided a medium for the public of one country to vent admiration for the achievements of the other, uninhibited by politics.

The awarding of the First Prize in the Tschaikovsky Competition to American pianist Van Cliburn and the reception given to the "Porgy and Bess" performing troup in the U.S.S.R. deserve comment. It is in no way to discount the excellence of these artists to surmise that their musical success in the Soviet Union had political overtones. They became focal points around which the deep-felt longing for people-to-people understanding was expressed. It was impossible in Russia to spark a spontaneous welcoming demonstration for a foreign government personage. (Consider the attempt to do so by Soviet Jews, and the gruesome consequences, in connection with Golda Meir's visit to Moscow in 1948.) Ovations for foreign performing artists, on the other hand, were perfectly safe. That they reached ecstatic heights is, in my opinion, as much an expression of Russia's desire for friendship with us as it is acclaim for American artistic talents.

I remember a comparable incident on the American side. A visiting Russian ballet company performed a surprise number as an encore, an American barn dance. The sight of "foreigners" in jeans and lumberjack shirts prancing to the tune of "Turkey in the Straw," together with the realization that these foreigners were Russians, probably triggered in the American audience powerful dormant feelings analogous to those of the other side. Very likely, the Royal Danish Ballet performing, say, a rumble from "West Side Story" before New York audiences would trigger an ovation equal in volume, but not, I think, of the same quality. The Danes aren't all that "foreign"; it's hardly a surprise, and not much of a heart-throbbing experience, that they understand and even admire our "ways." Besides, they aren't (and are not likely to be) "Communists," and our perceptions, because we "know better," are not readily susceptible to viewing them as savages or as enemies.

On a very different level of "exchange," the Pugwash Conferences were another channel for East-West meeting of minds.
These Conferences (so named after Pugwash, Nova Scotia,
where the first was held in 1957) were sponsored by private and
foundation funds. They reflected an initiative on the part of a
sector of the American public (mostly scientists) to arrange meetings between upper strata of technical, scientific, and intellectual circles of the Soviet Union and the United States
(prominent figures from other countries were also invited). The
idea was that away from the glare of publicity (the Conferences
were held in closed sessions) people accustomed to making and
attending to well-articulated statements of views, supported by
carefully reasoned arguments, could come to an understanding
at least on matters of mutual concern, such as the prevention of
war. Presumably it was hoped that the ideas emanating from
these discussions could provide the decision makers with opportunities for more productive communication and for conflict
resolution.

Since the proceedings were not published, it is difficult to
evaluate the effect of the Conferences. That there were some
effects is not unlikely since several of the participants were at
times quite close to centers of policy decisions. Whatever can be
discerned must be inferred from conversations, occasional articles (e.g. in the *Bulletin of the Atomic Scientists*) referring to
points raised in the Conferences, etc. It seems certain that matters pertaining to arms control were central in the discussions.
This is interesting because the official stand of the Soviet Union
toward arms control has been for the most part negative
("Nothing short of general and complete disarmament will al-
leviate the danger of war"). Thus the Conferences provided a
climate for discussing matters that could not be discussed in a
political setting of official government-sponsored meetings.

A question of importance is the extent to which Soviet scientists and intellectuals were able to express views departing from
those prescribed by official government policy. Opinions on this
matter differ. Some participants have reported instances where
Soviet participants have differentiated between the views of
their government and their own. Others had the impression that
Soviet participants never departed from stating and restating
the official publicized positions. At any rate, private evaluations

of the Conferences on the American side are varied. On the Soviet side, the Conferences seem to have had continued official approval.

This latter circumstance was, perhaps, a factor instigating the investigation of the Conferences by the U.S. Senate Subcommittee on Internal security (1961). The conclusions of the study were an echo of the McCarthy years.

> The Pugwash Conferences were initiated, in part, by individuals with significant records of support of Communist Causes, including one leading member of the Communist Party of France. . . . Among the sponsors and initiators . . . were individuals who have displayed a sharp, unreasonable, and sustained hostility to the U.S. . . . The Pugwash Conferences were approved by the Soviet Government. . . . The Soviet Government has extended flattering honors and recognition to some American scientists who attended the Pugwash Conference. . . . In general, the American scientists who participated . . . had no clear understanding of the nature of the international Communist Conspiracy, etc., etc.[1]

There was no discernible effect of the "study" on the Conferences which at this writing are still going on.

On the level of the military establishments, get-togethers have been the protracted disarmament negotiations. Obviously the positions of the main antagonists, the U.S. and U.S.S.R., were the determinants of the outcome of the negotiations. Although the United States formally supported the principle of "complete, general disarmament," there is no indication that any one on the American side seriously envisaged the implementation of that principle in the foreseeable future. American diplomatic efforts were directed solely at reaching some agreement on arms *control,* that is, at bringing about a situation where the levels of armaments would be stabilized and then perhaps eventually reduced; and even so, each reduction was to be undertaken jointly, and only provided ironclad guarantees could be worked out to prevent any military advantage from accruing to the Soviet Union from any such step. In point of fact, the so-called Arms Control and Disarmament Agency was set up under the U.S. Department of Defense for the express purpose of seeking out just those arms control measures that could not possibly result in a military advantage, however minimal, to the Soviet

Union, or those that would instead be to the advantage of the United States. The ACDA was to cue the U.S. negotiators at the disarmament conferences on such measures, that is, select those that it was permissible to propose or to support. Quite possibly the Soviet delegation was guided by an analogous agency of its own.

The Soviet Union on its part, largely resisted the very idea of arms control, arguing that only general, complete disarmament would eliminate the danger of war. Each side placed conditions on disarmament that were unacceptable to the other. The United States complicated the control issue by insisting that each step in the reduction of armaments be accompanied by inspections carried out by each side on the territory of the other. In particular, the *initial* step in the (hypothetical) disarmament program would have to be an inventory of existing weapons. The Russians refused to consider such procedures on the grounds, as they made quite plain, that they viewed them as a strategem designed for conducting espionage. They did not object, they maintained, to inspections, provided they were conducted *after* disarmament had taken place. The U.S. participants, in turn, viewed the Soviet conditions as a ruse. It may or may not have been taken for granted by Americans that the Russians would cheat any time an opportunity presented itself. It may or may not have been that the Russians were convinced that the Americans would spy whenever and wherever they could. At any rate, whether the Americans and the Russians trusted each other in any particular instance is not the issue. The issue was one of principle. For the Americans the central issue was, on principle, the matter of guarantees, and their main efforts were concentrated on working out elaborate systems to insure compliance *in advance* of any agreement. For the Russians the main issue was, on principle, the inviolability of military secrecy.

What the Russians consider to be jeopardizing to the security of the Soviet Union spans a range of information that is nothing short of fantastic. This conception of security is said to account for the absence of telephone books in major Soviet cities. American obsession with the possibility of Soviet cheating was no less extreme. Negotiations on the ban on testing nuclear weapons in the atmosphere were at last concluded successfully only when it became clearly impossible to point to what would be a method of "cheating"—no matter how farfetched. (The fact is that explosions of nuclear weapons in the atmosphere are immediately detectable everywhere throughout the world.) But it proved impossible to extend the ban to the testing of nuclear weapons underground, because, while underground explosions are detectable seismographically, occasionally earth tremors can be mistaken for explosions; so the detection is not foolproof. The Americans proposed elaborate inspection procedures to be conducted on the territories of both countries to make the identification of underground explosions more precise. The Russians repeated their usual objections to inspections. Yet, even after the Russians agreed to a limited number of on-site inspections, an impasse was reached on the *number* of these inspections. At one point specialists supplied evidence that, even with a limited inspection program, such as was acceptable to the Russians, the probability of getting away with undetected underground tests was minimal. An American expert then came up with a way to beat the system: it involved an excavation of fantastic size. When the tremendous cost of such an excavation was pointed out, the U.S. holdouts for security suggested that, well, then, the Russians would have an edge; they could use the Siberian salt mines for the purpose.

At this writing no agreement has been reached to extend the ban to the testing of nuclear weapons underground.

"Coexistence" negotiations on the military level produced two other tangible results that deserve mention. One is the Hot Line, the other the nuclear nonproliferation treaty. The latter will be taken up in Chapter 14 in connection with the role of China in Soviet-American relations. The so-called Hot Line, a direct telephone connection between Washington and Moscow, was adopted to establish instantaneous communication between the two heads of state who hold the fate of the world's population in their hands[2] in order to forestall a triggering of an "accidental" war by a "misunderstanding." If the Hot Line has already served this purpose, or whether it will in the future, who knows? If or when it works, we won't know it, because we cannot "rerun the scenario" of one of the past crises with the Hot

Line eliminated. If it fails, we probably won't know it either—except possibly for the terrifyingly short time we will have to ponder on what might have been if men purportedly concerned with the safety of their respective countries and their peoples were not so much more concerned with matters of "principle."

What have the aforementioned coexistence projects accomplished?

It seems that people-to-people contacts accomplished most, in the sense of creating feelings in broad sectors of both populations that not only peaceful coexistence but genuine friendship between the two countries would be possible if it were not for global politics. To an expert on international relations this expectation may seem naive, but there it is. It remains to be seen whether it becomes a factor to be reckoned with even in global politics. It can be said with certainty at least that it involves some mighty fundamental human urgencies that, from time to time, have unseated the powers that be.

It is more difficult to assess the contributions of scientific contacts, and of such collaborations as the above-mentioned Pugwash Conferences. When scientists meet as scientists, they are already at a far remove from the world of soldiers, statesmen, and diplomats. They do not have to grope for a common language; they already have one, and in addition accepted criteria, at least with regard to scientifically supported truths. For just this reason, however, the impact of these contacts on United States-Soviet relations is likely puny. A scientist is not shocked into a realization that his opposite number on the other side thinks as he himself does about matters that concern them both. He already knows this and is at home abroad. The question is how much of this long-established feeling of community that has persevered among scientists, despite personal foibles and world politics, can be transmitted to leaders who are preoccupied with a struggle for power. Not very much, it seems. For the scientist in another role, especially in a role close to the seats of power (that of an adviser, for example), thinks in categories relevant to that role. From his own world he brings at most technical expertise, and he places it at the disposal of people for whom the concept of a world community is at most a pious thought.

Professional soldiers, too, speak a common language. Could one expect that a sort of "cooperation" could develop between the military establishments of the two superpowers, at least to insure against mutual annihilation? The idea of arms control (espoused by a sector of military opinion in the United States) was directed toward this goal. An underlying more general idea of "cooperating with the enemy" has been given a theoretical formulation in the framework of game theory by Thomas C. Schelling.[3]

The theory of games can be defined as a theory of rational decision in conflict situations. It derives its name from the fact that so-called games of strategy, like chess, bridge, etc., are clear examples of conflicts where outcomes depend essentially on the opponents' strategic choices. A strategy is a plan of action in which choices of acts by a player are contingent on the possible choices of acts made by the other. Games of strategy are typically zero-sum games. In them the opponents have diametrically opposed preferences for the possible outcomes of the game. That is, the sum of the players' payoffs amounts to zero regardless of the outcome, so that the more one player wins the more the other (or others) must lose. Clausewitz's conception of war was essentially a zero-sum game; he held cooperation between enemies to be an absurdity, except possibly in matters of agreeing on the time and place of a forthcoming engagement.

Schelling noted that most human conflict situations, including even war, are not of the type represented by zero-sum games. Among the possible outcomes there may well be some that are preferred to other outcomes by both (or all) of the players. This is especially evident in the current global conflict. It is now impossible to deny, for example, that both the United States and the Soviet Union (conceived as players in a game) prefer the *status quo* to a nuclear war. Schelling cites other situations of this type; for example, both sides in World War II refrained from using poison gas, each being well aware that whatever advantage may accrue to the first users would be quickly canceled by immediate retaliation in kind.

When the interests of the opponents are not always diametrically opposed, they may engage either in tacit collusion or negotiations. The object of negotiations is to obtain an outcome most

advantageous to oneself while at the same time avoiding outcomes disadvantageous to both. Models of negotiated conflicts
are called bargaining games. Such a game is always a non-zero-
sum game, inasmuch as the interests of the players *partially*
conflict and partially coincide. Schelling urged the development
of a theory of rational conflict in mixed-motive situations. He
called particular attention to the role of communication (tacit
and explicit) in such contexts. His main thesis was that enemies
ought to learn how to communicate with each other, not so
much with the view of resolving their conflict of interests as
with the view of avoiding disasters that neither wants.

In Schelling's approach, another function of "improved communication" is to foreclose certain options, including one's own.
An example of this latter use of "communication with the enemy" is a message (by word or deed) that one is *irrevocably*
committed to a certain course of action (possibly contingent on
an action of the opponent). In certain cases this demonstration
of resolve prevents the opponent from entering on a collision
course from which he cannot swerve for fear of losing face. (It
may, of course, happen that the opponent adopts the same
strategy, which aggravates rather than attenuates situations of
this sort, as in so-called "eyeball to eyeball" confrontations. A
very real confrontation of this sort will be described in the next
chapter.)

For the most part, the Russians have shown little enthusiasm
for this kind of "cooperation between enemies." (By way of ex-
ception, there are the Hot Line, the limited test ban treaty, and
the nonproliferation treaty mentioned above.) The Russians' re-
luctance to "play the game" may be partially explained by their
chronic fear of being tricked into a disadvantageous agreement.
Another, perhaps more important, reason is the official stance of
the Soviet Union regarding a war which the U.S.S.R. might be
drawn into. They have invariably pictured such a war as an attack against the Soviet Union, hence a hideous crime against
humanity. It followed that, in their view, the military establishments of states hostile to the U.S.S.R. had no *legitimacy*. To
cooperate with these establishments (as in arms control agreements) would be tantamount to recognizing the legitimacy of
their existence: that is, granting that they exist for the same rea-

son as the Soviet military establishment—to deter or repel unprovoked attack. To grant this would imply a "moral symmetry" in the balance of terror, something American strategists (in
contrast to the politicians) have no compunction about accept-
ing but have not been able to get the Russians to accept. In
other words, while American diplomilitary strategists have, since
the late 1950s, acknowledged quite openly the Clausewitzian
view of international politics, the Soviet strategists have never
done so. In their writings, positive reference to Clausewitz (in
connection with the political content of military operations and
policies) are always coupled with an emphasis on the *asymmetry*
between the aims of Soviet foreign policy and those of capitalist
states.[4] This idea of "asymmetry" was utterly foreign to Clausewitz who never singled out the goals of Prussian foreign policy
as being any different from those of any other state.

Whether this admixture of ideology is only a vestige of an
earlier (pre-World War II) role of the Soviet Union in world
politics or a substantial component of current Soviet foreign policy is an open question. So far it seems to have inhibited the sort
of cooperation between enemies envisaged by American de-
ideologized strategists.

It remains to examine attempts to establish meaningful communication between the United States and the Soviet Union on
the level of heads of state.

Khrushchev believed in personal diplomacy, the sort that was
disdainfully dismissed in American government circles and in
most of the U.S. press ("summitry"). Possibly this apparently
genuine inclination of Khrushchev (there are ample reasons to
believe it was genuine, or, if you will, "sincere," as I believe)
was nurtured by a nostalgic remembrance of the war years
when the Grand Alliance was held together by the Big Three.
Or Khrushchev may have cherished a hope (which realists would
dismiss as fantastically naive) that the global conflict could be
resolved if only the leaders of the two superstates could "get
together" and "work things out." Evidently he had personal
regard for Eisenhower as a "simple, honorable man."

After considerable resistance on the part of the United States
Department of State, a second summit meeting finally was ar-
ranged to take place in Paris in May 1960. The meeting was

aborted by the U-2 incident. The United States had been systematically conducting espionage flights over Soviet territory. The purpose of these flights was apparently to spot any activity portending preparations for a surprise nuclear raid on the United States. Previous incidents of American planes shot down over Soviet territory took place near the Turkish-Soviet border. These incursions were represented by U.S. officials and the press as consequences of navigation errors and considerable public feeling was aroused against the trigger-happy Russians.

When the shooting down of the U-2 was announced by the Russians the location was not given, and the affair was at first routinely designated by Americans as another unintended violation of Soviet air space. When the Russians announced the location, about halfway between Pakistan and Norway, U.S. officials, supposing that the flier was killed, or at least had committed suicide as he was supposed to do to avoid capture, gave out the reason that the flier must have lost consciousness and was carried into the heart of Soviet Russia by the automatic pilot. Only then did the Russians announce that the flier (Francis Gary Powers) was alive and well and willing to talk. (Two years later the same technique of catching the enemy in a barefaced lie was used by John F. Kennedy on the Soviet foreign minister in connection with Soviet-installed missile bases in Cuba, about which more in the next chapter.)

Thus, at the first session of the summit meeting in Paris, Khrushchev tried to exploit the incident by appearing in the position of an injured party, demanding an apology from Eisenhower and a promise that the espionage flights would be discontinued. A way out was available to Eisenhower. Traditionally, governments renounce responsibility for the activity of their spies and abandon them to their fate. It is more than likely that Eisenhower could have truthfully denied knowledge of the Central Intelligence Agency; for it is difficult to believe that an espionage flight was scheduled, with Eisenhower's knowledge, to take place a few days before a meeting that was to be a prelude to understanding between the United States and the Soviet Union, or that Eisenhower had a hand in a deliberate sabotage of the summit meeting. At any rate, Eisenhower took a position understandably interpreted by Khrushchev as defiant and hostile. He acknowledged full responsibility for the espionage flights and refused to "apologize." The summit meeting broke up, and the scheduled visit of Eisenhower to the Soviet Union (which, it appears, was to have been a hero's welcome) was canceled.

Then in 1961 Khrushchev met with Kennedy in Vienna with both spouses also present. This was not a "summit meeting" in the sense such meetings were conceived, as carry-overs from the wartime meetings of the Big Three, where rulers were expected to arrive at agreements on the future course of history. The Vienna meeting was more of a social occasion, an opportunity for the new President and for the aging, harried Chairman to size each other up. Both were disappointed. Kennedy seemed determined to demonstrate to Khrushchev the calm firmness with which the United States, under new, young, progressive leadership, was facing up to Communist threats. Kennedy's self-confidence and diction must have irritated Khrushchev who had expected to "work things out" with Eisenhower, a "simple, honorable man," not with a dynamic, sophisticated, Ivy League type. Khrushchev was not one to disguise his chagrin, and his manners left much to be desired. The impression he made on Kennedy can easily be surmised. Alas, there went whatever hopes had lingered that peace could be brought to the world by "working things out" between the leaders of The Two.[5]

In summary, contacts between Russians and Americans, made with a view of "improving communications" and establishing a *modus vivendi,* enjoyed a degree of success inversely to the distance from the seats of power.

CHAPTER 12

The Last (?) Confrontation

To back up for a moment to the beginning of the post-Stalin period of relative relaxation of tensions, it is useful to remember that the Communist Empire was then still a solid land mass, one-fourth of the earth's land surface, with a population of nearly a billion, one-third of the world's. But there were two centers of power, one in Moscow, one in Peking. The alliance between the two was held firm by "capitalist encirclement," which, from the military point of view, was by no means a fantasy. Along the entire periphery of the Communist land mass were American bases with war-ready bombers carrying nuclear weapons. The encirclement stretched from Noway through Western Europe, Italy, Greece, Turkey; through Pakistan and Thailand (SEATO countries) and South Vietnam, which became a satellite of the United States in 1955, to the Philippines, Formosa, South Korea, Japan, and Alaska. From bases in Greenland and Iceland, the U.S.S.R. was accessible over the Pole. At a moment's notice, bombers might take off from all these bases and literally destroy the whole of the Soviet Union in a matters of hours. U.S. Secretary of State Dulles had declared in effect that the United States would hold the Soviet Union responsible for any political event anywhere in the world that the United States chose to interpret as "Communist aggression" and that a nuclear attack on the Soviet Union could be expected as a retaliatory measure if the United States chose to administer it.

177

Suppose under these circumstances the Soviet Union were to be led by someone who took literally the avowed aims of Soviet domestic and foreign policy. What would be the problems he would face, and how would he be expected to act?

Such a leader could not fail to see the ravages of Stalinism within the U.S.S.R. The country had become a police state wherein the life of everyone from the humblest strata to the pinnacles of leadership could be snuffed out by the despot's whim. Stalin's ideas of administration were akin to Frederick II's ideas of military discipline. Orders were to be obeyed by mechanical reflexes; motivation to obey was to be instilled by fear for one's life. I recall a story told to me in 1943 by a Soviet officer about how Tupolev designed one of his famous airplanes. He was told by Stalin to "invent" a plane with certain characteristics. The penalty for failure was death. (The story was told with pride in the way difficulties were overcome in the Soviet Union.)[1] An occasional tour de force may succeed under the drive of fear. On the whole, however, fear paralyzes. It certainly paralyzes a vast, bureaucratic machine where the only safety (of sorts) lies in following regulations to the letter and never taking initiative.

Xenophobia, emanating from Stalin's paranoia, threatened to undermine Soviet science. Agriculture, especially animal husbandry, was in a dismal state. The Eastern European satellites, emaciated by the parasitic role played by the Soviet Union with regard to their economies, were on the verge of revolt.

A man with understanding, and invested with Stalin's absolute power could have conceivably cut the Gordian knot by taking the following steps.

1. Administer a shock treatment by denouncing Stalin as a usurper.

2. Use the leverage of the denunciation to reverse the most pernicious features of Stalinism: clip the power of the secret police, encourage popular participation in the discussions of controversial questions, introduce civil liberties, remove censorship, etc.

3. Rationalize agriculture and decentralize economic decisions.

4. Press for a settlement with the United States with the view of removing sources of irreconcilable conflicts, normalizing trade

relations, seeking new formulas for reducing armament levels, etc.

5. Accord the satellites the status of equal partners.

This *may* have been the program that Khrushchev wanted to follow. Whether or not this is so, given the world he "inherited," inside and outside the U.S.S.R., it is difficult to imagine anyone doing more than he did. It must be remembered that, although in the decade after Stalin's death Khrushchev was still number one, his actual power was quite limited. He was not in a position to terrorize or liquidate anyone in his way by a mere look or word. To stay in power, he had to go through some fancy political contortions, and in the end he lost the game.

It goes without saying that Khrushchev's own political background severely limited his understanding of what ailed the U.S.S.R., namely the encrusted vested interests of the party bureaucracy. He himself must have shared the bureaucracy's nagging fear that a relaxation of its grip on all the aspects of national life might cost the bureaucracy not only its prerogatives but also its very existence. Therefore Khrushchev could not appeal to the populace over the heads of the bureaucracy. Himself a bureaucrat, he could hardly be expected to transcend the bureaucracy's way of thinking.

Another powerful constraint upon the relaxation of internal controls and of U.S.-Soviet tensions was China, now making a bid for leadership in the Communist Empire and especially in the impending revolutions in the Third World. China declared Khrushchev a traitor to Lenin's cause and seized upon every suggestion of liberalization and especially every attempt of accommodation with the United States to brand him a collaborator with the imperialists. China expected Russia to help her become a nuclear power in a hurry. When, to the Russians' way of thinking, it appeared that they were nurturing a viper, they precipitously withdrew, and that was the end of the monolithic Communist Empire. All Khrushchev could do was clutch his own power while his colleagues awaited their chance.

It seems that Khrushchev staked everything on "settling" the cold war. But if his stock was to go up, the "settlement" had to be at least a partial victory. *Some* concessions from the West had to be won. They might be no more than symbolic concessions, say neutralization of West Berlin or the dismantling of a few American bases in the encirclement. Khrushchev may have believed that, by taking an initial offensive, he could reach an advantageous bargaining position from which he could then retreat in return for concessions.

In any case, the offensive started shortly after the Vienna meeting with Kennedy. Atmospheric tests of nuclear weapons were resumed by Russia on a vast scale, breaking a tacit moratorium initiated by the Soviet Union in 1958. All that this accomplished was a resumption of testing by the United States. The sudden erection of a wall between West and East Berlin brought on the Berlin crisis of 1961, complete with an alerting of nuclear striking forces and a civil defense hysteria in the United States. The intended "message" was that the sealing off of Berlin was a prelude to the long-threatened "separate peace" between the U.S.S.R. and East Germany. Were this treaty concluded, the Soviet Union would no longer be responsible for guaranteeing free access to West Berlin through East Germany. This would force the Western Allies either to deal with East Germany—that is, accord her *de facto* recognition—or to force an access to West Berlin if the East Germans chose to seal it off. As has been said, West Berlin was of absolutely no strategic or economic importance to either side. It had become simply an "issue" over which each side could threaten the other by flexing its nuclear muscles and exhibiting "resolve."

There was no lack of "resolve" on the American side. In confrontations with Russia, the United States was usually willing to play the game of Chicken, as recommended by Herman Kahn. In playing this game in its original form (two cars on a collision course, each determined to make the other swerve), Mr. Kahn advised the following winning strategy: in full view of the opponent, tear off the steering wheel and throw it away. In this manner, the opponent will become convinced of your resolve, for now he knows that you could not swerve even if you wanted to. It may happen, of course, that just as you have yanked off *your* steering wheel, your opponent, guided by the same reasoning, has yanked off *his*. In that case, Mr. Kahn continues, you have a problem.[2] Having lost the game of Chicken in Berlin, Khrushchev played what turned out to be his last card: the installation of nuclear ground-to-ground missile launching sites in

Cuba. This ploy gave the American military the opportunity to enjoy the thrill of their lifetime.

To Americans who identified the goals of Soviet foreign policy with world conquest, Cuba was conclusive proof of the accuracy of their perceptions. For here was a country on America's doorstep "taken over" by the Russians. Or, to put it no less vividly, here was an injection of the virus of communism into the Western Hemisphere, America's hitherto undisputed security zone.

Cuba was already natural prime ammunition in the election campaign of 1960; and this time the Democrats could turn the tables on the Republicans, for it was not *their* administration that "lost" Cuba. Kennedy, in his election campaign, promised the American people that he would take proper measures to eliminate the incubus implanted by the Castro revolution. Nixon, his opponent, tried to get some campaign mileage by hinting that Kennedy was engaging in dangerous saber rattling. Later Nixon revealed that he, as Vice-President at the time, had been privy to concrete plans being made to eliminate the threat of a Communist state ninety miles from American shores, but that, naturally, he could not reveal military secrets just to score a debating point.[3]

At any rate, Kennedy was elected, and, upon taking office, was informed of those plans, which he proceeded to carry out. The result was the Bay of Pigs fiasco. The Cubans made short work of the American-sponsored invasion, and the United States returned to the slow, but presumably sure, method of eliminating communism from the Western Hemisphere by strangling Cuba economically.

Like West Berlin, Cuba became a battleground of wills. It was strategically worthless for the defense of the U.S.S.R. As for its offensive potential, even granting a successful installation of missile bases, it would be, of course, the first to go in a Soviet-American war. Only in the insane scenarios of the nuclear war strategists, with their Pandora's Box of surprise attacks, preemptive strikes, "exchange of cities," and the like, could Cuba be valued as so many chips in the game of mutual suicide. If such a game were to be played "for real" instead of on computers, no one would be around to count winnings and losses. However, there it was: Communist Cuba about to be armed with Soviet missiles, aimed at American cities with a combined population of 80,000,000.

Why did Khrushchev do it? To defend Cuba from further American attacks? Incredible. A nuclear response from Cuba would certainly initiate a general nuclear holocaust. Khrushchev had retreated on the Berlin issue (the peace treaty with East Germany was indefinitely "postponed" after the Berlin crisis of 1961). Cuba was a heavy economic liability to the Soviet Union. This burden could not be considered as an investment in a future communization of Latin America because, as I have repeatedly pointed out, the Soviet Union was no longer interested in the emergence of new Communist states, least of all in Latin America where Soviet influence was bound to be negligible. If Cuba was to be defended as a socialist state bullied by an imperialist power, surely there were other ways of deterring the United States, for example by a counterthreat against West Berlin, or even by a threat of nuclear retaliation against the United States from Soviet submarines. If a nuclear holocaust was to be started, there was no need to start it with a salvo from Cuba. Finally we must dismiss the idea that Khrushchev decided to arm Cuba with nuclear weapons simply in response to Cuban requests. Soviet largesse did not extend so far.

Only one explanation makes sense. Khrushchev was going to put the missiles there, then swap them for some concession by the United States, perhaps for the dismantling of some U.S. bases on Soviet borders, perhaps for neutralization of West Berlin, perhaps even for a firm promise to deny nuclear weapons to West Germany—the prize for which Khrushchev was apparently ready to give much in return but which had never been negotiable. The United States was determined to keep West Germany as a permanent threat against the U.S.S.R. and was not going to tie its hands by promises to limit Germany's military potential. In short, Khrushchev desperately needed to show that his coexistence policy paid off *something* besides ovations for Soviet artists.

Further evidence in favor of the conjecture that the missiles were meant to serve as bargaining chips was the failure to camouflage their construction. Recall the strategic principles of "nuclear exchanges" (cf. Chapter 10). If you plan a second strike, you want your opponent to know that you have a formidable nuclear capacity, but you do not want him to know its disposition, unless you want to provoke a first strike so as to destroy him by your second. Neither Castro nor Khrushchev can be seriously supposed to have intended to provoke the United States into a first nuclear strike. Therefore, failing to announce the presence of missiles and failing to camouflage them disposes of their second (retaliatory) strike purpose. Next, a first strike purpose of the Cuban missile sites must be dismissed, again owing to the absence of camouflage. If you plan a first strike, you must keep *both* the strength and the disposition of your nuclear capacity secret.

Only one conclusion is believable, namely that the missile sites were meant to be discovered by American espionage planes, as they indeed were. Possibly Khrushchev thought that the discovery would lead to negotiations initiated by the United States, in which he could strike a bargain, score a diplomatic success, and strengthen his tottering position. He thought wrong. The discovery of the missiles led to an ultimatum.

In American accounts, Kennedy appears as a hero of a blood-curdling drama. He is shown aerial photographs. Inexperienced, he is unable to read them. "Still looks like a football field to me," he is said to have remarked after examining a telltale spot on a picture. But the experts explain things to him as an X-ray specialist explains to a novice. The spots portend a dread malignancy, and there is no time to lose.

Kennedy acts. First he prepares the stage. He gets Soviet Foreign Minister Gromyko to repeat to him the assurance given some weeks earlier by the Soviet government to the effect that it had no need for missile sites beyond the boundaries of the U.S.S.R. Later, in his speech to the nation announcing the blockade, Kennedy could quote the Soviet assurances verbatim and dismiss them with the drama-laden terse comment, "That statement was false." To compound the cliff-hanging effect, he could quote Gromyko's repetitions of the assurances verbatim and dismiss *them* with the comment, "That statement also was false." In boxing, this feat is known as the "one-two punch."

From Tuesday, October 16, 1962, men who had the power of life and death over the population of the world met in almost continuous session discussing a course of action. Only two alternatives were seriously considered. One was a sudden air strike against Cuba designed to obliterate not only the uncompleted launching sites but also Cuba's entire military defense potential. The strike was to be followed by an invasion of the island (not to be bungled this time) and the liquidation of Castro's regime. The other course of action was a blockade of Cuba coupled with an ultimatum to the Soviet Union to remove the missiles immediately. If Russian ships tried to run the blockade, they would be attacked by the U.S. navy. If the missiles were not removed, the air strike against Cuba would follow.

Military chiefs for the most part favored the first alternative. Others, notably Secretary of Defense McNamara and Attorney General Robert Kennedy, favored the second.

In describing the sessions, Robert Kennedy[4] gives the impression that it was a gathering of wise, responsible, and dedicated men. The meetings themselves are described as the very essence of democracy in action. Rank was ignored. Everyone was respectfully heard. Everyone's opinions were carefully weighed. Above all, Robert Kennedy brings out the awesome responsibility weighing on the central figure in this drama. John F. Kennedy, to a Martian observer indistinguishable from any other featherless biped, has only to pronounce certain words to condemn tens of millions of other bipeds to instantaneous death without possibility of appeal. So it would appear to a Martian observer. But to Robert Kennedy, John is not just another biped. He is the embodiment of a whole civilization. He speaks and acts for that civilization. If he decides to stake that civilization in a game of Chicken, it means that history, possibly Providence, so ordained it. John's anguish is an ennobling ordeal, his decision a discharge of a sacred trust.

While the deliberations are going on, preparations are being made for the "surgical strike," as its proponents called the contemplated surprise aerial attack on Cuba. The malignancy must be removed. The instruments are laid out. The "surgeons," years of training and preparation behind them, are ready, nay eager, to show their skill. Everyone is at his post awaiting the Word.

In the meantime the ordinary mortals of Cuba, the Soviet Union, and the United States know nothing. There are no pub-

lished exchanges of notes, no press campaigns, no speeches, no
visible mobilizations. The war machine, several million times
more destructive than those of the Great Powers in the two
world wars, can be cocked in complete secrecy.

Finally the decision is made. Over the objections of the advo-
cates of "surgery," the President orders a more prudent course
of "treatment" for the time being, acknowledging that "surgery" may still be necessary. Cuba is blockaded. The Soviet
Union is to be ordered to remove the installations immediately
and unconditionally or see Cuba suffer the consequences.

John F. Kennedy speaks to his "fellow citizens." He is a strik-
ingly handsome man, magnificent in his cool confidence. First he
is like the hero-detective announcing to the murderer, caught
red-handed, that the jig is up. Then he reverts to the traditional
role of the war chief. So Caesar must have spoken to his legions,
bishops to Crusaders, Bonaparte to his hussars and grenadiers.
So the leaders of France, Germany, Britain, and Russia spoke to
"their people" in 1914. So spoke Hitler in 1939, Churchill in
1940, Stalin and Roosevelt in 1941.

> The path we have chosen [so speaks the Leader of the Free
> World] is full of hazards, as all paths are, but it is the one most
> consistent with our character and courage as a nation and our com-
> mitments around the world. The cost of freedom is always high—
> but Americans have always paid it. And one path we shall never
> choose, and that is the path of surrender or submission.
> Our goal is not the victory of might but the vindication of
> right—not peace at the expense of freedom, but both peace and
> freedom, here in this Hemisphere and, we hope, around the world.
> God willing, that goal will be achieved.[5]

Thereupon the United States National Anthem swells forth,
and the "fellow citizens" go about their business, convinced that
there is nothing, but absolutely nothing, for them to do but
"sweat it out." The Russians (as well as the Cubans, the French,
the British, the Italians, the Danes, and on and on and on over
the world) were also sweating it out.

That you and I are alive today may be due to the circumstance that Nikita Sergeevich Khrushchev, unlike John F. Kennedy,
was not cool, collected, and determined but, on the contrary,
perplexed, hesitant, and scared. He did not have the presence

of mind to throw Kennedy's accusations of mendacity back in his face, for example, by quoting Adlai Stevenson's denials of American involvement in the Bay of Pigs affair and capping it with the same chilling comment, "That statement was false." Had he been quick with repartee, he could have pricked Kennedy's indignation about being lied to by recalling the U-2 incident when Eisenhower's foreign ministry was coming up with lie after barefaced lie. Yes, Nikita could have told the Americans a thing or two about the "vindication of right," particularly about the rights of small nations to defend themselves. He could have recalled Russia's record in going to the aid of small, brave nations cowed by powerful, arrogant neighbors, as in 1914 when Russia refused to be intimidated by Germany's brazen warnings and went right ahead to the aid of little Serbia. Khrushchev could have cited chapter and verse from international law that defines blockade as an act of war; from Article 2 of the United Nations Charter which commits members to refrain from the threat or use of force against the territorial integrity or political independence of any state; and further from Article 53 which states that no enforcement action shall be taken under regional arrangements without the authorization of the Security Council. Khrushchev missed all these opportunities to score a resounding moral victory against the imperialists. Instead he backed down ignominiously, getting nothing from Kennedy except a promise not to invade Cuba, provided Cuba behaved and allowed on-site verification of compliance with the American ultimatum.

Not only did Khrushchev back down; he also *showed* a failure of nerve. On October 26 he sent two letters to Kennedy of which only one was published, the other being presumably too compromising of Khrushchev. Rumor has it that the unpublished letter is packed with sentiments and concerns unbefitting the head of a state and that for this reason its content was mercifully suppressed.

The published letter sufficiently reveals Khrushchev as less than ready to defend Russia's honor. It "explains," and it pleads for at least a token *quid pro quo*. "We agree to remove those weapons from Cuba which you regard as offensive. . . . The United States, on its part, bearing in mind the anxiety and concern of the Soviet state, will evacuate its analogous weapons from Turkey."[6]

But of course America could not be party to any such deal. Eventually the obsolete missiles in Turkey were removed, but only voluntarily, not as a discharge of an obligation. Similarly, when a state's prosecutor rewards a cooperative defendant, this is never a part of an explicit deal. It is beneath the dignity of a state to make deals with criminals.

And so the crisis was dissipated because Khrushchev violated an ancient code of national honor: he yielded to an ultimatum.

Kennedy, however, was not only resolute and proud. He was also magnanimous. He did not taunt Khrushchev with his cowardice, and he ordered his subordinates to avoid representing the outcome as a "victory."

All in all, the outcome of the Cuban crisis was for most Americans a boost of morale. Their confidence in the cool young man who led them was strengthened. The President himself must have derived considerable satisfaction with the course of events, in retrospect, that is. Robert Kennedy writes:

> President Kennedy was impressed with the effort and the dedicated manner in which the military responded—the Navy deploying its vessels into the Carribbean; the Air Force going on continuous alert; the Army and the Marines moving their soldiers and equipment into the southeastern part of the U.S.; and all of them alert and ready for combat.[7]

It must have been good to feel all that power and also that one was spared the necessity of using it. Not everyone, however, felt a sense of relief. Some of the Chiefs of Staff felt keen disappointment. One of them told Robert Kennedy that he believed in a preventive attack against the Soviet Union. "On that fateful Sunday morning when the Russians answered they were withdrawing their missiles, it was suggested by one high military adviser that we attack Monday in any case. Another felt that we had in some way been betrayed."[8]

President Kennedy was disturbed about these feelings of the military but also understanding. "We had to remember," he explained later to his brother, "that they were trained to fight and to wage war—that was their life. Perhaps we would feel even more concerned if they were always opposed to using arms or military means—for if they would not be willing, who would be?"

Now, *there* is a sobering thought.

CHAPTER 13

Accommodation

T he outcome of the Cuban missile crisis understandably bolstered the self-confidence of Americans. Those who viewed the United States conduct of the cold war as dangerous "brinkmanship" (the term coined from Dulles' "massive retaliation" threats) felt a sense of reprieve that Kennedy's ultimatum, thanks to Khrushchev's backdown, did not push the world over the brink. To the majority who shared the belief that the United States was the ordained leader of the Free World and so must give the Russians to understand that no "spread of communism" would be tolerated, the policy of containment was vindicated. Although plans for direct military intervention against the Castro regime had been shelved for the time being, still the United States policy had prevented the Soviet Union from deriving any advantage from a Communist state in the Western Hemisphere.

To most Americans, then, it seemed that in the Cuban crisis the United States had finally found the right "posture" vis-à-vis the Soviet Union. As against the extravagant threats of "roll back" (that is, driving the Russians out of Eastern Europe, such as was heard in the early fifties), of instantaneous "massive retaliation" (that was quietly dropped), American policy makers now perceived their posture as that of cool firmness.

Further, Americans nurtured a conviction that their policy promoted the rule of law as against that of force. This idea was predicated on the view that non-Communist governments of the

Free World were, by definition, legitimate; hence, protecting them against Communist aggression from without and overthrow from within was part of preserving the rule of law. Of course, it was difficult to reconcile some United States actions with the image of law versus force. There was, for instance, the U.S. CIA connivance in the overthrow of the elected government of Guatemala in 1954; but then, it was reasoned, this was done according to the American definition of "legitimate government." That is, to qualify as legitimate, a government in the Western Hemisphere had to be not only non-Communist but also anti-Communist.

John S. Pustay[1] goes a step further and identifies anti-Communist governments with *incumbent* governments. Since the Guatemalan government was not anti-Communist, it was not incumbent, even though it was in power. The *incumbent* government of Guatemala was the one replaced by the Communist-infiltrated regime. In this way, the prevention and cure of communism wherever it became manifest in the Free World was, by definition, the preservation of "legitimacy."

This view enabled United States leaders to feel that their action in the Cuban crisis was strictly within the bounds of international law. "We were able," writes Robert Kennedy, "to establish a firm legal foundation for our actions under the OAS Charter."[2] That is to say, experts in international law presumably were consulted as to whether, in announcing a blockade of Cuba, the United States was adhering to international law, and at least some of them replied in the affirmative.

An indication of the mentality prevailing in government circles during the Kennedy Administration was the attitude of leading political figures who a few years later were to become sharp critics of United States counterinsurgency policy spawned by the concept of "containment." An outstanding example was J. William Fulbright.[3] In October 1962, according to Robert Kennedy, Fulbright was an advocate of "military action against Cuba rather than such a weak step as a blockade."[4] However, statements by the President himself suggest that the sense of victory, of having stared the U.S.S.R. down, coupled with a profound conviction of the fundamental rightness of the American position, may have imbued him and those of his advisers who held out for a firm but measured response with a feeling that America could afford to be magnanimous as well as severe. (As remarked in Chapter 12, Kennedy eschewed gloating over the U.S.S.R.'s humiliation.) In any case, in his last major speech on American-Soviet relations, Kennedy struck a distinct note of coexistence:

> Among the many traits the peoples of our two countries [the U.S.A. and the U.S.S.R.] have in common, none is stronger than the mutual abhorrence of war. Almost unique among the major world powers, we have never been at war with each other.[5]

Khrushchev, some six months later, had this to say on the subject (the speech, incidentally, was made in the presence of Castro):

> Some comrades abroad claim that Khrushchev is making a mess of things, and is afraid of war. Let me say once again that I should like to see the kind of bloody fool who is genuinely not afraid of war. Only a small child is afraid of nothing, because he doesn't understand; and only bloody fools.[6]

Both passages may be reflections of an aftermath of the jitters brought on by the Cuban missile crisis. At the same time, it must be kept in mind that both Khrushchev and Kennedy oscillated with a rather large amplitude between conciliatory and arrogant postures. The probable political background of Khrushchev's sword rattling was discussed in Chapter 11. Kennedy's style was much more suave, apparently calculated to project an impression of poised confidence. It, too, had a political background. The return of the Democrats to power had been advertised as a signal to "get America moving again" after eight years of Republican lethargy. Pushing toward "New Frontiers" meant a rejuvenation, which in the usual American conception meant unimpeded and indiscriminate growth. Everything had to move ahead: science, GNP, foreign aid, the space program,[7] and, of course, U.S. military might.

One of the issues in the Kennedy-Nixon presidential campaign was the "missile gap," an alleged inferiority of the United States in the nuclear balance of terror. (Subsequently the missile gap proved to be a fiction; the base line, relative to which the "gap" was estimated, was never even defined. The United States simply decided to keep a three- or four-to-one superiority in the number of intercontinental ballistic missiles over the Soviet Union.)

So it seemed as if with the change of administration the long-sought "position of strength" from which to negotiate was in sight, an indication that America would resume her triumphal march into the future. It turned out, however, that there was little to negotiate about. The situation in Europe seemed stabilized, and American policy was certainly not going to jeopardize this stability by any reduction of the military potential of NATO. Western Germany, now the strongest state in Western Europe, economically and militarily, was firmly welded into the American defense system, and any diminution of her power was unthinkable. China, it was finally recognized, was not something to negotiate with the Soviet Union about. Besides, China did not loom as an imminent threat in 1960. She had just gone through an attempted accelerated industrialization ("The Great Leap Forward") and had her hands full extricating herself from its disastrous results. Communist subversion was to be dealt with locally, forestalled by "nation building" (that is, massive economic military aid to "incumbent regimes"), and put down by "measured response" if it flared up (that is, United States military force would go to whatever lengths necessary to crush insurgents). "Brushfire wars" was the name given to these actions.

The global strategy called for substantial increases in conventional forces, "conventional" including everything except nuclear weapons and biological warfare. Military spending, which had leveled off in the late fifties, spurted up once more by thousands of millions of dollars, but the country felt no pinch. On the contrary, increased spending contributed to the impression of renewed economic growth and was an additional reassurance that America was "moving ahead" once again.

One "negotiable" issue was the limited test ban treaty, concluded in 1963 with the U.S.S.R., signed, and ratified. This was the first United States accord with the Soviet Union relating to arms control. It was hailed in many quarters as a first step toward a gradual relaxation which, if properly followed up (still assuming that the United States posture was one of nonmalevolent firmness), would eventually bring the Soviet Union to its senses and usher in a peaceful era.

In this climate a peace movement arose, essentially a loose confederation of diverse groups, each pressing in the style most congenial to its membership for a more active policy of accommodation with the U.S.S.R. The positions of these groups ranged from pacifism and advocacy of unilateral disarmament to an acceptance of the avowed aims of American foreign policy as a basis on which "peace strategies" were proposed. Charles E. Osgood's proposal[8] is a good example of such a "peace strategy." Osgood envisages a reversal of the Richardsonian process of escalation (cf. p. 20). The reversal—a de-escalation—is to be initiated by a unilateral step on the part of the United States which, whatever the step, was in no way to jeoparize what is conventionally understood to be the security of the United States.

This first step is not to be expected to be immediately seized upon and reciprocated, Osgood cautions. The mistrust accumulated in the years of escalating hostility between The Two may not be readily overcome. Friendly overtures might be dismissed by the Russians as attempts to undermine Soviet vigilance. The important thing is not faintheartedly to give up the de-escalation strategy. Even if the first move is not reciprocated, it should be followed by others (still not jeopardizing American security). If no positive response is evoked, then nothing essential is lost. On the contrary, a gain may have been made in mobilizing the sympathy of world opinion. Moreover, in case the Russians too want to de-escalate but would not have the temerity to take the initiative for fear of losing face, then they will find in "our" persistence opportunity for responding with de-escalating steps of their own. This in turn will give the United States further openings to continue the process. Being self-reinforcing, the process can be expected to accelerate until, each side becoming reassured about the genuine intentions of the other, substantial bilateral agreements can be entered into. This strategy circumvents the difficulties of *starting* with bilateral agreements that, in an atmosphere of chronic distrust, is the usual hangup, since the two sides are likely to be adamant in bargaining, thus precluding agreement.

In some circles it was thought that the breakthrough in the limited test ban negotiations (going on then for two years) was the result of an official "experiment," inspired by the idea of gradual de-escalation. If so, we are not in a position to know what further steps, if any, may have been planned. John F. Kennedy was assassinated five months after his speech at the American University (cf. p. 190). Eleven months later Nikita S. Khrushchev, the apostle of the Soviet policy of coexistence, was fired. It was supposed that the successors to Kennedy and Khrushchev were committed to continue policies of gradual accommodation. However, the focus of global politics was soon to shift, and the confrontation between the United States and the Soviet Union was displaced from the center of attention.

The displacement was levered from China. After 1960, China's independence from the Soviet Union became too obvious to be denied. However, China, being a Communist power, in American eyes was an expansionist power. Regardless of whether or not Chinese and Soviet strategies were complicit, China, like Russia, had to be "contained." The problem posed to United States military strategy was the same whether the two Communist giants acted together or separately: United States strategy was to encircle the entire Communist land mass with military bases so as to offer a constant threat, just in case the Communists should attempt a sortie from their "fortress." Encirclement could not, of course, check the "spread of communism" outside that ring. There was Latin America, for instance. Still, proceeding on its own momentum, the encirclement program could include South Vietnam—a pivotal link in this chain of military bases.

South Vietnam is a part of what previously was known as Indo-China. When the French attempted in 1946–1954 to reconquer Indo-China, they were repulsed by the Viet Minh, a Vietnamese national force organized and led by Vietnamese Communists. In the aftermath of French defeat, a conference held in Geneva in the summer of 1954 produced an armistice agreement, signed by the Viet Minh and the French, that provided for a withdrawal of French troops south of the 17th parallel and of Viet Minh troops north of that line. Appended to the armistice agreement was a declaration by eight nations, since known as the Geneva Accord. The Accord stipulated that the French forces would be out of the country within two years and that a general election would then decide the political future of Vietnam. It further stipulated that the military demarcation line of the 17th parallel would in no way constitute a *political* boundary; it was to serve only to separate regions administered by erstwhile hostile forces, pending the withdrawal of the French and the holding of a general election. The Accord also stipulated that neither portion of the country was to enter into military alliances, nor were foreign military bases to be allowed on either territory, nor was foreign military aid to be used by either side.

The United States refused to join in this Accord, but it issued a separate statement in which it pledged:

> The Government of the United States of America declares with regard to the aforesaid Agreements and paragraphs that (i) it will refrain from the threat or the use of force to disturb them. . . .[9]

What the United States actually had in mind under this non-interference pledge is not clear. In any case, when the French withdrew from southern Vietnam (before the two years expired) one Ngo Minh Diem, who had been Prime Minister under Bao Dai, the French-installed puppet emperor, proclaimed an independent Republic of Vietnam. Thereupon American "aid" began to pour in. The United States idea was to build up South Vietnam into a viable "nation," politically stable, economically and militarily strong, and allied with the American defense system.

Objections that this move by the United States violated both the letter and the spirit of the Geneva Accord were brushed aside. The refusal by Diem, with United States support, to hold the agreed upon general election, or even to discuss it with the Northern sector, was justified on the grounds that Communists could not be expected to allow a free election on their territory. At first military "aid" from United States was camouflaged by the now well-known use of "advisers." Later, when the stream of military equipment became staggering in quantity and kind, it was justified on the grounds that the Communists had first violated the Geneva Accord. What this violation amounted to was that the "North" had allegedly organized in the South the opposition to the Diem regime. And besides, it was argued, South Vietnam, not having existed at the time of the Geneva Conference, had no obligation to carry out its provisions. As for the Americans' declaration of noninterference, who was there to hold them to it?

Diem was supported by his fellow Catholics who had fled from the North immediately after the armistice, by the army left over from the puppet army of the French, by upper economic strata fearful of the specter of communism, and, finally, by the might of the American "containment" policy.

Opposing Diem were the peasantry (whose traditional local self-government Diem had arbitrarily replaced with appointed officials), the Buddhists (whom Diem subjugated to religious persecution), and the democratically oriented professionals and intellectuals. Diem's response to the opposition was the establishment of a police state. The spontaneous local revolts that followed gradually coalesced into full-scale civil war. When the position of the South Vietnam Saigon regime became hopeless, Diem was assassinated. Quite possibly, from the evidence, his removal, if not also the actual assassination, was approved, if not instigated, by the United States Central Intelligence Agency.

Thereafter a quick succession of "governments," put together with United States "advice," culminated in the selection of a "strong man," Cao Ky, who was in the service of the French during the attempted reconquest of Vietnam.[10] Ky immediately undertook to vigorously prosecute the civil war and to put an end to attempts at creating a "democratic" government in Saigon. Massive American military intervention was now added to "aid," beginning with systematically escalated air attacks upon the North (February 1965) and the gradual building up of a major land war that by 1967 involved 500,000 United States troops and the "support" of two billion dollars per month.

From then on the Vietnam war completely dominated what constituted United States foreign policy. A solid opposition at home made itself known immediately after the bombing of North Vietnam began, and its growth kept pace with the momentum of escalation of the war. At first the opposition was ignored, as minority opinions often are in the United States; then the dissent made headlines when a wave of "teach-ins" beginning in March 1965 spread over college and university campuses. The teach-ins were a combination of mass meeting

and seminar, featuring, on the one hand, passionate denuncia-
tions of the war by rank and file academics and community participants and, on the other, sober and detailed analyses of social,
historical, political, and economic factors led by recognized
scholars and specialists.[11]

The teach-ins were something entirely new in the history of
popular opposition to war, anywhere. Traditionally opposition
to war manifested itself in two ways: one in individual attempts
to escape military service, as when, especially in Europe, peasants went into hiding from recruiting officers, or when in urban
societies, even in World War II, young men mutilated themselves to avoid being conscripted. The other kind of opposition
stemmed largely from religious or moral tenets, as with con-
scientious objectors and pacifist communities. Both these elements played a role also in the contemporary opposition in the
United States to the Vietnam war. A significant difference was
that with the teach-ins *intellectual* opposition to war made its
first appearance on a mass scale. Students and professors demanded debate with the Administration. Halfheartedly, the Administration responded. Here and there spokesmen for the State
Department, or the Pentagon, participated in the teach-ins.
They were assisted by a sector of the academic community
that supported the war. It goes without saying that, in this
new climate of dissent, proverbial appeals to patriotism, etc.,
would be of no avail because the country was not being invaded,
conscripts were not being called to defend it; this time the
country was the invader, and its citizens were called upon to
behave like conquerors. A rationale had to be invented by the
supporters of the war, and it was. The war was represented as
an incident in the containment policy; but, as it was impossible
in the circumstances of Asian politics to build up a credible case
of Soviet complicity, China was chosen as Enemy Number One.
Already in May 1964 (before the U.S. attack on North Vietnam),
China was being groomed for that role. Said a Department of
State policy paper:

> Communist China's interests are clear: It has publicly castigated
> Moscow for betraying the revolutionary cause whenever the Soviets
> have sounded a cautionary note. It has characterized the United
> States as a paper tiger and has insisted that the revolutionary
> struggle for "liberation and unification" of Viet-Nam could be con-

ducted without risks by, in effect, crawling under the nuclear and the conventional defense of the free world. Peiping thus appears to feel that it has a large stake in demonstrating the new strategy, using Viet-Nam as a test case. Success in Viet-Nam would be regarded by Peiping as vindication for China's views in the worldwide ideological struggle.[12]

A few days after the start of systematic bombings of North Vietnam, the State Department documented its case ("aggression from the north") by identifying no fewer than nine northerners (with photographs) fighting in the ranks of the southern insurgents against the Saigon regime[13] and by listing an inventory of captured weapons of Chinese manufacture, e.g., "One 90 mm. rocket launcher; 2 carbines (type 53); 120 rounds of 75 mm. recoilless rifle ammunition . . ." (photo supplied) etc.[14] In fairness, it should be mentioned that in the latter document other sources of weapons used by the insurgents were also recognized, for example, those captured from the French (in the earlier war for independence) and from the Saigon army (these, presumably, of American manufacture).

The situation in the middle sixties was quite different from that of even the late forties. Whereas the early "containment" of "communism" had been accomplished painlessly (the Greek revolution, for instance, was suppressed by British troops) and in Europe, except in countries occupied by Soviet troops and in Yugoslavia, the Communist wave receded with economic recovery, the war in Vietnam was costing the United States twenty to thirty billion dollars per year, plus a mounting casualty list and the most bitter internal strife since the Civil War.

The opposition was not confined to the campuses. It eventually mounted all the way up to the Senate where the Administration was challenged on its own ground. That is to say, senators like Fulbright, Morse, Gore, Young, and McGovern began to put questions to the Administration that, unlike questions concerning the "morality" of the policy, could not be dismissed by "realist" arguments about the primacy of "national interest," "security," and the like. The questions were precisely about whether the involvement in Vietnam (from its very inception) did in fact serve, or did contrarily jeopardize, the national interests of the United States. What developed therefrom was a national debate on geopolitics at the highest political levels—the first such debate in the United States.[15] This debate is a rich source of information on how thinking about American-Soviet relations underwent a profound change among people who expected automatically, by virtue of being elected representatives of a government by the people, to have a voice in the making of United States policies, including foreign policy, and who now discovered they were outsiders. They had not even been consulted. It became apparent that Lyndon B. Johnson had surrounded himself with people of one mind; and the deeper he got into the Vietnam mire, the more deaf he became to the warnings of those who suspected disastrous consequences from the involvement. Johnson's obsession with "winning" in Vietnam, at any cost, not unlike that of a gambler intent on recouping his mounting losses, contributed, in my opinion, a great deal toward a reevaluation on an unprecedented scale of the entire meaning of the cold war and its prospects.

The theme in this debate that is of most concern to the subject of this book is a recurrent one. The policy of containment was a very-near success. The time had come, by the mid-sixties, to reap its rewards—a gradual normalization of relations with a wiser, calmer Soviet Union, ready to join the "community of states" as a "normal" member. The Vietnam war undercut the opportunity. Witness the exchange between Senator Gore and Ambassador George Kennan (the Mr. X of Chapter 7):

> Senator Gore: Ambassador . . . to view this problem in the context of a decade hence, what is your assessment of its bearing upon the possibility that the Soviet Union may or may not continue on the course of rapprochement with the Western Powers which has been underway now since the confrontation of 1961,[16] thus possibly re-entering the European society or conversely becoming more closely aligned with Red China, not only in a push into the Pacific but aimed more closely in a more aggressive international Communist thrust?
>
> Ambassador Kennan: Senator Gore, a year ago this month in a public lecture at Princeton University . . . I tried to make the point that if we pressed our intervention in Vietnam, the Soviet Government would see no choice but to come down strongly against us and enter into a sort of a competition with the Chinese to see who could look most critical of our policies, most dedicated and violent in their defense of the Vietcong.
>
> I said that they would do this even if it [sic] had to proceed at the expense of Soviet-American relations.

Now this is exactly what has happened. The effect of the Vietnamese conflict is not to restore the unity between the Soviet Union and China. Things have gone too far for that. But it is to give their rivalry a form very understandable from the standpoint of our interests and the interests of world peace, namely, the form of a contest to see who can look the most anti-American, . . . who can appear to be the most violent defender of what they call national liberations movements. . . .

I think that we have more important problems than Vietnam to thrash out eventually with the Soviet Union, problems of disarmament, and problems of halting the proliferation of nuclear weaponry, and the still great and vital problem of Germany, which is, to my mind, the most specific political geographic problem in the world.

All this, as I see it, is in suspense while this Vietnam conflict proceeds, and the effect of the Vietnam conflict on the Soviet Union has been, I fear, to make it more difficult for us to discuss these things in a useful way with the Soviet leaders.[17]

The exchange with Senator Carlson is even more telling:

Senator Carlson: Why have the Soviets appeared to be reluctant to play any sort of peacekeeping role similar to the one that they played at Tashkent recently?

Ambassador Kennan: I believe it is because they are being pushed so hard by the Chinese.

The Soviet Government is, I think, very apprehensive if it does not take a very strong anti-American line, if it appears to be in any way aiding us in our purposes, it will lose its authority within the world Communist movement and its appeal to other nationalist semi-Communist movements in other developing countries. This, I think, explains its rather curious conduct in this respect.[18]

There has been quite a change in Kennan's view of the Soviet Union. In 1947 he saw the Soviet Union as seeking to promote strife everywhere in order to "fish in troubled waters." Now, in February 1966, it appears to him as a potential peacemaker whose hands are tied by the necessity of preserving the revolutionary image. True, the character of Soviet leadership had undergone profound changes. But the perceptions of Americans, concerned with foreign policy but excluded from decision on it, had also changed.

It is noteworthy that Kennan views the deterioration of Soviet-Chinese relations with alarm rather than with satisfaction. He sees a dangerous rivalry developing between the U.S.S.R.

and China as to which will appear to the Third World most violently anti-imperialist. Not many in the United States perceived this aspect of the Soviet-Chinese split. Most cold warriors welcomed it for obvious reasons and some went so far as to relish an eventual Soviet-American anti-Chinese alliance.

In summary, the Vietnam war produced radical changes in America's self-image and in American perceptions of global politics. The self-confidence that pervaded at least the government circles during the Kennedy Administration dissipated. Intense opposition to the war, starting on campuses, spread through the general population and reached high political strata. On the latter level, particularly among recalcitrant senators, searching questions began to be asked publicly, casting doubt on the entire conception of American foreign policy. Accommodation with the Soviet Union seemed now to have become a primary goal; China displaced the Soviet Union as the power that had to be "contained." But confidence in the standard methods of containment (aid to "incumbent" regimes, nuclear deterrence, military response) was shaken.

None of these changes, however, made the slightest dent in the stance of President Johnson, Secretary of State Rusk, and the military establishment. As far as they were concerned (at least in their public statements) the United States was fighting to protect the freedom of a small nation, to keep the Communist Chinese hordes at bay, and to preserve "faith" in American intentions to honor "commitments."

As for the Soviet Union, the change in its leadership occurred a few months before the massive American intervention in Vietnam. The obstacles that this intervention put in the path of Soviet initiatives toward accommodation of the United States were clearly pointed out in George Kennan's testimony at the Senate Hearings cited above. In my opinion, his estimate of the situation was entirely correct. In addition to his explanation, I offer these further considerations.

With Khrushchev's dismissal, all traces of the "personality cult" in the Soviet Union vanished. Whether during his tenure Khrushchev had stood a chance of acquiring dictatorial powers we do not know. Probably not. Yet he was still in the limelight, and the image of the Soviet Union was definitely stamped with his personality. His successors, on the other hand, were quiet men, discharging functions akin to those of chairmen of the board, and very little else. They no more qualified as heroes than Clement Attlee or Calvin Coolidge. The Soviet Union came under rule by committee.

Since the start of the five-year plans in 1928 the outlook of the upper strata of Soviety society has been increasingly a technocratic one. Indeed there was a strong overlap between the bureaucracy and the technocracy. Nevertheless the technocracy was severely handicapped by the sociopsychotic features of Stalin's regime. The technocracy (including the military) suffered not only from the ravages of mass liquidations but also from the crippling effect of political tyranny over initiative and inventiveness. The terror stopped with Stalin's death, but it took time for the technocracy to become an influential force in its own right. With the instatement of an engineer (Kosygin) as head of state, the technocrats seem to have arrived.

It is quite likely, then, that under other circumstances the new Soviet leadership would be extremely amenable to steps toward a dismantling of the cold war, with a view of turning full attention back to what had traditionally been considered the primary national interest of the Soviet Union, namely the building of communism in its own territory via the creation of material abundance and a universal raising of the "cultural level." In order to undertake this task, however, it was necessary to introduce two radical changes into Soviet political philosophy, and these have proved to be beyond the competence of the present Soviet leadership. Both changes have to do with "de-ideologization."

Concern with ideology enters Soviet policy in two ways. First, the U.S.S.R. is trying very hard to hang on to the role of ideological leader in the revolutionary and national liberation movements of the world. As has been pointed out, the fear of losing this leadership to China inhibited a more active policy of accommodation with the United States. Second, regarding the capitalist West, the present Soviet leadership cannot act in *total* disregard of Soviet public opinion, as Stalin could do since public opinion was obliterated during his rule. While it is true that Soviet leadership continues to exercise a near monopoly on public communication, the control of the party apparatus can now pass from one group to another, as has been demonstrated. So, there exists at least a trickle of influence on top leadership from the rank and file of the party. The rank and file, in turn, being recruited from the general population, is no longer mesmerized by a God-figure. In fact, public opinion of a sort has come into being, and, although it cannot exercise overt pressures by means of open debate on major domestic policies (open debate on foreign policy is still out of the question), the political leadership cannot any longer be completely unresponsive to it.

Now, in the Soviet Union, the support of public policy is mobilized exclusively by appeal to *ideological* tenets. Even in the Stalin era such support had to be mobilized, not that it was needed politically but because it was essential in order to channel social energy—as, for example, in marshaling superhuman efforts to rapidly industrialize, and for the war. These ideological tenets have remained unchanged: the Soviet Union, the first socialist state, is engaged in building an exploitation-free society; it is prevented from directing all its energy toward this admirable goal by the aggressive intentions of the imperialist bloc. Coexistence as a theme fits into this picture, wherein the imperialists are shown to be deterred from direct aggression by the military might of the U.S.S.R. Thus, as long as the would-be aggressors understand that aggression against the U.S.S.R. would be suicidal, there is no reason why states "with different social or political systems" cannot cooperate to the advantage of both.

But the Vietnam war precludes such cooperation with the United States.

The attack on Vietnam *is* direct aggression upon a socialist state. In the Soviet leaders' view, it cannot be ignored without violating fundamental ideological tenets and thus weakening the traditional basis of popular support. Related to these considerations is the continued obsessive need of Soviet leadership to preserve complete ideological hegemony of the Communist party over domestic affairs. A dissolution of the cold war would of necessity undermine this hegemony, as the increasing contacts with the West since "the thaw" have already begun to do. Of course, outside contacts are not the sole factor in this process. De-Stalinization, enlarged material aspirations stimulated by ris-

ing living standards, and the maturation of the postwar generation have all contributed to the evaporation of blind faith in the
infallibility of the party. Still, old shibboleths persist in the
minds of the leadership. They react, as does any aging leadership losing its self-confidence, or as an individual under intense
threat, by reverting to entrenched defense mechanisms. Suppres
sion of the democratization maturing in Czechoslovakia was
publicly rationalized by the Soviet leadership's concoctions of
falsehoods and by citing "hostile doctrines" (exactly as the
United States leadership rationalized its invasion of the
Dominican Republic). The real spur that urged the throttling of
Czechoslovakia must have been a Soviet version of the
"domino theory" invented by the United States to justify its
intervention in Vietnam: that is, a "defection" by one from the
course ordained by the master power would surely be followed
by others; in this case by the disintegration of the Soviet Empire
in Eastern Europe and, ultimately, of the hegemony of the party
bureaucracy.

Ironically, the Czechoslovakia affair may be responsible for
the revival of efforts on the part of the U.S.S.R. toward accommodation with the United States. The impotent American protests against that invasion may have been read as a signal that
"cooperation" on the basis of clearly delimited spheres of
influence was now possible—a basis that has always been a goal
of Soviet coexistence policy. Yet, it is clear that the Stalinist
conception of the "spheres of influence," as separated by an
Iron Curtain impervious to any cultural cross influence, is obsolete. In realizing this, Soviet leadership faces a dilemma. A division of the world into "spheres of influence" now seems realizable; but the division is no guarantee against the erosion of the
ideological hegemony of the Soviet Communist party. The dilemma is an obstacle to the Soviet leadership's understandable
striving to advance accommodation with the United States.

The problem of China is also a two-sided one. On the one
hand, China as a contender for leadership in the Communist
world inhibits accommodation between The Two; on the other,
her emergence as a nuclear power inimical to the Soviet Union
is pushing The Two toward each other. Obviously an accommodation between The Two on this basis portends no good for a

lasting peace. To begin with, China's social psychosis, as manifested in the fantastic Mao cult, is attributable to the intense anxiety felt in the face of the unrelenting military threat posed by the United States for the past twenty years. This threat has been much more real even than that posed to the U.S.S.R. by "capitalist encirclement." If a *de facto* Soviet-American alliance (no longer a fantasy) is added to this threat, China may well go over the brink.

It is ironic that enlightened Soviet thinkers, in revolt against the dictatorship of bureaucracy, seem not to be aware of this danger, if Andrei Sakharov, a physicist and credited as "father" of Russia's H-bomb, is representative of that group. In his pamphlet, privately circulated among Soviet intellectuals and published in the United States, Sakharov calls for complete intellectual freedom and the end of one-party rule.[19] But at the same time he plumps for an understanding with the United States based on the "convergence" of the two systems and, ominously, on a common response to the Chinese threat.

If such a development should occur (with or without democratization of the Soviet Empire), global politics would revert to the collective security idea—not, however, as envisaged in the peace-keeping role of the United Nations, based on an accord of all the Great Powers, but rather backwards, to the collective security idea of the thirties, to an alliance against a pariah, a specific state branded as "the aggressor." This kind of "collective security" made some sense a generation ago in the age of "conventional" warfare, when failure to *prevent* war still allowed the hope of ending it quickly and of bringing the aggressor to his senses. In the age of instantaneous annihilation, "collective security" is a misnomer. There is no security in the prospect of collective suicide.

CHAPTER 14

Prospects

A courtier of Catherine II of Russia once said, "What stops growing must begin to rot." Ulam quotes this aphorism on at least two occasions in support of his thesis that Soviet foreign policy is a continuation of imperial Russian foreign policy. Clearly, however, the commandment "to grow or perish" appears to govern not only the policies of all powers on the make but also the behavior of all systems engaged in a "struggle for existence" with other systems, be they business firms, political machines, or institutions. In particular, the commandment appears to govern the behavior of military establishments.

To push the biological metaphor further, one must find an analogue to the "survival of the fittest" principle. What makes an institution "fit to survive"? Sociologists of the "functionalists" school assume that institutions survive by virtue of their social utility. This notion, too, stems from a biological analogy. The organs of an organism have "survived" the evolutionary selection process because of their contributions to the survival of the organism. However, in these theories (both biological and social) there is no room for pathology, in particular for pathological autonomous growth of subsystems that have become uncoupled from the survival mechanisms of the system in which they are imbedded. A cancer does not contribute to the survival of the organism in which it grows; on the contrary, it kills it. However, while the organism is still alive, it nourishes the cancer. To put it crudely, the body "thinks" that the cancer cells are "its own" cells and so must be nourished rather than destroyed as invading cells usually are. Similarly, the viability of a social institution, that is, its ability to draw nourishment from the social system, depends not on its actual but on its perceived social usefulness.

In tribal wars, the whole tribe shared the spoils of victory or the burdens of defeat, and so the social utility of military groups was apparent to everyone. In the days when kings and statesmen boasted frankly of their conquests and openly planned future ones, war, hence military might, was universally recognized as a prerogative, first of princes, then of states. In our age, wars of conquest and dreams of national glory have ceased to be respectable. However, the military establishments did not thereby simply disappear for want of a rationale. In particular, even before World War II, the military establishments of the United States and of the Soviet Union were already perceived by their populations not as instruments of conquest but as insurance against the destruction of their very ways of life. When the common enemies of The Two were crushed, the military machines had already become firmly established in the minds of the people as the most vital of social organs, and so acquired perfect justification for their continued existence, and therefore growth. In fact, nowhere is the principle "grow or perish" more appropriate than with regard to military machines. What this amounts to is that the two machines have entered into a symbiotic relation to each other. Each is protected by the other.

Ask the average American why over half of his $180-billion federal budget has to be spent on means of destruction, and he will reply that national security depends on these means. Security against what? Against an attack. Attack by whom? Until a few years ago, the answer would invariably be "by Russia." Ask the average Russian why treasure and effort that might be spent in providing a better life for him is poured into armaments, and his reply will be a mirror image of the American's.

Establishment A must be maintained because establishment B exists, and vice versa. The argument is not unlike one that makes it appear impossible to solve certain elementary problems in arithmetic. Consider the following example. A man contracts to work for a firm for ten percent of the net profit per annum, the latter being the gross profit diminished by the man's salary. Even if the gross profit is known, one can argue that it is impossible to determine the salary, because in order to calculate the salary one must know the net profit, and in order to know the net profit one must know the salary. An obvious way out occurs only if one learns to solve two equations *simultaneously*, as every high school student knows. The problem is trivial, but appears insoluble as long as one is mesmerized by the "incontrovertible logic" of the vicious cycle.

The malignant nature of the unimpeded growth of military establishments is painfully apparent even to the policy makers of The Two. Yet it is impossible to show *either* of The Two a way out of the impasse. This can be done only if somehow *both* realize the impasse into which "incontrovertible logic" has led them and seek a way out jointly. However, while *each* of the powers is an "entity" of sorts, that is, a quasi-organism with a sensorium, some reasoning habits, and a decision center, *both* of them are not *an* entity and so cannot absorb information as a unit, process it, organize it into perceptions, draw conclusions, and act on them.

The realists in effect assert this when they portray the states and their interests as *the* actors in international relations. In the light of their analysis, much of what states do becomes understandable. In the light of Clausewitz's theory, for example, it becomes understandable why Europe became an armed camp when its civilization reached a pinnacle at the end of the nineteenth century. In the light of Ulam's and Aron's analyses, it becomes clear why the "cooperation" between the Soviet Union and the West did not survive their common victory over the Axis, and why the rule of world law, to which the West presumably aspired, could not be established. (Both writers wrote in the Clausewitzian framework of thought.)

However, "understanding" international relations is not the only result of this analysis. Another result is that its framework of thought about international relations is perpetuated *because* it makes so much sense. In this way, not only do the realists start with the "world as it is," they also end up with it. Their descriptive theory ("the world as it is") merges with a prescriptive (or normative) theory ("keep it so").

Now, a descriptive theory should be judged by its correspondence with reality, and here the realists are on fairly safe ground, at least with regard to recent history. A prescriptive theory, however, presupposes values. The values presumably served by prescriptions of *realpolitik* are subsumed under "national interests." To judge the worth of the realists' prescriptive theory, it is necessary to examine the extent to which the "national interests" are actually furthered by policies derived from the theory. To do this, however, one must first establish what the national interests of particular states are at particular times. The realists frequently specify them, but do not pursue the matter further. For example, they do not raise the question of whether "national interests," as they define them in particular situations, represent the aspirations of the populations concerned, or of special groups or strata, or, perhaps, only of the policy makers.

Here Clausewitz was on much more solid ground. He projected the Europe of the eighteenth century onto the nineteenth. Indeed, the "national interests" of the nineteenth century European states were those of the eighteenth century continued. Primarily they were the appetites of the rulers for more territory, more power, more prestige, etc. The difference between the eighteenth and nineteenth century international relations was that in the nineteenth century nationalism was added. That is, the aspirations of the princes became those of their peoples. I do not here raise the question of whether those aspirations were in the "true" interests of the people. It suffices to note that in the age of nationalism the populations (or at least the articulate strata) did identify their aspirations with those of the states; so "national interests" could be fairly well defined in terms of the predominant perceptions of the time.

Nineteenth century developments that undermined the Clausewitzian system in Europe were discussed in Chapter 3: (1) new war technology that changed wars of decision into wars of attrition; (2) ambiguity of the "nation states"; (3) the rising tide of social revolutions. In the aftermath of World War I it looked for a while as if nationalism, the prime mover of wars as depicted (and glorified) by Clausewitz, collapsed. It made a comeback as fascism, but now with strong admixtures of eschatological ideology, something not found in the classical Clausewitzian nationalism. In the Soviet Union, eschatological thinking had become the mortar of social cohesion. (Under Stalin, classical nationalism was revived, but the eschatological component was never completely submerged, at least not on the level of ritualistic rationalization.) In the West, especially in the United States, pure nationalism was no longer sufficient for mobilizing total national effort. It was necessary to invoke a vision of a "non-Clausewitzian" world after victory. And this ideological component had to be retained even in the realists' definition of "national interest" after the Axis was in fact defeated. We have seen it in Walter Lippmann's definition of American war aims (see pp. 54–55). It is evident in Raymond Aron's "world sociology," as he calls it, even though he attempts to root his analysis in Clausewitz's ideas.[1] An ideological component must be tacitly assumed also by nuclear strategists, otherwise the risks of nuclear war cannot be justified, since the costs exceed any conceivable gains of victory or losses from defeat in the conventional diplomilitary game.

So it seems that, just as nationalism was the new factor in international affairs at the opening of the nineteenth century, ideology (dormant since the religious wars) reappeared as the new factor in the twentieth.

Ideology creates difficulties for the realists' normative theories. On the one hand, ideology must be included in the definition of "national interest" if only because the classical interests of individual states can no longer suffice as a catalyst when frankly stated as determinants of foreign policy. Power-wielding units are now *blocs* of states; and even though the power of each bloc resides predominantly in its leading member (the United States and the Soviet Union, respectively), still "national interest" has to be somehow identified with the interest of the whole bloc. Thus it is generalized in terms of ideological goals: "peaceful economic development of the world under law and order" or "protection of the achievements of the socialist revolutions."

On the other hand, ideologically expressed goals, being vague, do not indicate concrete diplomilitary strategies, which are the end products of the realists' normative theory. The realist prides himself on his "realism," which, in his framework of thought, means the taking into account of the existing distribution of power in formulating immediate goals. These calculations must often push ideological considerations into the background. This presented no problem to Stalin who could always count on instantaneous, unanimous acceptance of everything he did, both by his henchmen and by the population. It is becoming a problem for the present Soviet leadership, however, as popular faith in their infallibility wanes. American leaders are facing a most serious problem in this respect, as reiterations of the hitherto unquestioned "national interests" of the United States and their ideological rationalizations can no longer serve as bases for "consensus."

The most serious difficulty facing the realists, at least in the United States, is the emergence of the systemic component in the conduct of foreign policy, one that no longer can be ignored. Richardson's mathematical models of arms races could well be dismissed as mere intellectual exercises. Lenin's emphasis on the expansion pressures of capitalist economics as determinants of policies in capitalist states could likewise be attributed to specific ideological bias. However, the self-propelled burgeoning of the American war machine is neither a formalistic theory nor an eschatological fantasy. And for the first time since the rise of militarism, many a realist finds himself in opposition to the militarist. As C. Wright Mills pointed out, the surest way to convince oneself of the reality of the power elite is to try to buck it. Realists like Robert McNamara (U.S. Secretary of Defense, 1961–1968), who attempted to apply "rational" principles in defense policy, eventually learned the futility of such exercises. The war machine, once an instrument of foreign policy, has become an autonomous system within the body politic. Like a malignant growth, it has escaped the control of the supersystem within which it grows.[2] It is of no avail to the realists to point out that *further* escalation of the arms race is no longer in the "national interest" of the United States. The U.S. military has demanded, and will get, its "anti-Chinese" "thin" anti-ballistic-missile-missile system. Once this "thin" system is installed, it will fatten. The consequences are obvious to anyone, but the military continues to have its way. It is not necessary to conclude on that account that the military establishment, as a separate body, "dictates" to the civilian authority. The lines are not sharply drawn, as they also are not drawn between the government, the industrial, and the research circles. Personnel is freely shifted among all of them; and the ideas have ample opportunity to diffuse through the whole complex.

Why do the ideas of the military usually prevail? It seems to me that in the United States these ideas are most virulent because they evoke images that are most appealing to the traditional American elite, namely business and growth. Therefore, although when put in terms of expense (an estimated eighty billion dollars in 1969) the new role of the military may evoke some misgivings, when seen in terms of bustling activity (booming production, jobs, contracts, research grants, etc.) "defense" is a firmly embedded, welcome aspect of American life, quite aside from its alleged protective role. Not many will define the social role of the military in these terms. But when it comes to *specific* situations (job, contract, expense account, and so on), unbeknown to oneself, one searches for ways of rationalizing the cornucopia. One may not even use such rationalizations explicitly, may even join with others in cursing the insatiable monster. Nevertheless, one is *less* ready to take an active part in meaningful efforts to combat it. On the national scale, the summation of these inhibitions is all it takes to make the military politically unassailable.

The military framework of thought is technocratic, that is, completely occupied with means, not with goals. Once an ultimate goal is given and sufficiently well defined, the technocrat is able to make his contribution, but not otherwise. Therefore he is most comfortable when his work can be demonstrably related to the furtherance of a given, fixed, and well-defined goal. The task of the engineer is the clearest example. He must design a physical system (a bridge, an airplane, a chemical plant) to given specifications. His is not to reason why, nor to consider the possible effects of the bridge, or the aircraft, or the plant on people who will use it or will not use it or who will be affected by the uses to which it is put.

In some contexts, the task of the physician is also well defined. He must save or prolong a life or restore a human organism to a "normal" state. To the extent that these goals are not questioned, and to the extent that the criteria of "normality" are universally accepted (as they usually are with regard to physiological functions), the physician can be comfortable in the role of the technician. In other contexts, however the desirability of the goals, or even their meaning, can be questioned. In some cases it is difficult to say *whether* a given life *ought* to be prolonged. Likewise, normal psychological function is by no means as clearly defined as normal physiological function. Faced with such situations, the physician can either join in extratechnocratic explorations of the social role of medicine or disclaim competence and remain a technician.

However, unlike the engineer, the physician is not as clearly justified in retreating to the technocratic point of view, since he is in much more intimate contact with the beneficiaries (or victims) of his expertise than is the engineer. It is more difficult for him to hold that decisions governed by values (the worth of a life, the meaning of "normality") are properly outside the scope of his competence.

Nevertheless, both the engineer and the physician can still rationalize a technocratic attitude, because *so much* of their purely technocratic functions can be ethically defended. While all technology may be rejected in principle by some (like the Amish) and all medicine by others (like the Christian Scientists), powerful arguments can still be made to the effect that technology and technocratic medicine have, on the whole, benefited humanity. (The conclusiveness of the argument is not the issue here.)

Let us now examine the implications of the technocratic orientation of the military. Seemingly the usual arguments apply here: Foreign policy questions are political and must be decided by political authorities. The armed might of a nation is a necessary adjunct to foreign policy; armed might depends essentially on technology. Consequently the technocratic attitude of the military is socially justified. To know whether war technology is of ultimate benefit to humanity is a legitimate question in philosophy, but it falls beyond the scope of military competence (recall Clausewitz's disclaimer). So, a military establishment, it can be argued, serves at least a portion of humanity, and thereby discharges its social function.

The argument may have had some validity when armed might served as an instrument of conquest or an instrument of defense against conquest. This function, however, has been lost, at least by the military establishments of the Great Powers, because, as has been pointed out, conquest of the opponent's territory cannot any longer possibly justify itself economically or politically; even existing empires (results of past conquests) became political and economic burdens and had to be abandoned. What faces us is the most fundamental fact of global politics today: the *only* justification for the existence of the military establishment —especially of a great power that neither needs nor (paradoxically) can undertake conquests—is the military establishment of another. That is to say, the only "protection" a military establishment of a great power can provide its population is that of deterring a *senseless* attack by another.

The way out of this dilemma is suggested by the solution of simultaneous equations. We must fix our attention on the social function, if any, of the *global* military machine, not on that of a particular component of it. If we do this, we see that the technocratic attitude can no longer be justified by an appeal to the division of responsibilities: "Someone else has chosen the ends, our job is to provide the means."

The goal served by the *global* military establishment could have been chosen only by someone intending to exterminate the human race. If we reject a devil, and if we are skeptical about Freud's hypothesized "death wish," we must conclude that *no one* chose this goal. The goal of total destruction is being served not by design but as a consequence of the technocratic orientation of the human components of the global military machine. Each one does his job. The individual jobs coalesce into team tasks, these into "system" functions. The total is a supersystem of men and machines *whose sole function can be discharged only in the extermination of man and his works.*

If we view this global organization in terms of its goal, we arrive at a sardonic but defensible conclusion, namely that there is no longer any problem of getting the United States and the Soviet Union to "cooperate." They are already cooperating. The leadership of each protects the military machine of the other against possible doubts by the other's population concerning its *raison d'être.* Thus the policy of massive retaliation was announced by the United States Secretary of State just at the time (shortly after Stalin's death) when the circumstances were most favorable in the Soviet Union for a basic reevaluation of its diplomilitary policies. Similarly, when, as a consequence of the Vietnam war, European public opinion was swinging away from supporting United States policy, when, following France's *de facto* withdrawal from NATO, Denmark and possibly Norway were seriously contemplating formal withdrawal, the Soviet leaders gave NATO a new lease on life by invading Czechoslovakia.

What are the prospects?

The art of war is now in the "baroque" period of its development, the stage of exuberant growth and elaboration. The immediate prospects for the practitioners of the art are bright. The continued dominant position of the Soviet military is assured both by the reinvigorization of NATO and by the new Chinese threat. Since Stalin's death there has been a progressive "technocratization" of the Soviet military. According to R. Kolkowicz[3] the trend will reflect itself in increased emphasis on defense spending at the expense of economic development. To any technocrat, "progress" means essentially a burgeoning growth of his own gadgetry; to the military technocrat "progress" means "a bigger bang for a buck" or "more rubble for a ruble."

The American military technocrats have much to be thankful for, in particular for a Secretary of Defense (Laird) more appreciative of expanding horizons that his cost-accounting predecessor. Especially encouraging is the fact that the development of new weapons can proceed along several lines at once. While the "enemies of progress" direct their agitation against a highly publicized development like the ABM, projects like CBW and the MIRV can proceed unmolested. The latter is especially promising because, once it is deployed, self-policing arms agreements become virtually impossible.[4]

It is noteworthy that the prospects for continued growth of military machines have become independent of shifts in the global political situation. Formerly a political *rapprochement* between The Two spelled dangers for the war machine such as being saddled with arms limitations or even disarmament. Now these "dangers" have receded. Political *rapprochement* between the United States and the Soviet Union, if it now occurs, is most likely to be a military alliance against China. In that case, nothing will change except the identity of the actors. There might even develop a cyclic process described by Orwell, where two of The Three are always aligned against the third; but when it looks as if the coalition is "winning," one of the partners shifts sides, so that the game can continue.[5] Or, the alliance of The Two may spell the end of China. In that case, The Two will again be left facing each other.

All of these prospects point to war—not a politically instigated war by a *systemically* generated one, a war that no one wants, not even the military, for after *that* war they will be out of business too.

Through all this, the strategic community, discharging its responsibility of planning for contingencies, depicts possible futures by means of "scenarios." There are imagined sequences of politicomilitary events and responses of the several "actors" to them. In the same way, a chess player thinks several moves ahead and, taking the consequences of his and the opponent's possible choices, plans his strategies.

These exercises make sense only if one identifies with the players. If, however, one identifies with the chess pieces, the situation looks very different. One then wonders whether the pieces can undertake anything to prevent moves that will take them off the board or indeed to prevent the game from being played at all. This is the chronic question that plagues the ordinary person who becomes aware of the ultimate meaning of the cold war and of global power politics in general. In answer to his plaintive question "What can *I* do?" the answer must, of course, remain "Nothing, if you expect *your* action to turn the attention of the players away from the game and toward the pieces." Such an answer, however, becomes a self-fulfilling prophesy, since if everyone is convinced of his individual impotence the collective remains impotent. What, then, are the prospects for collective action and its outcome?

In the United States, events since 1965 have demonstrated the near-futility of conventional political action in matters of foreign policy. Not only is geopolitics far removed from most people's immediate concerns; regardless how vividly the dangers of global power politics are portrayed, the consequences still remain outside of ordinary experience, and the imagery of the horrors is dulled by repetition. Thus, even though the obscenities of a nuclear holocaust have been widely publicized, and deep anxieties have been aroused in the American population in the fifties and early sixties, still no effective political action could be mobilized that could make an impact on the policy makers.

To begin with, the rationalizations of the cold war and the optimistic prognoses of the containment policy and of its variants were accepted by the overwhelming majority. Second, even if rejection of current policies became widespread, this would not guarantee significant and timely changes. This is amply demonstrated by the weak effects of the comparatively strong opposition of the Vietnam war. Barring impeachment, the American President is assured four years of tenure. Congressional elections are two years apart. Nomination of candidates is for the most part tightly controlled by political machines whose active workers are motivated less by issues (let alone ideologies) than by patronage rewards for "regularity." Occasional grass roots revolts against local party organizations do take place. But these are only isolated events with little impact on the national political apparatus. Uphill political action requires not only strenuous but also sustained effort *outside* of the average citizen's business or professional involvements. The style and habits of American life are not conducive to such efforts on the part of the general population.

Needless to say, in the Soviet Union even these opportunities do not exist. Consequently, little or nothing can be expected from conventional political action at the grass roots level in the U.S.S.R.

Can policy makers come to their senses? The pocket of resistance in the United States Senate has been mentioned. Starting with opposition to the Vietnam war, some dissenting senators and congressmen have gone on to challenge the entire policy of global containment.[6] At a conference held in March 1969, they gave voice to ideas far beyond the usual arguments of the realists ("a wrong war at a wrong time"). In particular, the thrust of the appeal was to turn attention away from "global strategic problems" in order to focus it on the internal sources of frustrations.

> Eventually, we must recognize that the factors which determine our massive military budget are to be found less abroad than they are here at home. The reason we are able to move a wounded Marine from the jungles of Vietnam to the finest medical care in minutes, yet cannot do the same for a sick child on the Mississippi delta or on an Indian reservation, is very much bound up in our image of ourselves.
>
> Being the greatest power in the world carries not only political and economic implications, but psychological elements which many of us have not yet truthfully faced. We do a great deal to buttress that image of power. Other sacrifices we find harder to make. We are six percent of the world's population using more than sixty percent of its goods and developed resources. We are convinced that the American way of life is the best in the world, that American management and enterprise are the best in the world, and that capitalism is the best tool for development. The result is that our foreign policy is not dictated as much by external threats, as we should like to think, but is an extension of our own economic, political, and social institutions.
>
> The questions we must ask ourselves are not who are the Russians or what are the Chinese or Vietnamese about, but who and what are Americans? If anti-Communism is all we can agree on as a national credo, we will never be able to break the psychosis of force and destruction which is the American tragedy.[7]

Statements of this sort are a novelty in high political strata in the United States. In the fifties they would have sealed the political death warrant of anyone who made them. The breakdown of inhibitions against public statements of this sort certainly bespeaks a change in political climate. One is reminded of Khrushchev's de-Stalinization speech in 1956, also a harbinger of a radical change in the political weather.

In the Soviet Union at that time the question was how far the momentum of de-Stalinization could carry. It carried quite far, but not far enough to break the grip of party bureaucracy on Soviet life, which of course it was not meant to do. In the United States, the revolt in high political strata does not even presage a change of course. It is no more than an echo of popular dissent. It is extremely doubtful whether it will carry any political punch, whether, for example, it can marshal sufficient political support to bring to power people with fresh views on international relations. An even more crucial question is whether, if this were to happen, the new leadership could exercise its power to bring about decisive changes in American foreign policy.

The dissenting senators and congressmen give evidence of understanding the difficulty: the *de jure* political power, as defined in the Constitution, has been replaced by the *de facto* power of the monstrous bureaucratic machine through which the military-industrial complex exercises its hegemony. When John Kennedy, after the Cuban missile crisis, remarked that had he acted less energetically he would certainly have been impeached, he was giving evidence of an awareness of this power. His impeachment would not have been a result of popular pressure on Congress. The pressure would have come from the centers of *de facto* political power.

De facto political power in the United States resides in an elite. At one time it was fashionable to deny its existence. However, evidence of its decisive role in determining the *major outlines* of American policy, both domestic and foreign, is overwhelming. This elite, like its Soviet counterpart, is arrogantly antidemocratic. By democracy I mean here a state of affairs where the policies, domestic and foreign, of states grow out of the aspirations of ordinary people and out of conditions under which ordinary people can become aware of their aspirations through collective political action. Both the American and the Russian Revolutions, and the social orders that they were supposed to establish, were conceived in these terms. Both were eventually subverted by the emergent power elites whose aspirations became incompatible with the needs of ordinary people.

The needs of the overwhelming majority of the world's people are exceedingly simple and highly visible. They revolve around the problems of living out a biologically normal life span, reasonably free from anguish and fear, and assuring the same for the children. In addition, there are certain spiritual needs manifest in all cultures: the need for perceiving an order in the scheme of things, the need for human affection, the need for communion with beauty. Upon closer examination, the apparent diversity of ethical and esthetic values and of conceptions of reality in different cultures and societies does not adumbrate their common origins in psychic needs but merely reflects the different ways in which attempts were made to satisfy these needs.

The aspirations of the power elites are, for the most part, unrelated to the basic needs of the bulk of humanity. The aspirations of the elites develop in the process of consolidating and exercising power. With regard to these activities two observations can be made. First, they are undertaken by people whose biological needs are amply satisfied; second, characteristic human feelings of compassion, loyalty, remorse, etc., must be suppressed in playing the power game, whether in business, in politics, or in war. The outcomes of these games (essentially who is to control what and whom) are of no more relevance to the needs of ordinary people than were the ambitions of the contenders for thrones, titles, and domains, the primitive issues of eighteenth century international politics.

True, in the era of nationalism, large sectors of European publics identified their aspirations with those of the power elites, and this identification is still strong, particularly in the United States where the bulk of the population has not yet experienced directly the ravages of war. However, the parasitic role of the military machine and, above all, its *systemic* origin has become apparent even in the higher political strata to those who have retained a sense of loyalty to the principles on which this republic was founded and which are now being subverted.

> This [military-industrial] complex is not a conspiracy, it is an enormous, self-perpetuating institutional organism. It receives such a disproportionate amount of Federal funds that there is no effective counter-balance to it, and such decisions as those on Vietnam and the ABM are generated from institutional momentum rather than conscious policy decisions.[8]

I do not know whether a direct political analogue to the American industrial-military-research complex exists in the U.S.S.R. One would think not, because all investment of capital is controlled centrally so that greed, the psychological prime mover of big business operations, must manifest itself in other forms. For instance, in the prewar decade of rapid Soviet industrialization, practically all capital investments were in producer goods that produced materials (for example, steel) for more producer goods or machines to make other machines. The population was exhorted to suffer privations by appeals to the needs of defense and promises of prosperity to come. The actual driving force, however, may have been a sort of intoxication with burgeoning industrial power. The erstwhile revolutionaries became tycoons, that is, potentates of a vast industrial complex. Nevertheless, it must be kept in mind that strenuous social effort could be mobilized in Russia as readily (perhaps more so) by invoking the heroics of peaceful construction as by appeals to military security. That is how the Stalinists derived both their actual power and their sense of power from the entire process of industrialization; and there is no reason to attribute special significance to its military sectors. On the contrary, emphasis on peaceful construction provided a genuine ethical prop for the Stalinist regime, both at home and abroad. Peaceful construction was at the time the only concrete manifestation of Communist ideals.

It is more likely that the Soviet military exerts influence on policy by demanding certain conditions as prerequisites for discharging its responsibilities. A case in point is the difference in the treatment accorded to Poland and to Hungary in the anti-Stalinist revolts of 1956. In Poland, the Soviets yielded, and a wave of liberalization swept the country. In Hungary, the anti-Stalinist revolt was crushed. The common explanation is that, whereas in Poland Communists never lost control of the revolt, in Hungary they did. Another possible explanation (which I have from Polish and Soviet sources) is that Hungary borders on a non-Communist state (Austria) while Poland does not; and so the stationing of Soviet troops is seen by the Soviet military to be imperative in Hungary but not in Poland (troops in East Germany can defend Poland from an attack by NATO). Perhaps this factor was also decisive in Czechoslovakia which borders on West Germany. A "political explanation" of the crushing of the Czechoslovak revolt (the Soviet version of the domino theory) need not be dismissed on that account, however.

There is little doubt that the Soviet military, like its American counterparts, exerts pressures on the Soviet position in disarmament negotiations. With the best intentions, it is immensely difficult for any professional group to adopt views that diminish the significance of their profession. The military man, like any other professional, constantly seeks and finds ways of bolstering the importance of his social role.

The militarist's principal political weapon for making himself indispensable is fear:

> It is fear that gave [the bureaucracy] this enormous power and autonomy in the 1950's and early 1960's. This fear caused us to consolidate and delegate power—in effect to say, "Here, we will give you all the money you can use, all the authority you need, and you deal with the danger of the Soviet Union and the Communist world."
>
> It is interesting proof of the role of fear that the Secretary of Defense [Laird], when he was up here talking about the ABM, when he was seeking approval of the so-called "Safeguard" system, immediately resorted to the tactic of trying to scare the hell out of everybody. I think one can say of the Secretary of Defense that he is a man who fully learns his business.[9]

One can well imagine similar ploys used by Soviet marshals and generals to cut the ground from under the opposition (of which there is evidence) to the invasion of Czechoslovakia in the highest political organs of the U.S.S.R. The military may have described to them all the dire consequences of allowing Czechoslovakia to go "soft." Appeals to "hard realities," dismissal of sentiments—in short, bringing into focus a "man's world," the world of the power struggle, usually wins the day in the decision-making bodies of great powers. In this way the needs and aspirations of ordinary people, in particular of women and children who are least of all concerned with distributions of global power, strategic advantages, and the rest of the baggage of "realistic" foreign policies, are given weight zero in the deliberations of policy makers.

Three-fourths of the people on earth are hungry, and two-thirds are women and small children. The gap between these people and those who wield power of life and death over them remains abysmal for all the revolutions and "social progress" of the past two centuries. The gap is as wide today as it was in the eighteenth century when men were sent to kill and to be killed to "decide" the legitimacy of the successor to the

Spanish throne. The only difference is that then the gap was perceived only locally, between lord and serf; now it is perceived globally. Chinese revolutionary rhetoric, for all its bombastic nonsense, comes closest to providing an understanding of the immensity of the gap.

We are now witnessing a revolt against the Old Order. Its thrust is directed not along the clogged channels of normal political process but at the social foundations of the order—at the elites whose power stems neither from divine nor constitutional authority but simply from the dynamics of power accumulation—a system process. The revolt amounts to a denial of the legitimacy of this power and to the regimes that wield it.

We do not know in what forms the revolt will be manifested. It is not likely that in the West the issue will be decided by "classical" armed uprisings (although these may well occur sporadically). Actually, even the revolt against the *ancien régime* in France (and subsequently in all of Europe) was not defined by the storming of the Bastille. It was defined rather by the disintegration of loyalty to the Old Order in the minds and hearts of the people. In the revolt of the young in the West, we may be witnessing the same phenomenon. The war-waging state no longer commands loyalty. Tear gas, tanks, and improved tactics of riot control will disperse demonstrations but they will not restore loyalty. A similar revolt is incubating in the Soviet Empire. Neither the tired old phrases nor the secret police will restore in the minds of the people the infallibility of their leaders.

The historical meaning of the revolts within their empires is still not apparent to the American and Soviet power elites. The American policy makers, however, are becoming aware of their helplessness against the armed revolts of hungry lands. Can we hope that the successors of Clausewitz worthy of the title will draw the appropriate analogy from their master's explanation of how the untrained citizen army of France was able to beat the precise Prussian war machine? Will they then explain how it happened that pajama-clad "gooks" were able to frustrate the modern version of military perfection? Will they go where Clausewitz refused to tread, delve into the psychology of power, and show how the rice peasants drove the leaders of the most powerful state in the world to such a frenzy that they forgot the master's impregnable principle (war is a *political* instrument) just after they learned it?

Will the Soviet disciples of Clausewitz understand the new type of people-war waged by the "nonresisting" Czechs against their "protectors"? If so, will they see a new factor emerging in global politics that will, at long last, make the master's theories as obsolete as Frederick's marching orders of battle?

Our question "Will the policy makers come to their senses?" is not really relevant to these more searching questions. "To come to one's senses" means to take more cognizance of reality (as in regaining consciousness). But so-called reality is invariably perceived in a given framework of concepts and categories. As long as the concepts and categories of the policy makers remain the same, all that can be expected of them, should they "come to their senses," is attempts to find more effective means to achieve their own goals or, at best, to make these goals somewhat more "realistic" by taking into account the constraints under which they must be pursued. The infusion of "realism" into American foreign policy means little more than circumscribing the portion of the world over which United States political, cultural, and economic hegemony can be established without incurring unacceptable risks. Likewise, when Soviet leaders "came to their senses" and removed the excesses of Stalinist terror in the Soviet Union, they undertook these measures with a view of reestablishing confidence in the leadership of the Communist party and of revitalizing the economy. Whatever further pressures for "liberalization" exist with the Soviet establishment are similarly motivated. In both cases the elites "come to their senses" only to the extent of removing the immediate dangers to their continued role as elites.

The more searching questions raised do not concern a better awareness of reality within the old frameworks of thought. They concern fundamental changes of perception. Such changes cannot be expected of the elites, because radically changed perceptions would destroy the ideological basis of the elites' social role. Of course individual perceptions sometimes change, even, as we have seen, within the ranks of the elites. In 1968 an entire ruling group, the bulk of the Czechoslovakian Communist party, gave evidence of a radical change of perception when it attempted to redefine the meaning of Communist leadership, that is, the role of the Communist party in a Communist state. If this revolution of perception had succeeded, it would have constituted an unprecedented case: a liquidation of centralized power initiated by the elite itself. What was demonstrated, however, was that the rulers of Czechoslovakia ruled only with Moscow's permission. In the eyes of their masters, they failed to discharge their duty as local representatives of central power and were, in effect, dismissed.

In the United States, changes in perception demonstrated by some politically prominent persons still do not threaten entrenched power. There is no way of knowing how the power elite will protect its prerogatives when and if these prerogatives are seriously menaced by erosion from within.

In contrast to the perceptions of the elites, strongly immunized to change by their very social role, perceptions in the populations are undergoing deep and pervasive changes. Historically such changes have been the most far-reaching. They are irreversible and end up by destroying habits of thought and behavior on which the exercise of power over the populations depends. It is, however, much too early to identify these changes in perception with a nascent world revolution. The rebels, the dissidents, and the alienated have no common ideology (such as Marxism had been for the revolutionary sector of the European labor movement), no common leadership (such as the Communists had between the two world wars). They do not even have a concrete common grievance. The Latin-American peasant is rebelling against economic bondage. The Southeast Asian guerrilla is fighting against a murderous war machine devastating his country. The dissident Soviet intellectual feels most keenly the stifling enforcement of orthodoxy in the spiritual life of his country. In the United States, the alienated youth and intelligensia do not have even the grim satisfaction of defying officially imposed orthodoxy. Instead they must suffer the frustration of enjoying intellectual and political freedom which, however it is exercised, remains ineffectual against the arrogance and mendacity of the ruling elite. In their despair the angry young are driven to "direct action," as are the Blacks who have turned their backs on "integration." Neither the immediate

nor the ultimate consequences of all this ferment (agrarian revolts, guerrilla warfare, dissidence and alienation of the intellectuals, student and minority uproars) can be foreseen. Only one
common by-product is discernible: a universal disruption of the
mechanisms of rule, what the rulers call "law and order." The
weaponry of the rulers is defied; their shibboleths are scorned.
Never before have the mighty of the earth been for so many
people objects of contempt.

We might suppose, therefore, that we are witnessing another
collapse of an *ancien régime,* and the thought may be a source
of satisfaction to those who have lost faith in the efficacy of
"normal political processes" and of routine reforms. Some, including the Chinese leadership (on the face of their rhetoric),
seem to welcome even the prospect of World War III, which
they expect to be a catalyst of a Leninist world revolution.
There is no reason, however, to suppose that these prognoses
will be realized any more than those of the U.S. nuclear strategists who make glib calculations of "rates of recovery" after
nuclear holocausts of different magnitudes. We simply do not
know what will happen in conditions without meaningful prece-
dents and all attempts to draw historical analogies between a
nuclear-biological world war and earlier upheavals or disasters
are likely to be profoundly misleading. Already the first two
world wars initiated processes totally unforeseen by either the
erstwhile power elites or the revolutionaries of the time. A holocaust exceeding its forerunners by several orders of magnitude
may introduce systemic (including mass-psychological) disloca-
tions that will make all current social doctrines as irrelevant to
the resulting human condition as medieval eschatological doctrines are to the present.

Shortly after World War II, Stringfellow Barr[10] suggested
that, even though the United States and the Soviet Union
emerged as the most powerful states in the world, it is well to
keep in mind that most people do not live in either of them. It
is true that the combined populations of The Two comprise no
more than fifteen percent of the world's population. And it is
true that resistance against U.S. imperialism is stiffening and
that Soviet orthodoxy is rapidly losing its ideological grip. None-
theless the absolute power of life and death over everyone on

this planet that is vested in the Soviet-American elites cannot be ignored. The mobilization of this power does not depend on the fervor or the loyalty of populations (as did ordinary military power of only a generation ago). The present genocidal power can be mobilized by a few words of command by either of The Two. And it makes little difference whether this power is used in a paroxysm of mutual destruction (as has been hitherto feared by both Russians and Americans) or in collusion against the rest of the world (as much of the rest of the world is beginning to fear). The very existence of that power is a threat to humanity.

This threat must be dealt with quite apart from the other dangers to humanity that it overshadows: overpopulation, chronic poverty, pollution, depletion of resources, etc. Regardless of the steadily eroding authority of the contemporary descendants of absolute monarchs, the fact remains that the global infernal machine is under their complete control. Somehow they must be restrained from activating it. And since they are impervious to any arguments except those related to their prime concerns (relative destructive potentials of the war machines, dangers of accidental wars, possibly at times the long-range economically debilitating effects of an unlimited race for military supremacy), the help of the "moderates" and the "realists" within the power elites must be enlisted. Even the expertise of the military (irrelevant as it is to collective human needs) has a place in this immediate task, which is like the task of dismantling a time bomb without exploding it.

In particular, the importance of makeshift arrangements by The Two, such as the Nonproliferation Treaty aimed at preventing the terror weapons from falling into "unreliable hands," must not be minimized. While the measures are pitifully insufficient, they are indispensable. The Third World contains not only the innocent victims, past and future, of The Two but also their leaders. Whatever these leaders were while they led liberation struggles, when they become policy makers of states, they begin to think and act like them. A case in point is the militarization of India, the land of Gandhi, where pressure for acquisition of nuclear weapons is mounting. Indian leaders have so far staunchly pursued a nonalignment policy. India and China together could have become a mighty voice of the dispossessed demanding an end to the psychopathic games of the rich. Apparently it seemed more important to the Chinese leaders to undermine India's influence in the Third World and so make an enemy of India. Ironically, it is the Chinese already in possession of nuclear weapons who denounce the Nonproliferation Treaty that may deny these weapons to their "enemy." Such is the perverse logic of condemming everything that originates in the enemy's camp.

The leaders of the Third World emulate those of the Great Powers and learn from them. As they adopt the entire baggage of diplomilitary "realism," they may embark on the same policies that as revolutionary leaders they had rightfully condemned. And so World War III may start between India and China, or between India and Pakistan, or between Israel and Egypt, or in Balkanized Africa. So far such outbreaks in the Third World have been reduced to smoldering by a tacit collusion of The Two, but the danger of embroiling the nuclear powers is always there and will increase as the new nations "mature," i.e., become more militarized. The responsibility for this morbid "development" of underdeveloped countries can be put squarely on The Two from whom the poor learn, to whose status as "powers" they aspire, and by whom they are armed.

For these reasons, even if a world revolutionary movement against entrenched power becomes a political reality, it cannot simply evoke a plague on both houses on the strength of the insight that the "national interests" of both are destructive to the needs of man. It cannot dismiss expertise in conventional international relations on the grounds that obsolete political techniques are powerless in the face of the dangers that threaten humanity. Revolutionary leaders must never forget that the inhabitants of the entire world are still completely at the mercy of the two military establishments, not only physically but also spiritually. Consequently Soviet-American relations, irrelevant as they are in themselves to the substantive world issues, will nevertheless determine whether these issues can ever be faced at all.

NOTES

Chapter 2

1. Lewis F. Richardson, *Arms and Insecurity* (Chicago: Quadrangle Books; Pittsburgh: The Boxwood Press, 1960).
2. *Leninsky Sbornik* (a serial publication), Moscow-Leningrad: Institut Lenina, 1924–, vol. XII, pp. 389–452.
3. Isaac Deutscher makes a point of the fact that before World War II Stalin denounced "spheres of influence" as a product of a "nationalist frame of mind . . . which aims at doing away with the foreign policy of the October Revolution." After the war "spheres of influence" became the basis of Stalin's foreign policy. Cf. Isaac Deutscher, *Stalin, A Political Biography* (New York and London: Oxford University Press, 1949), pp. 412–13.

Chapter 3

1. Notably Henry A. Kissinger, at this writing special adviser to the President of the United States. See his series of articles in *Foreign Affairs:* "Reflections on American Diplomacy," October 1956, vol. 35, no. 1; "Strategy and Organization," April 1957, vol. 35, no. 3; "Missiles and the Western Alliance," April 1958, vol. 36, no. 3; also *Nuclear Weapons and Foreign Policy* (New York: Harper, 1957; Oxford University Press, 1957).
2. Quoted in *Makers of Modern Strategy*, Edward Mead Earle, ed. (Princeton, N.J.: Princeton University Press, 1952), p. 56.
3. *Ibid.*, p. 55.
4. Karl von Clausewitz, *On War* (New York: Barnes and Noble, 1966), vol. I, p. 2.
5. Karl Schwartz, *Leben des Generals Karl von Clausewitz und der Maria von Clausewitz* (Berlin: Fred Dümmlers Verlag, 1878), p. 219 (my translation—A.R.).
6. *Ibid.*, p. 226 (my translation—A.R.). The forthcoming battle was at Jena, where Prussia suffered a disastrous defeat.
7. Examples: Browning's "Incident of the French Camp," Lermontov's "Borodino," Tennyson's "Charge of the Light Brigade."
8. Clausewitz, *op. cit.*, vol. II, pp. 341–42.
9. During Napoleon's invasion of Russia, Clausewitz was at first adjutant to General Phull, a Prussian in the service of Russia, later a member of General Pahlen's staff at Vitebsk and Smolensk.

Chapter 4

1. Reginald Horsman, *The Causes of the War of 1812* (Philadelphia: University of Pennsylvania Press, 1962).
2. *Ibid.*, p. 266.
3. Amaury de Riencourt, *The American Empire* (New York: The Dial Press, 1968), pp. 13–14.
4. Horsman, *op. cit.*, p. 267. "Orders in Council" were in effect a blockade of Europe and a system of embargoes which were England's answer to Napoleon's continental system, that is, a measure in the economic war between England and France.
5. R. W. Van Alstyne, *The Rising American Empire* (Oxford: Basil Blackwell, 1960), p. 69.
6. Samuel E. Morrison and Henry S. Commager, *The Growth of the American Republic* (New York: Oxford University Press, 1950), vol. 2, p. 325.
7. *Ibid.*, p. 315.
8. Senator Albert J. Beveridge of Indiana, quoted in Van Alstyne, *op. cit.*, p. 187. Source: R. J. Bartlett, *The Record of American Diplomacy*, 3rd ed. (New York: Knopf, 1956), pp. 385–88.
9. In our own day, the theme is echoed in *The Ugly American*, a novel by William J. Lederer and Eugene Burdick (New York: W. W. Norton, 1958). The action is in a southeast Asian country. Through ignorance, arrogance, or indifference of its emissaries, the United States is "losing the country to the Communists." Here and there individual Americans succeed in winning the admiration and loyalty of the natives by treating them "as equals" and, above all, by introducing modest but practical technical innovations which yield immediate and locally visible payoffs. (Example: long handles on brooms that eliminate the bent backs of the aged.)
10. The traditional American outlook on war is clearly described in Robert W. Tucker, *The Just War. Exposition of American Concept* (Baltimore: The Johns Hopkins Press, 1960; New York: Oxford University Press, 1961).
11. Cf. F. von Bernhardi, *Germany and the Next War* (New York: Longmans, Green, 1914), pp. 18–28.
12. Walter Lippmann, *U.S. Foreign Policy, Shield of the Republic* (New York: Pocket Books, Inc., 1943), p. 6.
13. Cf. Alfred T. Mahan, *The Interest of America in Sea Power, Present and Future* (Boston: Little, Brown and Co., 1898).
14. Lippmann, *op. cit.*, p. 21.
15. *Ibid.*, p. 105.
16. *Ibid.*, p. 106.
17. *Ibid.*, p. 115.
18. *Ibid.*, p. 116.
19. *Ibid.*

20. B. Ts. Urlanis, *Voiny i Narodoselenie Evropy (Wars and the European Populations)* (Moscow: Izdatelstro Sotsialno-ekonomicheskoi Literatury, 1960), pp. 8–9.

21. The Zinoviev Letter was purported to contain instructions to the British Communist party on the conduct of Communist propaganda in the British armed forces.

22. Quoted in Adam B. Ulam, *Expansion and Co-existence. The History of Soviet Foreign Policy 1917–1967* (New York: Frederick A. Praeger, 1968), p. 213. Source: *Soviet Documents on Foreign Policy, III, 1933–41,* Jane Degras, ed. (London and New York, 1953), p. 36.

23. *Ibid.,* p. 181. Source: Degras, *op. cit.,* II, p. 243.

24. The end of the Soviet policy of collective security is often associated with the Munich Pact (September 1938), concluded by Germany, Italy, Britain, and France without the participation of either Czechoslovakia or the Soviet Union. Czechoslovakia was forced to cede the Sudeten territories to Germany, a prelude to her subjugation by Hitler six months later.

25. Ulam, *op. cit.,* p. 570.

26. H. S. Dinerstein, *War and the Soviet Union* (New York: Frederick A. Praeger, 1959).

27. Alexander Solzhenitzyn describes how an experienced Soviet bureaucrat reads a newspaper which to him has come to mean not so much a source of news as an intricate, subtle code. In this code (the arrangement of the articles, the turns of phrase, the choice of words, the order in which officials are named) the bureaucrat senses the slightest shifts in the political wind and readjusts both his professional and social behavior accordingly. Alexander Solzhenitzyn, *The Cancer Ward* (New York: Bantam Books, 1969), p. 207. For an extensive study of Kremlinology, see Michel Tatu, *Power in the Kremlin. From Khrushchev to Kosygin* (New York: The Viking Press, 1969).

28. A. V. Kirsanov, *S. Sh. A. i Zapadnaya Evropa (U.S.A. and Western Europe)* (Moscow: Mezhdunarodnyie Otnoshenia, 1967).

29. Example: Ralph K. White, "Misperceptions and the Vietnam War," *The Journal of Social Issues,* July, 1966, vol. 22, no. 3.

30. Example: C. Wright Mills, *The Causes of World War III* (New York: Ballantine Books, 1958, 1960).

31. Examples: Philip Noel-Baker, *The Arms Race* (New York: Oceana Publications, 1958); J. David Singer, *Deterrence, Arms Control, and Disarmament* (Ohio State University Press, 1962), chap. 7; and "Feedback in International Conflict: Self-Correcting and Otherwise," in *Essays in Honor of Ludwig von Bertalanffy,* Ronald G. Jones, ed. (New York: George Braziller, Inc., in press).

32. See Charles A. Beard, *The Economic Basis of Politics and Related Writings,* compiled and annotated by William Beard (New York: Random House, Vintage Book V-42, 1957).

33. William Appleman Williams, *Roots of the Modern American Empire* (New York: Random House, 1969).
34. Lloyd C. Gardner, *Economic Aspects of New Deal Diplomacy* (Madison: University of Wisconsin Press, 1964).
35. Gabriel Kolko, *The Politics of War. The World and United States Foreign Policy, 1943–45* (New York: Random House, 1968).
36. Gabriel Kolko, *The Roots of American Foreign Policy* (Boston: Beacon Press, 1969).
37. *Ibid.*, p. 55.
38. *Ibid.*, pp. 60–61.
39. Kolko, *op. cit.* (*The Politics of War*), p. 624.
40. *Ibid.*, p. 626.

Chapter 5

1. The severe criticism leveled against Simonov's and Fadeyev's plays about Russian guerrillas behind German lines in World War II is revealing. The gist of the criticism was that the guerrillas were portrayed as improvising amateurs, lacking the organizational precision characteristic of "true Communists." In particular, Fadeyev was taken to task for having failed to point out that "in reality" the guerrillas were directed by the party, that is, essentially from Moscow. Alexander Werth, *Russia at War, 1941–1945* (New York: Avon Books, 1965), p. 387, ftnt.
2. *Ibid.*, p. 937.
3. In a conversation with the actor Nikolai Cherkasov, who was to portray Ivan the Terrible on the screen, Stalin expressed two reservations with regard to Ivan's character and policy. One was that the czar periodically succumbed to remorse following his blood baths (a weakness); the other was that he did not complete the extermination of Russia's noble families. (Personal communication from an acquaintance of Cherkasov.)
4. Adam B. Ulam, *Expansion and Co-existence. The History of Soviet Foreign Policy 1917–1967* (New York: Frederick A. Praeger, 1968), p. 297.
5. After World War I, the group of Eastern European states allied with France were referred to by anti-Communist statesmen as the *cordon sanitaire*, that is, a barrier against Bolshevik infection.
6. Molotov's speech, October 31, 1939, quoted in Werth, *op. cit.*, p. 84.
7. Stalin "wrote off" the Chinese Communists on several occasions. In particular, during World War II he promised to back Chiang Kai-shek as the only "sufficiently strong" leader of China. Cf. Robert E. Sherwood, *Roosevelt and Hopkins. An Intimate History*, rev. ed., (New York: Harper and Bros., 1950), p. 902. On another occasion, Molotov declared that the Soviet Union was not interested in

the Chinese Communists, "who were not really Communists at all": Edward R. Stettinius, *Roosevelt and the Russians* (Garden City, N.Y.: Doubleday, 1949), p. 20.

Accounts of Stalin's apprehensions of the revolutionary movements in Western Europe at the close of World War II appear in several sources, e.g., in Gabriel Kolko, *The Politics of War* (New York: Random House, 1968), chap. 17.

Stalin's decision to "liquidate" the Greek revolutionary movement is reported in Milovan Djilas, *Conversations with Stalin* (New York: Harcourt, Brace & World, 1962), p. 181.

The shooting of nearly the entire Central Committee of the Polish Communist party is mentioned in Isaac Deutscher, *Stalin, A Political Biography* (New York and London: Oxford University Press, 1949), p. 380, ftnt.

Chapter 6

1. Herbert Feis, *Between War and Peace: The Potsdam Conference* (Princeton, N.J.: Princeton University Press, 1960).
2. *Ibid.*, p. 73.
3. *Ibid.*, p. 77.
4. Herbert Feis, *Churchill, Roosevelt, Stalin,* 2nd ed. (Princeton, N.J.: Princeton University Press, 1967), p. 599.
5. H. Stuart Hughes, "The Second Year of the Cold War. A Memoir and an Anticipation," *Commentary*, August 1969.
6. *Ibid.*, p. 28.
7. *Ibid.*, p. 29.
8. Gar Alperovitz, *Atomic Diplomacy: Hiroshima and Potsdam* (New York: Random House, Vintage Books, 1967).
9. Letter to Cecil Lyon, May 2, 1945, quoted in Joseph Clark Grew, *Turbulent Era* (Boston: Houghton Mifflin, 1952), vol. 2, p. 1485 ftnt
10. *Ibid.*, p. 1446.
11. Quoted in *New York Times,* June 24, 1941.
12. This extraordinary exchange was reported by Harry S. Truman himself in *Memoirs, Vol. I: Year of Decision* (Garden City, N.Y.: Doubleday, 1955), p. 82.
13. Stimson's serious reservations against the Truman-Byrnes version of atomic diplomacy are revealed in a letter and a memorandum to Truman, dated September 11, 1945. Both are published in Appendix III of Alperovitz, *op. cit.*
14. Alperovitz, *op. cit.*, p. 101. Source: J. Stalin, *Stalin's Correspondence with Churchill, Atlee, Roosevelt and Truman, 1941–45* (Moscow, 1957).
15. Quoted by Carl Oglesby in "Vietnam: This Is Guernica," *The Nation,* June 5, 1967, vol. 204, p. 720.

16. Feis, *op. cit.* (*Between War and Peace*), p. 179.
17. *Ibid.*, p. 179.
18. See, for example, Norman Cousins and Thomas K. Finletter, "Why Did We Drop the Atomic Bomb?" in *The Shaping of American Diplomacy, Vol. 2, 1950–55*, William Appleman Williams, ed. (Chicago: Rand McNally and Company, 1951, 1963).
19. Quoted in Alperovitz, *op. cit.*, p. 199.
20. Alexander Werth, *Russia at War, 1941–1945* (New York: Avon Books, 1965), pp. 849–50.

Chapter 7

1. How Stalin thought about the future of Germany is much more difficult to infer. This question will be touched upon in Chapter 8.
2. Gar Alperovitz, *Atomic Diplomacy: Hiroshima and Potsdam* (New York: Random House, Vintage Books, 1967), p. 139. Sources: *Foreign Relations: Conference of Berlin (Potsdam) 1945* (Washington: U.S. Government Printing Office, 1960), vol. I, pp. 367, 369–70, vol. II, p. 729; *Central and South East Europe, 1945–48*, R. R. Betts, ed. (Liverpool: Royal Institute of International Affairs, 1950), p. 29, 207.
3. Winston S. Churchill, *The Second World War* (London: Cassell & Co., 1954), vol. VI, p. 198.
4. H. S. Dinerstein, *War and the Soviet Union* (New York: Frederick A. Praeger, 1959), p. 174.
5. The leading Soviet journal of military theory. Raymond L. Garthoff states that it is one of several Soviet security-classified sources: *Soviet Strategy in the Nuclear Age* (New York: Frederick A. Praeger, 1958), p. 270.
6. From an article by P. A. Rotmistrov in *Voyennaya Mysl*, March 1955; quoted in Dinerstein, *op. cit.*, pp. 171–72.
7. *Military Strategy: Soviet Doctrine and Concepts*, Marshall V. D. Sokolovsky, ed. (New York: Frederick A. Praeger, 1963), p. 198.
8. P. A. Rotmistrov, "On the Role of Surprise in Contemporary War," *Voyennaya Mysl*, February 1955; quoted in Dinerstein, *op. cit.*, p. 187.
9. Sokolovsky, *op. cit.*, Preface.
10. Among the authors who give accounts of the clash over Eastern Europe, there is general agreement that the issue of Poland overshadowed those of other East European countries. Aside from the strategic importance of the invasion routes through Poland, Stalin probably had reason to fear a future hostile regime in Poland more than anywhere else. Russia had been a partner in four partitions of Poland. Like the earlier partitions, the last was justified by declaring the Polish state to be an unviable monstrosity (cf. Molotov's remark, p. 79).
11. X, "The Sources of Soviet Conduct," *Foreign Affairs*, July 1947.

12. F. C. Schwartz, *You Can Trust the Communists (To be Communists)* (Englewood Cliffs, N.J.: Prentice-Hall, 1960).
13. *Ibid.*
14. Archibald MacLeish, "The Conquest of America," *The Atlantic Monthly*, August 1949.
15. Quoted in Walter and Miriam Schneir, *Invitiation to an Inquest* (Garden City, N.Y.: Doubleday, 1965), p. 170.
16. Letter from Stalin to Churchill, February 16, 1943; quoted in Winston Churchill, *The Hinge of Fate* (Boston: Houghton Mifflin, 1950), p. 745.
17. According to Alexander Werth, who spent the war years in the Soviet Union, the ill feeling against the Allies for failing to open the second front was most intense in the summer of 1942, the time of the Germans' deepest penetration. Following Stalingrad, the mood changed to one of resignation mixed with a growing pride kindled by the victories that the Red Army was achieving "unaided." Alexander Werth, *Russia at War, 1941–1945*, Part Four, "The Black Summer of 1942," and Part Six, "1943: Year of Hard Victories" (New York: Avon Books, 1965).
18. Frederick C. Barghoorn, *The Soviet Image of the United States: A Study in Distortion* (New York: Harcourt, Brace, 1950).
19. *The Situation in Biological Science*, Proceedings of the Lenin Academy of Agricultural Sciences of the U.S.S.R., Session July 31–August 7, 1948 (Moscow: Foreign Languages Publishing House), p. 602.
20. The Russian word *razgrom* (with the same root as *pogrom*) means violent destruction, as of an enemy force. In the purge of the late forties, the word was freely used to describe (with approval) the liquidation of university departments, research institutes, etc., allegedly corrupted by "alien ideas"—a sort of orgy of intellectual lynchings. The similarity to "de-Jewification" *(Entjudung)* in Germany in the 1930s was striking.
21. *Voprosy Sovremionnoi Fiziki (Problems of Modern Physics)* (Moscow: Izdatelstvo Akademii Nauk SSSR, 1952).

Chapter 8

1. Raymond Aron, *Peace and War. A Theory of International Relations* (Garden City, N.Y.: Doubleday, 1966).
2. Milovan Djilas, *Conversations with Stalin* (New York: Harcourt, Brace & World, 1962), p. 153.
3. *Ibid.*, p. 153.
4. James V. Forrestal, U.S. Secretary of Defense (1947–1949), finally became obsessed by the notion of a Communist invasion of the United States. He committed suicide during a psychotic episode in 1949.

5. Adam B. Ulam, *Expansion and Co-existence. The History of Soviet Foreign Policy 1917–1967* (New York: Frederick A. Praeger, 1968), p. 535.

6. Aron, *op. cit.*, pp. 672–73.

7. The Rapacki Plan, proposed in 1957 by the Polish foreign minister (naturally with the support of the Soviet Union), provided for a "denuclearized zone" to include both Germanies, Poland, and Czechoslovakia, that is, a prohibition against manufacture and stockpiling of nuclear weapons in those regions. The plan was rejected by Americans on the grounds that it would make it impossible to supply West Germany with tactical nuclear weapons and so would give a military edge to the Russians.

Chapter 9

1. A view of the consequences of capitalist economic penetration to the populations of underdeveloped nations is cited by Noam Chomsky in his *American Power and the New Mandarins* (New York: Random House, Vintage Book V-555, 1969), p. 135, in this statement by H. D. Malaviya, speaking of India: "The systematic destruction of Indian manufacturers; the creation of the Zemidari [landed aristocracy] and its parasitical outgrowths; the changes in agrarian structure; the financial losses incurred by tribute; the sharp transition from a pre-monetised economy to one governed by the international price mechanism—these were some of the social and institutional forces that were to bring the apocalypse of death and famine to millions—with few or no compensatory benefits to the ryot [peasant]." Source: F. Clairmonte, *Economic Liberalism and Underdevelopment* (Bombay and London: Asia Publishing House, 1960).

2. Owen Lattimore, *The Situation in Asia* (Boston: Little, Brown and Co., 1949).

3. Gen. Joseph W. Stilwell, *The Stilwell Papers* (New York: William Sloan Associates, 1948).

4. John Foster Dulles, Speech before the Council on Foreign Relations, New York, January 12, 1954. Published in *Readings in American Foreign Policy*, American Foundation for Political Education, 1952–55, vol. 2, p. 188.

5. Press and Radio News Conference, Washington, March 16, 1954. *Ibid.*, p. 190.

Chapter 10

1. Here it is important to note the developments in strategic thinking as the strategists became acclimatized to the idea of nuclear war, or, better said, as people who took the idea of nuclear war in stride joined the strategic community. The neo-Clausewitzians among them thought in terms of extending Clausewitz's ideas to

encompass the new developments, that is, of enriching the "art of war" with nuclear diplomilitary strategy. Herman Kahn, an outstanding representative of this school, opposed the notion that a nuclear war would necessarily be a "spasm war" of short duration. He argued that even in a nuclear war fought with intercontinental missiles there would be many opportunities for strategic refinements, for control of its intensity, and even for a continuation of diplomatic dialogue, essentially bargaining, blackmail, etc. Cf. Herman Kahn, *On Thermonuclear War* (Princeton, N.J.: Princeton University Press, 1960); *Thinking about the Unthinkable* (New York: Horizon Press, 1962); *On Escalation. Metaphors and Scenarios* (New York, Washington: Frederick A. Praeger, 1965).

2. Cf., for example, *Science and Citizen,* a publication of the St. Louis Citizens Committee for Nuclear Information (CNI), St. Louis, Mo.

Chapter 11

1. U.S. Senate Committee on the Judiciary, *The Pugwash Conferences,* a staff analysis prepared for the Subcommittee To Investigate the Administration of the Internal Security Act and Other Internal Security Laws (Washington: U.S. Government Printing Office, 1961).
2. The grotesquerie of the anatomical figuration, I declare, was not contrived; by accident it turns out to be horribly appropriate.
3. Thomas C. Schelling, "The Strategy of Conflict: Prospectus for a Reorientation of Game Theory," *The Journal of Conflict Resolution,* 1958, vol. 2, no. 3, pp. 203–64.
4. Cf. *Military Strategy: Soviet Doctrine and Concepts,* V. D. Sokolovsky, ed. (New York: Frederick A. Praeger, 1963), pp. 42–50.
5. The meeting between Kosygin and Johnson in New Jersey (1967) against the background of the Vietnam war was an occasion for an exchange of pleasantries and apparently nothing else.

Chapter 12

1. The practice of extorting "creativity" by terror is the principal theme of Alexander Solzhenitzyn's novel *The First Circle* (New York: Harper & Row, 1968).
2. Herman Kahn, *On Escalation. Metaphors and Scenarios* (New York, Washington: Frederick A. Praeger, 1965), p. 11.
3. As Nixon put it, "I was in the position of a fighter with one hand tied behind my back." Richard M. Nixon, *Six Crises* (Garden City, N.Y.: Doubleday, 1962), p. 352.
4. Robert F. Kennedy, *Thirteen Days, A Memoir of the Cuban Missile Crisis* (New York: W. W. Norton, 1969).

5. Address by President Kennedy, October 22, 1962; in Robert F. Kennedy, *op. cit.*, p. 171.
6. *Ibid.*, p. 199.
7. *Ibid.*, p. 118.
8. *Ibid.*, p. 119.

Chapter 13

1. John S. Pustay, *Counter-insurgency Warfare* (New York: The Free Press of Glencoe, 1965).
2. Robert Kennedy, *Thirteen Days, A Memoir of the Cuban Missile Crisis* (New York: W. W. Norton, 1969), p. 51.
3. In his book, *The Arrogance of Power* (New York: Random House, Vintage, 1966), Senator Fulbright sharply attacks the policy of establishing U.S. hegemony over global politics.
4. Kennedy, *op. cit.*, p. 54.
5. Speech by President Kennedy at the American University, Washington, D.C., June 10, 1963; quoted in Alexander Werth, *Russia at War, 1941–1945* (New York: Avon Books, 1965), Introduction, p. xv.
6. As quoted in Werth, *op. cit.*, Introduction, p. xvi.
7. During the moon journey of the U.S. astronauts in July 1969, political commentators in Europe recalled that the Apollo program was initiated a few days after the Bay of Pigs fiasco. The race to the moon, they pointed out, was a deliberate attempt to "reestablish the prestige" of the United States. The flag-waving demonstration in the Houston Control Center at the conclusion of the journey offered a dramatic confirmation of this aspect of the space program.
8. Charles E. Osgood, *Alternative to War and Surrender* (Urbana, Ill.: University of Illinois Press, 1962).
9. Quoted in David Schoenbrun, *Vietnam: How We Got In, How To Get Out* (New York: Atheneum, 1968), p. 41.
10. According to an account by Jonathan Randal *(New York Times,* June 11, 1967) cited by Noam Chomsky, *American Power and the New Mandarins* (New York: Random House, Vintage Book V-555, 1969), ftnt. 25, p. 130, "only one officer [among South Vietnam's military leaders] above the rank of lieutenant colonel did not serve in the French army against the Vietminh in the French–Indo China war."
11. *Teach-in U.S.A. Reports, Opinions, Documents,* Louis Menashe and Ronald Radosh, eds. (New York: Frederick A. Praeger, 1967).
12. "United States Policy in Viet-Nam," Bureau of Public Affairs, Department of State, Foreign Affairs Outline (Washington: U.S. Government Printing Office, May 1964), no. 6, p. 4.
13. "Aggression from the North, the Record of North Viet-Nam's Campaign to Conquer South Viet-Nam," Department of State

Publication 7839, Far Eastern Series 130, Office of Media Services, Bureau of Public Affairs (Washington: U.S. Government Printing Office, February 1965), pp. 6–10.

14. *Ibid.*, p. 19.
15. Cf. *Congressional Record*, Senator Morse, September 23, 1965; Senator Hartke, June 30, 1966; Senator McGovern, April 25, 1967; Senator Fulbright, December 8, 1967.
16. Possibly the Senator means 1962 (the Cuban missile crisis).
17. *Report on the U.S. Senate Hearings—The Truth About Vietnam*, Frank M. Robinson and Earl Kemp, eds. (San Diego, Calif.: Greenleaf Classics, 1966), p. 200.
18. *Ibid.*, p. 202.
19. Andrei Sakharov, *Progress, Co-existence, and Intellectual Freedom* (New York: W. W. Norton, 1968).

Chapter 14

1. Chapter 1 of Raymond Aron's *Peace and War, A Theory of International Relations* (Garden City, N.Y.: Doubleday, 1966; London: Weidenfeld & Nicholson, 1967) begins with the quotation from Clausewitz cited on p. 31 of this book. However, the amoral symmetry of Clausewitzian conception of international relations is abandoned. "The West tends to recognize, albeit unconsciously, the primacy of peace; also faced with a conflict, it looks for a peaceful solution or settlement. . . . If the Soviets renounce the destruction of the West, the West will gladly let them live as they wish. . . . The Soviets, on the other hand, cannot even conceive of what a peace without victory might be" (pp. 672–73). Of course the mirror image of this perception is readily found in Soviet writings, e.g., *Military Strategy: Soviet Doctrine and Concepts*, V. D. Sokolovsky, ed. (New York: Frederick A. Praeger, 1963), chap. II.
2. It is interesting to observe that Kolko, an exponent of a systemic theory of international relations, specifically denies the autonomous role of the "military-industrial complex" which he calls "mythical." He pictures the military establishment as a pliable tool of business interests. While Kolko marshals impressive evidence in support of his view, I believe he would face difficulties in extending it to encompass the role of, say, the Soviet military establishment in perpetuating the arms race.
3. Murray Thomson, *Militarism 1969: A Survey of Trends* (Dundas, Ont.: Canadian Peace Research Institute, Peace Research Reviews, October 1968), vol. 2, no. 5. Source: R. Kolkowicz, *The Soviet Military and the Communist Party* (Princeton N.J.: Princeton University Press, 1967).
4. ABM—antiballistic missile, designed to intercept intercontinental ballistic missiles (ICBM). CBW—chemical and biological warfare. MIRV—multiple independently targeted reentry vehicles, aptly

described by an MIT physicist as "A 'missile bus' whose 'passengers' are nuclear bombs. It enables a single booster to deliver as many as fourteen bombs, each one accurately aimed at a different target. The targets can be 50 to 100 miles apart, perhaps even more." Leo Sartori, "The Myth of MIRV," *Saturday Review*, August 30, 1969, p. 10.

5. George Orwell, *1984* (London: Secker & Warburg, 1959).
6. See Note 15, Chapter 13.
7. George S. McGovern, Gaylord A. Nelson, *et al.*, "The People vs. the Pentagon," *The Progressive*, June 1969, vol. 33, no. 6, pp. 6–7, introductory essay to the edited transcripts of the Congressional Conference on the Military Budget and National Priorities, Washington, D.C., March 28–29, 1969.
8. *Ibid.*, p. 5.
9. John Kenneth Galbraith, *ibid.*, p. 16.
10. Stringfellow Barr, *Let's Join the Human Race* (Chicago: University of Chicago Press, 1950).

INDEX

absolute monarchy, 9, 26
accustomed frameworks of thought, 14
Adams, John Quincy, 46
aggression against U.S.S.R., 202
"aggressions," 149
aggressiveness of states, 128
aggressive urges, 111, 128
"aggressor nations," 49
"alien ideas," Soviet purges of, 124
alliances, ad hoc, 46, 53; as concordance of interests 53; permanent, 53; use of, 38
Alperovitz, Gar, 87, 88, 89, 94, 95
America (*see* U.S.)
American conception of foreign policy, 48; —of war, 49
American economic potential (as "trump"), 92; historical experience, 91; ideology, 112; isolationism, 43, 51, 91
American imperialist ambitions, 44, 46, 47, 70, 142; expansion of, 45, 141; foundations of, 138; practicality of, 47; resistance against, 225; role in Pacific, 46
American naval strength, 52; political ideology, 144; security, 92; strategy, 90
"[The] American Way," 114
America's leadership, mission, 115; safety, belief in, 51
ancien regime, 225
anti-communism in U.S., 114–115; Congressional committees, 117; espionage trials, 114, 117; labor union purges, 117; "security system," 116; "subversive organizations," 117
anti-Communist hysteria, 114, 115–116; neurosis, 112
anti-Western purge of Soviet science,

124, 125, 126
apocalyptic view of struggle, 19
"appeasement," 92
Arab nationalism, Soviet support of, 145
armies, "citizen" (also "people's"), 29, 37; conscripted, 34; democratization of, 37; 18th century, 26; French Revolutionary (Grande Armee), 29; morale, 137; professional, 34, 37; Prussian, 29; soldiers' impulse to obey, 29; standing, 29
armaments, levels of, 20
armed might, 11
arms budgets, 20
arms control, 167, 191; agreement on, 168, 174
arms races, 20, 23; dynamics of, 69; "equilibrium," 20; mathematical model of, 20; Richardsonian process, 131, 210
Aron, Raymond, 127, 132, 207
aspirations of [the] masses, 77; ordinary people, 72, 221; populations, 138, 208, 219; power elites, 219; princes, 208
atomic attack, hypothetical, by U.S. against Soviet Union, 103, 104
atomic bomb, 64, 92, 93, 95, 96, 148; as "trump," 92; Soviet development of, 103, 115, 126, 150; "ultimate weapon," 88, 118
atomic bombing, strategic, 102
atomic diplomacy, 95; partnership, 92, 96
atomic strike, 102; "pre-emptive," 105
atomic weapons, as threat, 92; U.S. buildup of, 102; —monopoly of, 87, 88, 98, 99, 101, 118, 148, 150
attack by Russia, 206